Publications of
The Colonial Society of Massachusetts
Volume 48

BOSTON FURNITURE
OF THE
EIGHTEENTH CENTURY

A CONFERENCE HELD BY THE
COLONIAL SOCIETY OF MASSACHUSETTS
11 AND 12 MAY 1972

BOSTON
The Colonial Society of Massachusetts
Distributed by The University Press of Virginia

PRINTED FROM THE INCOME OF THE
SARAH LOUISE EDES FUND

Title-page illustration: Detail of pediment of Chest-on-Chest.
Made by John Cogswell. (Museum of Fine Arts, Boston,
William Francis Warden Fund, 1973.289.) See also figs. 125, 139, and 143.

Foreword

BOSTON furniture of the eighteenth century has long interested informed collectors and students of furniture history.
Yet, no book has been devoted to the subject. While cata-
logues and scholarly works have appeared on the eighteenth-century
furniture of New Hampshire, Rhode Island, Connecticut, New
York, New Jersey, Pennsylvania, Maryland, and South Carolina,[1]
little has been written on Massachusetts and particularly Boston. Today such an obvious research need in the field of American art does
not long remain fallow. Even before this book was begun, preliminary work had commenced. In 1948 Mabel Swan published the first
major list of Boston craftsmen.[2] Subsequent researchers such as Rich-

1. Major regional studies are in chronological order by state: *The Decorative Arts of
New Hampshire 1725–1825* (Manchester, New Hampshire, 1964); *The Decorative Arts
of New Hampshire: A Sesquicentennial Exhibition* (Concord, New Hampshire, 1973);
Ralph E. Carpenter, Jr., *The Arts and Crafts of Newport, Rhode Island, 1640–1820* (New-
port, Rhode Island, 1954); *The John Brown House Loan Exhibition of Rhode Island
Furniture* (Providence, Rhode Island, 1965); *Three Centuries of Connecticut Furniture
1635–1935* (Hartford, Connecticut, 1935); *Connecticut Furniture, Seventeenth and Eigh-
teenth Centuries* (Hartford, Connecticut, 1967); Joseph Downs and Ruth Ralston, *A
Loan Exhibition of New York State Furniture* (New York, 1934); V. Isabelle Miller,
Furniture by New York Cabinetmakers, 1650–1860 (New York, 1956); *New York Furni-
ture before 1840 in the Collection of the Albany Institute of History and Art* (Albany, 1962);
Margaret E. White, *Early Furniture Made in New Jersey, 1690–1870* (Newark, New
Jersey, 1958); William M. Hornor, Jr., *Blue Book, Philadelphia Furniture: William
Penn to George Washington* (Philadelphia, 1935); *Baltimore Furniture: The Work of
Baltimore and Annapolis Cabinetmakers from 1760 to 1810* (Baltimore, 1947); William
Voss Elder III, *Maryland Queen Anne and Chippendale Furniture of the Eighteenth Cen-
tury* (Baltimore, 1968); E. Milby Burton, *Charleston Furniture, 1700–1825* (Charleston,
South Carolina, 1955).

2. Mabel Munson Swan wrote numerous articles on New England furniture of the
eighteenth century. Her most important study of Boston is a two-part article entitled
"Boston's Carvers and Joiners," *Antiques*, LIII (March and April, 1948), 198–201, 281–
285. Other material by Mabel Swan is cited in a bibliography at the end of this
volume.

1. CHEST-ON-CHEST. Made by Benjamin Frothingham (paper label), Charles-town, Massachusetts, c. 1765–1790. Mahogany and white pine; H. 88⅜ inches, W. 45¼ inches, D. 25 inches. (Private collection.)

ard Randall, Benno Forman, and Vernon Stoneman have contributed to the picture of the Boston furniture industry.[3] More recently
four students in the Winterthur Program in Early American Culture, Brock Jobe, Margaretta Lovell, Gilbert Vincent, and Mary
Ellen Yehia, began to examine various aspects of the subject.

In 1972 the Colonial Society of Massachusetts offered to sponsor
the conference "Boston Furniture of the Eighteenth Century" as
their second annual meeting on early New England culture. At their
first conference, chaired jointly by Sinclair Hitchings and Walter
Muir Whitehill, eight papers were presented on Boston prints and
subsequently published in *Boston Prints and Printmakers 1670–1775*,
volume 46 of the *Publications* of the Colonial Society of Massachusetts. For the furniture conference, the Colonial Society turned to
the newly established Department of American Decorative Arts and
Sculpture at the Museum of Fine Arts, Boston. Jonathan Fairbanks,
Curator of the Department, with the encouragement and advice of
Walter Muir Whitehill, developed the format for the conference.
Eight speakers were invited and an exhibition of Boston furniture
was planned to coincide with the conference. Although focussing
on Boston proper, the co-ordinators of the conference chose to include a paper on Benjamin Frothingham of Charlestown because of
the numerous pieces of extant furniture signed or labelled by this
important Boston area craftsman (fig. 1).

On May 11, 1972, the conference opened at the headquarters of the
Colonial Society at 87 Mount Vernon Street. After introductory
remarks by Walter Muir Whitehill, papers were presented by Brock

3. While Richard Randall has several outstanding articles to his credit (see the
bibliography), his best-known work is *American Furniture in the Museum of Fine Arts,
Boston* (Boston, 1965). This catalogue includes well-documented pieces of Boston
furniture made throughout the century. Benno Forman and Vernon Stoneman have
contributed specific studies on furniture produced at the beginning and end of the
century, respectively. See Benno M. Forman, "Urban Aspects of Massachusetts
Furniture in the Late Seventeenth Century," *Winterthur Conference Report 1969:
Country Cabinetwork and Simple City Furniture* (Charlottesville, Virginia, 1970); Vernon C. Stoneman, *John and Thomas Seymour, Cabinetmakers in Boston, 1794–1816*
(Boston, 1959) and *A Supplement to John and Thomas Seymour, Cabinetmakers in Boston,
1794–1816* (Boston, 1966).

Jobe and Mary Ellen Yehia. During the afternoon, conference members moved to the Museum of Fine Arts to hear lectures by Gilbert Vincent and Margaretta Lovell and to view the exhibition "A Bit of Vanity, Furniture of Eighteenth-Century Boston." Many documented examples were brought together in Gallery T-2, including a William and Mary style slate top table (fig. 2), a desk-on-frame and pier table (fig. 3), both with mask-carved knees, and a blockfront chest of drawers originally owned by Thomas Lamb (c. 1753–1813) of Boston (fig. 4). Unfortunately one of the best-documented and most unusual pieces of Boston furniture, an enormous orrery made by Joseph Pope between 1776 and 1788 (fig. 5), could not be moved from the basement of Houghton Library, Harvard University, to the

2. DRESSING TABLE. Boston area, c. 1700–1720. Walnut, white pine, and slate; H. 30⅛ inches, w. 44⅛ inches, D. 30¼ inches. (Dietrich Brothers Americana Corporation: photo, Richard Cheek.) *According to family tradition, this table was owned by Thomas Hinckley (1618–1706) of Barnstable, Massachusetts.*

3. PIER TABLE. Boston area, c. 1740–1770. Mahogany and white pine; H. 29 inches, W. 28½ inches, D. 17⅛ inches. (Museum of Fine Arts, Boston, M. and M. Karolik Collection, 41.586.)

4. CHEST OF DRAWERS. Boston, c. 1760–1790. Mahogany and white pine; H. 30 inches, W. 36 inches, D. 21⅜ inches. (Private collection: photo, Richard Cheek.) *According to family tradition, this chest was owned by Thomas Lamb (c. 1753–1813), a merchant of Boston.*

5. ORRERY. Made by Joseph Pope, Boston, 1776–1788. Mahogany; H. 78 inches, Diameter 78 inches. (Historical Scientific Instruments Collection, Harvard University.) *In March, 1789, Harvard College purchased this orrery from Pope for £450.*

Museum. Portraits by Robert Feke, Joseph Badger, and John Singleton Copley (fig. 6) enriched the exhibition with views of friendly, confident faces and costly, decorative furniture.

On May 12, the participants in the conference returned to the Colonial Society headquarters to listen to papers by Richard Randall, Gordon Saltar, Sinclair Hitchings, and Dean Fales. The conference ended with a luncheon at the Club of Odd Volumes, 77 Mount Vernon Street.

This book, issued as volume 48 of the Colonial Society's *Publications*, contains the papers presented at the conference.[4] Many were

4. Gordon Saltar who spoke on wood analysis as an aid to the study of New England furniture submitted the most useful portions of his highly specialized paper for publication: a list of New England cabinet woods and an annotated bibliography on the identification of woods.

6. MRS. EZEKIEL GOLDTHWAIT. Painted by John Singleton Copley, Boston, 1770–1771. Oil on canvas; H. 50 inches, W. 40 inches (excluding frame). (Museum of Fine Arts, Boston, Bequest of John T. Bowen in memory of Eliza M. Bowen, 41.84.)

transformed afterwards by additional research stimulated by the lively exchange of thought generated at the conference. A list and bibliography of furniture craftsmen working in Boston during the eighteenth century have been added as appendices.

Photographs of 132 objects appear throughout the volume to amplify the text. While many have been illustrated before, never has such a large number been compiled for one publication. Some are shown here for the first time: a pair of armchairs (fig. 7) owned by Thomas Lamb of Boston and stamped "S.F," probably the initials of the chairmaker,[5] an early blockfront bureau table with string inlay (fig. 18), and a bombé desk and bookcase signed in pencil by Benjamin Frothingham and D. Sprage and dated 1753 (figs. 97 and 162). Partly as a result of the increased interest generated by the conference, one of the most important but rarely seen pieces of Boston furniture, a chest-on-chest signed by John Cogswell, was acquired by the Museum of Fine Arts and is handsomely illustrated in color in figure 125.

The purpose of the conference was to foster comparison and distribution of recent scholarship. In doing so, it provided new insights into Boston eighteenth-century furniture and summarized past information in light of modern discoveries. It also pointed towards further research needs in the field. The study of Federalist Boston (c. 1788–1815) and its furniture has hardly begun. Little is known about the introduction of the neoclassical style in Boston, the influence of Boston furniture of the Federal period on other urban centers such as Salem, and the changing craft practices in late eighteenth-century Boston. For the entire century many questions remain unanswered. What was the relationship between Boston craftsmen and those in surrounding towns? What effect did the Revolution have on

5. A side chair and lolling chair in the Winterthur Museum bear the stamps of Stephen Badlam, a cabinetmaker of Dorchester, and the unidentified S. F. Charles Montgomery speculated that S. F. may have been the initials of a Boston journeyman working for Badlam during the 1790s. A likely candidate is Samuel Fisk, a Boston cabinetmaker who died in 1797. Charles F. Montgomery, *American Furniture, the Federal Period in the Henry Francis du Pont Winterthur Museum* (New York, 1966), nos. 30, 110.

7. ARMCHAIR. Stamped "S.F" (probably the initials of the maker), Boston, c. 1770–1795. Mahogany and maple; H. 35¾ inches, W. 22 inches, D. 21 inches. (Museum of Fine Arts, Boston, Gift of the Misses Aimée and Rosamond Lamb, in memory of Miss Rose Lamb, 1972.927: photo, Richard Cheek.) *According to family tradition, this chair was owned by Thomas Lamb (c. 1753–1813), a merchant of Boston.*

the furniture industry? How influential were patrons in determining style changes in Boston? What effect did imported furniture have on Boston styles? This book is but a beginning—a beginning, it should be added, that emphasizes the Queen Anne and Chippendale periods (c. 1725–1788). It is hoped that as a result of this effort more information will become available and eventually a more comprehensive history of the furniture trade will be written.

It is curious that in our twentieth-century push-button age precise knowledge about the past still generates slowly. Patient sifting, sorting, and gathering of facts for this volume came about because many persons willingly contributed their talent, time, and effort. The Colonial Society of Massachusetts must be credited with providing the impetus for the conference. The Henry Francis du Pont Winterthur Museum, its research facilities, library, staff, and certain fellows and graduates also did much to make the conference possible. Advice from Albert Sack of Israel Sack, Inc., was essential in preparing the Boston furniture exhibit at the Museum of Fine Arts. Lu Bartlett, Assistant to the Curator, with the assistance of the following graduate students from Boston University's American and New England Studies Program installed the exhibit and wrote the captions for the catalogue: Anne Farnam, Sheridan Germann, Joyce Goldberg, John Herzan, Mary Beth Hornbeck, Eugenia Kaledin, Robert MacKay, Betsy Mankin, Brian Pffeifer, Clarisse Poirier, Ned Reynolds, and Mary Ellen Yehia.

Several persons loaned or helped to arrange for loans of articles to the exhibition. Charles F. Montgomery, who constantly supported and encouraged the conference, provided several important objects from the Yale University Art Gallery. Dietrich Brothers Americana Corporation, William du Pont, Mr. and Mrs. Edward C. Johnson, John P. Kinsey, the Misses Aimée and Rosamond Lamb, the Massachusetts Historical Society, and Israel Sack, Inc., loaned pieces of furniture for the show.

The content and organization of this book were improved by the assistance of six readers: Barry Greenlaw, Morrison Hecksher, Darrell Hyder, Myrna Kaye, Andrew Oliver, and the late Clifford Shipton. Darrell Hyder and Barbara Jobe ably provided special editorial work for individual articles.

The list of furniture craftsmen at the end of this volume was compiled by many different individuals. Brock Jobe completed research on craftsmen active between 1725 and 1760. Myrna Kaye with the assistance of Eleuthera du Pont, Carole Karnath, Elodie Loraamm, Lee Mobbs, Mary Noone, and Priscilla Sloss compiled information on craftsmen working at the beginning and end of the century. Myrna Kaye then prepared the entire list for publication in this volume and Joyce Goldberg added a bibliography of books and articles on Boston eighteenth-century furniture craftsmen.

Innumerable details of putting this volume in order were conducted with vigor by Brock Jobe as part of his internship experience in Boston University's American and New England Studies Program. We gratefully acknowledge not only his major contribution to the content of this volume, but also his great ability to direct essential correspondence and photographic needs down to the last detail. As ready assistants helping with every need throughout the final six months of the project, Eleuthera du Pont and Lynne Spencer are to be thanked as well.

Design of this volume and its final appearance are due to the combined talents of Roderick D. Stinehour of The Stinehour Press and E. Harold Hugo of The Meriden Gravure Company, both of whom participated in the conference.

WALTER MUIR WHITEHILL
Editor

BROCK JOBE
Editorial Assistant

JONATHAN FAIRBANKS
Curator of American Decorative Arts and Sculpture Museum of Fine Arts, Boston

February 25, 1974

EXPLANATORY NOTES

FOR THIS PUBLICATION the geographical borders of Boston are defined according to their eighteenth-century limits. Boston, a hilly, treeless peninsula, was bounded on the north by the Charles River, on the west by extensive salt marshes, on the south by a neck of land linking the peninsula to the Roxbury mainland, and on the east by the harbor and mud flats (fig. 8). Five towns, Dorchester, Roxbury, Brookline, Cambridge, and Charlestown, encircled the peninsula on three sides. Craftsmen from surrounding towns, no doubt, produced furniture quite similar to Boston examples. For this reason, only documented pieces of Boston furniture are ascribed to "Boston" in the captions while those with similar characteristics but lacking histories or makers' marks are identified as "Boston area."

In the captions signed or labelled examples are identified by the term "made by." The work of Benjamin Frothingham is further divided by type of documentation: paper label, ink inscription, signature in pencil, or signature in chalk. Attributions are based on well-documented histories or specific stylistic and constructional evidence. *Circa* dates (designated as "c.") are used for examples without a precise date of manufacture. The identification of woods is based on visual analysis. The primary wood is listed first, followed by secondary woods and other materials. Different views and details of an object are noted. Complete information is provided only for the primary illustration, usually an overall view. Special caption comments have been contributed by individual authors for certain objects.

All dates appearing in the captions and text are in Old Style, but with January 1 being used as the beginning of the year rather than March 25 for the period before 1752. Thus a date of January 10, 1728/9 becomes January 10, 1729. The original spelling of manuscript material is retained in all quotations; however, superior letters have been brought down to the line. Monetary values before 1750 are listed in Old Tenor; those afterwards are in the devalued currency, Lawful Money.

Contents

BOSTON FURNITURE
OF THE
EIGHTEENTH CENTURY

◆ BROCK JOBE ◆

The Boston Furniture Industry

1720–1740

The Artificers in this Place Exceed Any upon ye Continent And are here also Most Numerous as Cabinet Makers, Chace & Coach Makers . . . Watchmakers, Printers, Smiths, &C.[1]

IN 1750 James Birket, a traveller from the West Indies, found Boston filled with craftsmen. To him, their number surpassed that in any other American town. Today, as one passes through museums and historical societies, he is likely to agree with Birket. Hundreds, if not thousands, of pieces of furniture made in the Boston area during the eighteenth century have survived. Their makers are, for the most part, unknown. However, the quantity of objects attests to the activity of many craftsmen. This paper is concerned with these men—their number, their opportunities for work, their homes, and the economy in which they operated. Such information provides new insights into not only the men themselves but also their furniture.

Between 1725 and 1760 approximately 127 joiners and cabinet-makers,[2] 38 chairmakers, 23 upholsterers, 16 carvers, 11 turners, and 9 japanners worked in Boston. These 224 craftsmen comprised a total larger than that of any other American town during this period.

1. *Some Cursory Remarks Made by James Birket in his Voyage to North America 1750–1751*, ed. Charles M. Andrews (New Haven, 1916), p. 24.

2. In this paper no distinction is made between joiners known to have made furniture and cabinetmakers. For more information on the use of the two terms in colonial Boston, see Benno M. Forman, "Urban Aspects of Massachusetts Furniture in the Late Seventeenth Century," *Winterthur Conference Report 1969: Country Cabinetwork and Simple City Furniture* (Charlottesville, Virginia, 1970), pp. 17–20.

Philadelphia, Boston's nearest competitor, contained about thirty percent fewer craftsmen.[3]

An increase in shipbuilding during the early eighteenth century provided abundant work for many of these craftsmen. Queen Anne's War (1702–1713) had proved especially profitable for local merchants.[4] Their desire to enlarge the home fleet and the willingness of foreign entrepreneurs to purchase Boston vessels created jobs in every branch of the furniture industry. For example, Samuel Grant, an upholsterer, often supplied chairs and stools for the cabins of newly constructed ships.[5] Joseph Ingraham, a local carver, completed the carved details for five ships during 1739. His bill of over £300 included £30:5:0 for an "11 foot Lyon for ship Dragon."[6] Such accounts are typical for carvers and suggest that they were far busier with shipwork than with furniture. Joiners often outfitted the interiors of vessels. Two such craftsmen, Daniel and Joseph Ballard, were often involved in civil litigation and were forced by the courts to account for their work. According to one law suit, Joseph Ballard constructed panelling, cupboards, chests, lockers, cornice moldings, window sashes, and "ye hen & goose coop" for a ship.[7] Other joiners provided similar services, sometimes building tables and desks in addition to performing finished carpentry work.[8]

Besides shipwork, merchants offered cabinetmakers and chairmakers the opportunity to export their goods in vessels bound for Nova

3. An appendix at the back of this volume includes these workmen in a list of furniture craftsmen active in Boston during the eighteenth century. For comparable statistics for Philadelphia, see Arthur W. Leibundguth, "The Furniture-Making Crafts in Philadelphia, c. 1730–1760" (unpublished M.A. thesis, University of Delaware, 1964), pp. 132–136.

4. Bernard and Lotte Bailyn, *Massachusetts Shipping, 1697–1714: A Statistical Study* (Cambridge, 1959), pp. 42–47, 49–50, 74–76; Wesley Frank Craven, *The Colonies in Transition 1660–1713* (New York, 1968), pp. 307–310.

5. Thomas Hancock, Daybook, May 27 and December 29, 1738 (Baker Library, Harvard University).

6. Suffolk County Inferior Court of Common Pleas, Boston, Massachusetts, December 21, 1741 (hereafter Suffolk Common Pleas).

7. Ibid., January 18, 1750.

8. For example, see Peter Faneuil, Daybook, May 11, 1732, p. 389 (Baker Library, Harvard University).

Scotia, the coastal ports of New York, Philadelphia, and Charleston, or the West Indies. That craftsmen took advantage of the mercantile activity is demonstrated by the statements of Plunkett Fleeson, a Philadelphia upholsterer. In 1742 he advertised chairs "cheaper than any made here, or imported from Boston." Evidently, hundreds of Boston chairs were flooding into the area because two years later Fleeson chastised "the Master Chair Makers in this City . . . [for] Encouraging the Importation of Boston Chairs."[9] Even in 1762, when Philadelphia cabinetmakers were beginning to produce their finest furniture, Ebenezer Call asked his brother in Boston to have chairs made by a Mr. Lampson and shipped to Philadelphia.[10]

In addition to ship construction and an export trade, the merchants themselves were excellent clientele for craftsmen. Though occasionally importing furniture from England, local merchants usually relied on Bostonians for their home furnishings. Samuel Abbot, who began his mercantile career in 1760, kept an "Accompt of Household Furniture."[11] In it he noted the purchase of his household goods for the next thirty years. With the exception of four Philadelphia (Windsor) chairs[12] and two looking glasses, all of Abbot's furniture was made in Boston. Chairmakers Henry Perkins, William Fullerton, and George Bright provided mahogany tables and chair frames. John Forsyth, William Gray, and Ziphion Thayer upholstered these chairs and furnished bed mattresses, pillows, curtains, and window cushions. Adino Paddock, a coachmaker, billed Abbot £40 for a chaise "Carved Gilt & Laced"[13] while John Gore, a successful japanner,

9. Quoted in Richard H. Randall, Jr., "Boston Chairs," *Old-Time New England*, LIV (Summer, 1963), 12–13.

10. Ebenezer Call to William Call, Philadelphia, January 15, 1762, Gratz Papers (The Historical Society of Pennsylvania [photostat copy, Henry Francis du Pont Winterthur Museum Libraries, Joseph Downs Manuscript Collection]).

11. Samuel Abbot, Account Book, 1754–1808, pp. 21–22, 41–42 (Baker Library, Harvard University).

12. It is possible that these chairs may also have been of Boston origin, since the term "Philadelphia chair" was a generic one for any type of Windsor chair.

13. In this context, "Laced" could either mean "diversified with streaks of color" (*A New English Dictionary on Historical Principles*, 10 vols. [Oxford, 1905], VI, part I, 11) or be an abbreviation for "lacquered."

8. THE TOWN OF BOSTON IN NEW ENGLAND BY JOHN BONNER 1722. Drawn by John Bonner, engraved by Francis Dewing. Copperplate engraving, first state; H. 16 13/16

Barton's Point.

Copper Works.

Charles River

Ferry to Charles=Town

Rope Walk

Lei's Ship Yard

E&N. Mill Dam m

Mill Pond.

N.Water Mill

Goes Ship Yd

Ferry Way

Print & Whites Ship Yd

Burying Place

Baker

Salem Street

Water Mill

Hill Street

Cap. Gree nough's Shipy.

Treamont S

Hanover St

Middle Street

North Street

Lyn Street

Thornton's Shi'p Yard

Cornhill

Fish Street

Ship Street

N.Battery.

King Street

Lee's Ship Yd

Greenwood's Ship Yd & Wharfe.

Wentworth's Wharfe.

Scarlett's Wharfe

Clarks Ship Yt

Old Wharfe.

Clark Wharfe.

We hall the Long Wharfe

Pool's Wharf

Olivers Dock

Long Ware H.

HARBOUR

Wing's Sh.Yd

Olivers Sh.Yd

Gates Wharfe.

Old Wharfe.

FortHill.

S.Battery.

ving. Boston N.E.1722.

inches, w. 23 inches (engraved surface only). (I. N. Phelps Stokes Collection, Prints Division, The New York Public Library.) See also figs. 9 and 10.

9. DETAIL OF BONNER MAP SHOWING AREA BETWEEN UNION AND PRINCE STREETS. (I. N. Phelps Stokes Collection, Prints Division, The New York Public Library.) See also figs. 8 and 10. *Many furniture craftsmen lived on Ann, Middle, and Back Streets in the North End.*

painted and framed a coat of arms for £2. Such complete documentation is nonexistent for the first half of the eighteenth century. However, individual references to purchases by Daniel Henchman, Matthew Bond, and other merchants suggest that they, too, primarily patronized local craftsmen.[14]

The homes of furniture craftsmen were located throughout the city. Samuel Wheeler, a chairmaker, lived on Orange Street[15] near the neck of land leading to Roxbury. Thomas Luckis, a carver, owned a portion of a home almost two miles away on Lynn Street in the North End (fig. 8). Many lived in craftsmen's districts either in the North End between Union and Prince Streets or in the South End between Cornhill and Battery March (figs. 9 and 10). John Brocas, John Corser, Samuel Ridgway, and Job Coit resided on Anne and Union Streets. A block away on Back and Middle Streets were the homes of cabinetmakers Nathaniel Holmes, Thomas Sherburne, James McMillian, Thomas Johnson, and William Johnson. In the South End on Battery March lived at least five chairmakers. Occasionally these individuals owned their dwellings, but as the century progressed more and more men chose to rent houses, portions of tenements, or just rooms. Indeed, evidence suggests that middle-class property-owning craftsmen of the late seventeenth and early eighteenth centuries were gradually replaced by increasingly wealthy merchant-craftsmen and poor journeymen.[16]

Boston furniture makers worked in an economy based on commodity and credit exchange. Foreign coin did not circulate in the city and even the paper money printed by the Massachusetts government was scarce among craftsmen. As a result, a type of bartering

14. See accounts between Henchman and William Downe, a Boston upholsterer, xv, Domestic Bills, January 24, 1743, Hancock Papers (Baker Library, Harvard University). See also accounts between Bond and Thomas Gibbons and Lanier Kenn, two cabinetmakers in partnership, Suffolk Common Pleas, December 15, 1733.

15. For complete documentation on the shop locations of Boston's furniture craftsmen, see Brock Jobe, "The Boston Furniture Industry 1725–1760" (unpublished M.A. thesis, University of Delaware, 1975).

16. James A. Henretta, "Economic Development and Social Structure in Colonial Boston," *William and Mary Quarterly*, 3rd ser., XXII (January, 1965), 81–88.

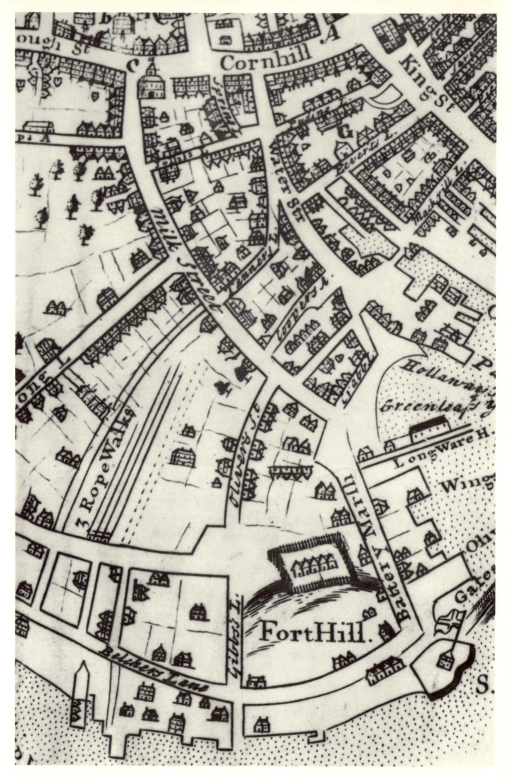

10. Detail of Bonner Map Showing Area between Cornhill and Battery March. (I. N. Phelps Stokes Collection, Prints Division, The New York Public Library.) See also figs. 8 and 9. *Many furniture craftsmen lived on Milk Street and Battery March, near the wharves of the South End.*

system prevailed where workmen traded small amounts of cash, goods, services, and notes of obligation in lieu of money. A note written by William Randle, a japanner, is typical of the latter form of exchange. On July 15, 1724, he promised to pay "Mr John Greenwood or order Fourty five Pounds on or before the first day of April next, it being for Sundry Prints of ye City of New York Bought & Received of him."[17]

In this economy, personal trust played an important role. No man wanted to sell goods to another unless he believed that he would eventually be repaid. Artisans especially needed good credit reputations because of the many items required in their work. Cabinetmakers turned to merchants and ship captains for imported lumber and to braziers and shopkeepers for imported brassware, tools, nails, and glue. Furthermore, in an urban environment, they depended on victuallers and innholders for food and drink. To succeed in such an atmosphere required hard work and reliable connections within the craft and the community. Apprenticeship and kinship ties were the easiest ways of securing these connections. In both, masters and fathers provided assistance for younger men to begin their careers. For this reason, successive generations of families followed the same trade and became trusted members of the community. The Coit family, comprised of Job, Sr., and his three sons, worked as cabinetmakers. The Perkins family included five chairmakers in two generations. The most extended family, the Frothinghams of Boston and Charlestown, contained sixteen woodworkers in four generations.[18] Some craftsmen married into the families of furniture makers. Ebenezer Clough, a Boston joiner, married Elizabeth Welch, the daughter of a Charlestown joiner. Robert Davis, a Boston japanner, married the daughter of William Randle, another local japanner.

These complex kinship ties may have contributed to the general conservatism of Boston furniture when compared to that of Phila-

---

17. Suffolk County Superior Court of General Sessions, Boston, Massachusetts, docket 21711.

18. Thomas B. Wyman, *The Genealogies and Estates of Charlestown*, 2 vols. (Boston, 1879), I, 381–395.

delphia. The prolonged use of stretchers or the continued appearance of Queen Anne style furniture in the 1760s and 1770s could have resulted from traditional family training.

Family ties not only provided security for Bostonians who trained locally as apprentices, but also made it extremely difficult for immigrants to break into the furniture industry. Between 1730 and 1760 no inventory of an immigrant craftsman exceeded £100 while those of several native workmen surpassed £2000.[19] Family connections by no means insured success, but they seem to have been at least a prerequisite for the attainment of wealth in the furniture industry.

Boston's faltering economy after 1740 further decreased the immigrants' opportunities. A drop in population during the thirty years prior to the Revolution reflected the deteriorating condition. As the Reverend Andrew Burnaby stated in 1760, "The province of Massachusetts-Bay has been for some years past, I believe, rather on the decline. Its inhabitants have lost several branches of trade, which they are not likely to recover again."[20] Growing competition from other coastal ports, the Molasses Act, and high local taxes created little need or attraction for additional craftsmen.

The best example of the immigrant craftsman's problems is Charles Warham. Born in London in 1701,[21] he travelled to Boston sometime before 1724.[22] The young cabinetmaker, who had apparently completed an English apprenticeship, discovered hard times in his new home. Numerous court cases reveal that he was unable to pay

19. The only records documenting immigration into Boston between 1700 and 1760 are ship impost records for the years 1715 and 1716. These incomplete records list the names of eight newly arrived joiners and cabinetmakers from London, Bristol, Ireland, Barbados, Long Island, and North Carolina. Obviously, many others ventured to Boston, but unfortunately their names rarely appear in town records. *A Volume of Records Relating to the Early History of Boston Containing Miscellaneous Papers,* XXIX (Boston, 1900), 229–242 (hereafter *Miscellaneous Papers*).

20. Andrew Burnaby, *Travels Through the Middle Settlements in North-America in the Years 1759 and 1760,* 2nd ed. (1775; rpt. Ithaca, New York, 1960), pp. 103–104. For information on the decline in trade, see Carl Bridenbaugh, *Cities in the Wilderness* (1938; rpt. Oxford, 1971), pp. 303, 330–336.

21. E. Milby Burton, *Charleston Furniture 1700–1825* (Charleston, 1955), p. 127.

22. Warham purchased goods from Samuel Gardner, a Boston shopkeeper, on October 9, 1724. See Suffolk Common Pleas, December 14, 1730.

for food or rent.[23] Without any means of solving his dilemma, Warham evidently became a poor risk to his creditors. In 1731, he sold his
household possessions and moved to Charleston, South Carolina.[24]
On November 2, 1734, he advertised in the *South Carolina Gazette*
"all sorts of Tables, Chests, Chests-of-drawers, Desks, Bookcases &c.
As also Coffins of the newest fashion, never as yet made in *Charlestown*."[25] He purchased lots for his home and shop on Tradd Street
and during the ensuing years established a prominent cabinetmaking
trade in Charleston. As a result of his newfound prosperity, he turned
later in life to land speculation. In 1776, for example, he offered for
sale 5000 acres of South Carolina real estate. He died on July 20, 1779,
leaving a substantial estate.[26] Debt-ridden in Boston, a city glutted
with craftsmen, Warham succeeded in Charleston where demand for
his work was far greater.

In contrast to this immigrant, several of Boston's native sons prospered in the furniture industry. The career of Nathaniel Holmes, a
cabinetmaker, is illustrative of how men with strong local kinship
ties manipulated the credit economy to their best advantage. Holmes
was born in Boston on December 29, 1703.[27] His father, Nathaniel,
Sr., had worked as a joiner and mason during the late seventeenth
century. Young Nathaniel was only eight when his father died, and
presumably his mother apprenticed him a few years later to one of
Boston or Charlestown's many cabinetmakers. By 1725 he had
opened his own cabinet shop near the Mill Bridge in Boston.[28] Three
years later he married Mary Webber, the daughter of a lumber dealer
and sawmill owner, a connection which obviously served his best
interests, and during the next decade expanded his cabinetmaking
business by employing workmen from the Massachusetts Bay area.

In 1735 Holmes purchased a distillery on Back Street and for five

23. Ibid., March 22, 1731, August 28, 1732.
24. Ibid., March 3, 1733.
25. Quoted in Burton, *Charleston*, p. 126.
26. Ibid., pp. 126–127.
27. For information pertaining to Holmes's life, see George Arthur Gray, *The
Descendants of George Holmes of Roxbury 1594–1908* (Boston, 1908), pp. 16, 28–30.
28. *Miscellaneous Papers*, p. 223.

years prospered through the production of both rum and furniture. At the same time he began to hire vessels to carry his goods up and down the coast. His rum business and carrying trade proved so profitable that after 1740 he abandoned his cabinetmaking operation. To complement his distillery, Holmes built a sugar baking house in 1748[29] and for the next twenty years shipped sugar, molasses, and rum on his own sloops and schooners to Newfoundland, the Middle Colonies, and the South. When he died in 1774, he left an estate valued at almost £4000 which included land and houses throughout Massachusetts and Maine. He owned dwellings on Back, Charter, Middle, and School Streets in Boston as well as a farm in Malden and land in Falmouth and Kennebeck.[30] Holmes succeeded far better than any other cabinetmaker in Boston. His biography indicates that a craftsman could become wealthy, but only by changing occupations could he amass a great fortune.

Fortunately, surviving documentation permits a detailed analysis of Holmes's furniture business.[31] During the 1730s Holmes served as a merchant-middleman for numerous craftsmen in Boston and surrounding towns whom he supplied with food, clothing, brassware, lumber, and glue. In return, they constructed furniture which they delivered to Holmes who then sold it to ship captains for export or to private customers in Boston.

Holmes employed ten joiners and cabinetmakers, only four of whom worked in Boston. Robert Lord, Richard Woodward, and Thomas Johnson lived in Boston. Woodward, in fact, boarded with Holmes. Another local cabinetmaker, Thomas Sherburne, helped Holmes manage the business in 1736 and 1737. John Mudge and Jacob Burdit resided in Malden, a small village on the Malden River,

29. Thomas Atkins to Nathaniel Holmes, Boston, VIII, Bills, March 16, 1748, Bourn Papers (Baker Library, Harvard University).

30. The inventory totalled £3885:0:3. Suffolk County Registry of Probate, Boston, Massachusetts, docket 15727 (hereafter Suffolk Probate Records).

31. The following information is based on accounts between Holmes and John Mudge, Jacob Burdit, and Mary Jackson, 55.523–525, 55.764.2 (Winterthur Libraries, Joseph Downs Manuscript Collection) and two folders of bills and receipts in the Bourn Papers, VI, Accounts Current 1727–1738, and VIII, Bills 1728–1759 (Baker Library, Harvard University).

north of Boston. Thomas and Chapman Waldron lived in Marble-head, a coastal settlement about sixteen miles northeast of Boston. James Hovey worked for Holmes for nine months in either Plymouth or Boston. The home of Timothy Gooding, Jr., the last of Holmes's workmen, has not been located. The majority of these men were between twenty-one and twenty-eight years of age,[32] suggesting that Holmes was responsible for aiding them at the start of their careers, when they needed credit to purchase household and shop goods.

Holmes dealt with three turners, two bed bottom makers, and a japanner, all presumably of Boston. The turners, John Underwood, Daniel McKillister, and Daniel Swan, produced lathe-turned legs, drops, finials (called flames in the accounts), pillars, and balls which were later used by the joiners to embellish their furniture. Pillars and balls were produced in sets and probably used in the upper portion of tall case clocks as columns and finials, respectively (fig. 11). The bed bottom makers, William Bulfinch and Elias Thomas, laced canvas to bed frames made by Holmes or his workmen. A typical cloth bottom is illustrated in *The Cabinet Dictionary* by Thomas Sheraton (fig. 12).[33] Holmes's japanner, William Randle, performed an assortment of services, including the gilding of pillars for a clock and the japanning of a pedimented high chest.

The personal papers of Nathaniel Holmes reveal that these fifteen craftsmen constructed 338 pieces of furniture for their employer between 1733 and 1739. Unfortunately, only a portion of the business is documented in the bills and receipts. We have no information, for instance, on how much furniture Holmes constructed himself. Nor do we have complete accounts for each craftsman's work. The total number of objects probably far exceeded those recorded in the papers.

32. Birth records have only been found for Johnson, Mudge, Burdit, and Sherburne, all of whom were born after 1708. Woodward was called Holmes's apprentice in 1736 and must have been in his early twenties when hired by his former master. Jeremiah Townsend to Nathaniel Holmes, Boston, VI, Accounts Current, February 1, 1739, Bourn Papers (Baker Library, Harvard University).

33. Thomas Sheraton, *The Cabinet Dictionary* (London, 1803), plate XV.

11. DETAIL OF TALL CLOCK SHOWING PIL-
LARS AND BALLS. Works by Benjamin Bagnall,
Boston, c. 1715–1730. Case, walnut and white
pine; H. 98½ inches, W. 20⅞ inches, D. 10⅜
inches. (Collection of Mrs. Charles L. Bybee
and the late Charles L. Bybee: photo, Richard
Cheek.) For an overall view of the clock, see
Antiques, XCIII (January, 1968), 77.

Tables and desks constituted the great majority of their work. Of
the documented objects, 62 were desks and 225 were tables. Many
were simple utilitarian pieces of furniture made of maple or pine
(fig. 13). However, these craftsmen also made elaborate card and tea
tables as well as veneered desks with inlaid stringing and stars. On
June 15, 1738, John Mudge billed his employer £3:3:0 for a "Larg
Sedor desk with a star and scolup dros, no well rume, Lap beeded
and pilor dros."[34] Such a desk probably resembled one owned by the
American Antiquarian Society (fig. 14). "No well rume" indicates
that insufficient space was available for a concealed well, a feature
often found in New England desks of the William and Mary style.
"Scolup dros" may refer to either the shell carved drawers of a desk
interior (fig. 80) or the small arched drawers above the pigeon-

34. John Mudge to Nathaniel Holmes, Malden, Massachusetts, January 6, 1738,
55.524 (Winterthur Libraries, Joseph Downs Manuscript Collection).

CAMP BED.

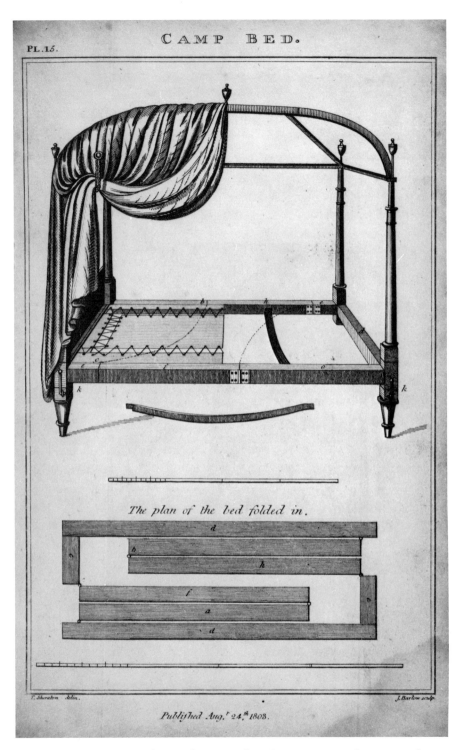

The plan of the bed folded in.

Published Aug.ᵗ 24.ᵗʰ 1803.

12. CAMP BED. From Thomas Sheraton, *The Cabinet Dictionary*, plate xv. London, 1803. (The Metropolitan Museum of Art, Rogers Fund, 1952.)

13. TABLE. Eastern Massachusetts, c. 1730–1760. Maple and white pine; H. 25½ inches, W. 31 inches (open), D. 31⅞ inches. (The Henry Francis du Pont Winterthur Museum.)

holes.[35] The reference to pillared drawers describes the narrow document drawers with applied pilasters, seen on many Boston eighteenth-century desks (fig. 15).

Holmes's workmen constructed 16 desks and bookcases and 16 chests of drawers. To decorate these large pieces of furniture, they often applied carved or inlaid shells. In 1733 William Randle was paid for gilding two carved shells, probably for a high chest (fig. 16).

35. A desk at the Museum of Fine Arts, Boston, has small arched drawers above the pigeonholes and a concealed well in the desk interior. See Richard H. Randall, Jr., *American Furniture in the Museum of Fine Arts, Boston* (Boston, 1965), fig. 55.

14. DESK. Eastern Massachusetts, c. 1730–1760. Cherry and white pine; H. 46½ inches, W. 36 inches, D. 19½ inches. (American Antiquarian Society: photo, Richard Merrill.) *According to family tradition, this desk was owned by Governor James Bowdoin (1726–1790) of Boston. Feet and brasses are replaced.*

Four years later Richard Woodward charged Holmes eighteen shillings for "putting in a Shell" and one pound for "Setting 2 Shells."[36] These later references document the difficult and expensive task of in-

36. Richard Woodward to Nathaniel Holmes, Boston, VI, Accounts Current, December 12, 1737, Bourn Papers (Baker Library, Harvard University).

15. INTERIOR OF DESK-ON-FRAME SHOWING PILLARED DRAWERS. Boston, C.
1740–1770. Mahogany, maple, tulipwood, and white pine; H. 42⅛ inches, W. 35¾ inches,
D. 22⅞ inches. (Museum of Fine Arts, Boston, Gift of Mr. and Mrs. Henry Herbert Edes,
36.34: photo, Richard Cheek.) For an overall view of the desk, see Richard H. Randall, Jr.,
American Furniture in the Museum of Fine Arts, Boston (Boston, 1965), p. 74. *According to
family tradition, this desk was owned by Jedidiah Parker (born 1736) of Boston.*

laying strips of wood in a radiating pattern (fig. 17). String inlay was
an even more common decorative motif. John Mudge constructed
"a Case of dros and tabell stringed" in October, 1738, and a month
later made "a Case of drawers soled ends and stringed."[37] The earlier
reference suggests a matching high chest and dressing table with
string inlay. The latter may refer to a veneered high chest with solid
sides decorated with stringing.

Holmes's workmen enumerated only twelve other pieces of furniture in their bills. In 1737 Richard Woodward constructed wall
brackets and a bureau table (fig. 18).[38] His Boston colleague, Thomas

37. John Mudge to Nathaniel Holmes, Malden, Massachusetts, January 6, 1738,
55.524 (Winterthur Libraries, Joseph Downs Manuscript Collection).

38. This is one of the earliest references to an American bureau table. According to
Nancy Goyne Evans, the form did not become popular in New England until after
1750. Evidently Woodward constructed an elegant table, for he charged Holmes six
pounds, a sum equivalent to that for a large desk. Richard Woodward to Nathaniel
Holmes, Boston, VI, Accounts Current, December 12, 1737, Bourn Papers (Baker
Library, Harvard University). See also Nancy Goyne Evans, "The Bureau Table in
America," *Winterthur Portfolio III* (Winterthur, Delaware, 1967), pp. 25–27.

16. HIGH CHEST. Boston area, c. 1730–1750. Walnut and white pine; H. 89½
inches, W. 43¾ inches, D. 22 inches. (The Metropolitan Museum of Art, Gift of
Mrs. Russell Sage, 1909.) *This chest has carved and gilded shells, probably similar to the
type of work performed by William Randle for Nathaniel Holmes.*

17. HIGH CHEST. Eastern Massachusetts, c. 1730–1750. Walnut and white pine; H. 86⅛ inches, W. 43¾ inches, D. 23⅛ inches. (The Henry Francis du Pont Winterthur Museum.) *This chest is decorated with inlaid shells, probably similar to those set in by Richard Woodward.*

Johnson, made a tea chest and frame, a tankard board, and a double chest of drawers. None of Holmes's craftsmen working outside the city produced similar one-of-a-kind items.

These workmen charged Holmes for the amount of labor involved in making or assisting on a piece of furniture. A standard cost was often set for each form. Tables, for example, were priced according to their length. Richard Woodward charged eleven shillings per foot for tables in 1736. A year and a half later he demanded an extra shilling per foot, no doubt reflecting inflation in colonial Boston. The price of desks also varied according to size. John Mudge charged £2:10:0 for his standard desk and £1:1:0 for a smaller version. Any

18. BUREAU TABLE. Boston area, c. 1730–1750. Walnut and white pine; H. 31¼ inches, W. 33¾ inches, D. 19⅜ inches. (Gore Place Society, Waltham, Massachusetts: photo, Richard Cheek.) *This bureau table decorated with string inlay is representative of early bureau tables made in Boston during the 1730s and 1740s.*

ornamentation increased the cost. For a desk with pillared drawers, Mudge added two shillings to his standard sum. Veneering, a popular form of decoration on Boston furniture, increased the cost of construction. In 1734 Mudge built both solid wood and veneered chests of drawers. The price of the former amounted to £3:2:0 while the latter was £4:0:0. Occasionally the accounts refer to other details such as stringing, inlaid stars and shells, bracket feet, and toes.[39] These motifs varied greatly in price and probably were custom ordered.

Often a single object entailed the work of many craftsmen. According to the Holmes papers, a veneered high chest, similar to that made by Ebenezer Hartshorne (fig. 19), required the work of five men. Holmes himself supplied the lumber, brassware, and nails to a cabinetmaker who constructed the case. A turner furnished the cabinetmaker with drops, flame finials, and columns for the front of the chest. After the case was completed, a highly skilled craftsman inlaid the star and may have carved the two shells. Finally, a japanner put on the finishing touches by gilding the shells.

In summary, the papers of Nathaniel Holmes provide much important data on the cabinetmaking trade in the Boston area during the third decade of the eighteenth century. Although no extant furniture can be traced to Holmes or his workmen, the accounts attest to the quantity of their output. Hopefully, examples will be found, so that we may some day more accurately judge the skills of these men and the characteristics of their work.

No discussion of the furniture industry could be complete without considering the role of the upholsterer. During the eighteenth century the upholstery trade was deemed the most lucrative and prestigious craft profession. Its members not only made and sold bedding, bed curtains, and upholstered furniture, but also imported all types of textiles and dry goods for resale. Thomas Fitch and Samuel Grant were two of Boston's wealthiest upholsterers. A study of their

39. Toes probably refer to the unusual adaptation of the Spanish foot seen on the japanned high chest made by John Pimm (fig. 37). Similar feet appear on dressing tables at Historic Deerfield and the Museum of Fine Arts, Boston.

19. HIGH CHEST. Made by Ebenezer Hartshorne, Charlestown, 1739. Walnut and white pine; H. 90 inches, W. 41½ inches, D. 21½ inches. (Museum of Fine Arts, Boston, Julia Knight Fox Fund, 31.432.) *A chest such as this required the work of many craftsmen.*

careers demonstrates the reasons for their success as well as the activities and products of the upholsterer in colonial Boston.

The son of a local cordwainer, Thomas Fitch was born on February 5, 1669.[40] His father died when he was only nine. Apparently his mother apprenticed him to a Boston upholsterer, perhaps Edward Shippen, an eminent English-born merchant-upholsterer who moved to Philadelphia about 1688. Fitch later corresponded frequently with Shippen and often sold goods in Boston for his Pennsylvania friend. In 1694 he married Abiel Danforth, the daughter of the Reverend Samuel Danforth of Roxbury. During the following years he established a highly profitable upholstery business and became a respected man in the community. He held numerous public offices including selectman, moderator, town auditor, and representative to the General Court. His daughters married men of high standing. Martha married James Allen, a prosperous merchant, and Mary wedded Andrew Oliver, later a lieutenant governor of the colony. When Thomas Fitch died in 1736, he left a personal estate of £3388:8:11. He also owned several houses in Boston and thousands of acres in many newly established towns in Massachusetts.[41]

Fitch trained Samuel Grant in the upholstery trade.[42] Born in 1705, Samuel was the son of Joseph Grant, a local boat builder.[43] He married Elizabeth Cookson in 1729 and they raised six children over the next twenty-five years. Like his former master, Grant held several important town positions. Between 1747 and 1757 he served as town selectman, in 1768 as town moderator. At his death in 1784,

40. For genealogical material on Fitch, see Ezra S. Stearns, "The Descendants of Dea. Zachary Fitch of Reading," *New England Historical and Genealogical Register*, LV (July, 1901), 289, 291.

41. Fitch's immense estate was never completely settled. He owned land in forty towns in addition to all of Gallops Island. Suffolk Probate Records, docket 6868.

42. In a letter of October 20, 1725, Fitch described Grant as "my Young man," a phrase often used for an apprentice. Thomas Fitch to Silas Hooper, Boston, Fitch Letterbook (Massachusetts Historical Society).

43. For genealogical information on Grant, see W. Henry Grant, *Ancestors and Descendants of Moses Grant and Sarah Pierce* (Lebanon, Pennsylvania, n.d.), pp. 3, 9–10, 12.

he gave the bulk of his estate to Moses Grant, his only surviving son.[44]

Fortunately for historians of the decorative arts, several volumes of the account books and letterbooks of Thomas Fitch and Samuel Grant have survived.[45] With these documents it is possible to focus on the lives of two Boston upholsterers during the years 1720 to 1740. Fitch established an extensive trading network throughout the colonies, specializing in the distribution of English textiles. In addition, he sometimes imported other goods which might sell well in the colonies. In a letter to a New York merchant he stated that "besides all Sorts of Upholstery goods as rugs blank[e]ts quilts ticks broadstrip &c," he also offered for sale "a Pcill [Parcel] of Ironware and nails."[46] Further correspondence shows that Fitch sold spectacles, penknives, candlesticks, stockings, caps, clothing materials, and other dry goods to merchants in every coastal port from Halifax to the West Indies. To transport these goods he owned shares in several ships.

In addition to his mercantile pursuits, Fitch operated an upholstery shop where he or his workmen produced beds, bolsters, mattresses, curtains, and furniture. Some jobs were done for his clients in their

44. No inventory was taken of Grant's personal property and real estate. In his will he left £466:13:4 to his grandson, John Simpkins, £400 to his granddaughter, Mary Thatcher Simpkins, and cancelled the debts owed to him by his son-in-law, John Simpkins. The remainder of the bequest went to Moses Grant. Suffolk Probate Records, docket 18314.

45. The author is aware of ten volumes which span the first seventy years of the eighteenth century. For the purposes of this paper, only portions documenting business activities between 1720 and 1740 will be considered. See Thomas Fitch, Letterbook, 1702–1711 (American Antiquarian Society); Letterbook, 1714–1717 (New England Historic Genealogical Society); Letterbook, 1723–1733 (Massachusetts Historical Society); Account Book, 1719–1732 (Massachusetts Historical Society); Account Book, 1732–1736 (Massachusetts Historical Society); Samuel Grant, Account Book, 1728–1737 (Massachusetts Historical Society); Receipt Book, 1731–1740 (The Bostonian Society); Account Book, 1737–1760 (American Antiquarian Society); Petty Ledger, 1755–1762 (Boston Public Library); Petty Ledger, 1762–1771 (Boston Public Library).

46. Thomas Fitch to Isaac DeRiemer, Boston, August 7, 1704, Fitch Letterbook (American Antiquarian Society).

20. BED VALANCE. Salem or Boston, c. 1720–1740. English cheyney, w. 12½ inches. (Essex Institute, Salem, Massachusetts.)

homes. In 1724 he charged George Cradock £0:1:6 for "puting up a bedstd & Curts."[47] A year later Fitch completed the wallpapering of a room for John Jekyl. The cost was £2:12:9 for seventy-eight and a quarter yards of binding, papering tacks, and labor. Jekyl had purchased the paper himself and employed Fitch only to hang it.[48]

The great majority of Fitch's patrons were wealthy merchants, lawyers, and physicians of Boston, Newport, and New York. The list included John Read, Esquire, of Boston, Edmund Quincy, Esquire, of Braintree, Isaac Lopez of Newport, and William Beekman of New York. For such a prominent clientele, Fitch made every effort to provide fashionable furnishings. He sometimes wrote to his friends in England for patterns for bed hangings. In 1725 he instructed John East, an upholsterer in London, to "Get your best draughtsman to draw a few of ye newest fashion'd & pretty neat airy Val:ts [Valances] headcloths headboards & Testers and a cornish [cornice] or two: and ye figure of a counter pane if they are in fashion."[49] Several times in the next five years, Fitch requested additional patterns. In an illuminating letter on the taste of Bostonians, he asked

47. Thomas Fitch, Account Book, May 22, 1724, p. 281 (Massachusetts Historical Society).

48. Ibid., September 11, 1725, p. 351.

49. Thomas Fitch to John East, Boston, April 6, 1725, Fitch Letterbook (Massachusetts Historical Society).

East "to send me a pattern or figure of Fashionable Vallance & the figure of a headboard & headcloth done by some ingenious workman to be put on a flat headcloth & as the fashion I think is very plain, he may send some with a little more work, our people too generally choosing them somewhat showy."[50]

Fitch's letters explain the close similarity between English and American bed hangings. An example at the Essex Institute (fig. 20) resembles the end of a valance illustrated in a scene from *A Harlot's Progress* by William Hogarth (fig. 21). Another valance, originally

50. Ibid., December 8, 1731.

21. A HARLOT'S PROGRESS, plate II. Drawn and engraved by William Hogarth, London, 1732. Copperplate engraving; H. 11⅞ inches, w. 14⅝ inches (engraved surface only). (Museum of Fine Arts, Boston, Harvey D. Parker Collection, P11991.)

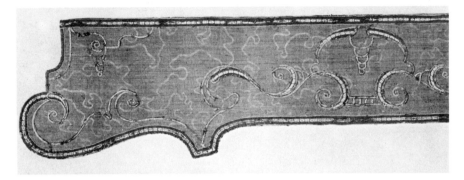

22. BED VALANCE. Boston area, c. 1730–1760. English harrateen; w. 13 inches. (Society for the Preservation of New England Antiquities.) *According to family tradition, this valance was owned by the Robbins family of Arlington and Lexington, Massachusetts.*

owned by the Robbins family of Lexington, Massachusetts (fig. 22), relates to an English example, also engraved by Hogarth in the two prints, *Before* and *After* (fig. 23). Such comparisons demonstrate the attempts of American upholsterers to follow English designs. Using imported fabrics and patterns, they were able to copy the most recent fashions in London.

Fitch occasionally collaborated with English upholsterers on elaborate bed hangings. A letter to Silas Hooper, a London merchant, in December, 1725, records the joint efforts of two men on different continents to complete a set of hangings:

Now I desire Yo to apply to some Upholder that's a neat Workman and get him to Match this Camblet very exactly with enough of it only for one sute of outside Vallane and to Cover one set of Cornishes, and make up the outside vall and Cover the Cornishes handsomely and fashionably, and cover the head board, wood head Cloth and Testr. with some . . . Satten and make the Inside Vall thereof, Let the whole be of a good Air or fancy for a room 10 feet high, and trim'd with the same lace of the Inclosed pattern packing up for me full Enough of the Same binding and breed suitable to finish ye Curtains bases and base moldings here.[51]

51. Ibid., Thomas Fitch to Silas Hooper, Boston, December 15, 1725.

23. BEFORE. Drawn and engraved by William Hogarth, London, 1736. Copperplate engraving; H. 14 11/16 inches, w. 11 15/16 inches (engraved surface only). (Colonial Williamsburg Foundation.)

Fitch intended to use this set of hangings as a model for another "sute of the Same which I shall wholly make up here."[52] Such lengthy correspondence suggests the importance of bed hangings in the eighteenth century. For Boston's gentry they provided a symbol of status

52. Ibid.

as well as comfort. Feather mattresses weighing up to sixty pounds, curtains with over thirty-five yards of expensive worsted material, and elaborately carved high-posted frames made beds the most costly objects in the colonial home.[53]

Fitch succeeded in business by capably serving an elite clientele. Evidence indicates that his apprentice, Samuel Grant, sought to do the same. In 1728 Grant had completed his indenture and was working at the Crown and Cushion in Union Street (fig. 24). Fitch helped him to begin business by selling him upholstery materials on credit. Of additional importance were the contacts that Grant had made while under his master's guidance. After his apprenticeship he patronized a London upholsterer used by Fitch, employed the same chairmaker to make bedsteads and chair frames, and sold goods to many of the same persons.[54] After his master's death in 1736, Grant, in effect, inherited both the business and reputation of Thomas Fitch.

The scale of his activity, however, never reached the magnitude of his master's enterprise. Grant never developed the extensive export trade which characterized Fitch's career. Perhaps increasing competition from Newport and New York merchants impeded his chances of success in the coastal business. More likely he simply lacked the capital to finance a complex mercantile operation.

Grant rarely imported his textiles directly from English merchants. Whereas Fitch had dealt with as many as five London factors at one time, Grant requested upholstery from only one man and, in this case, the orders were small. Without a far-reaching export trade, Grant had no means of repaying English merchants with goods marketable in London. Fitch had sent furs from New York, tar from the Carolinas, logwood and sugar from the West Indies, and whalebone to his factors in England. He also collected bills of exchange

---

53. Florence M. Montgomery, *Printed Textiles: English and American Cottons and Linens 1700–1850* (New York, 1970), pp. 49, 55–56.

54. The upholsterer was John East. See Samuel Grant, Account Book, April 11, 1735, p. 383 (Massachusetts Historical Society). The chairmaker was Edmund Perkins. See Thomas Fitch, Account Book, January 15, 1725, p. 312 (Massachusetts Historical Society); Samuel Grant, Account Book, February 12, 1730, p. 35 (Massachusetts Historical Society).

24. TRADE CARD OF SAMUEL GRANT. Attributed to Thomas Johnston, Boston, 1736. Restrike of copperplate engraving; H. 4 inches, W. 6⅜ inches (engraved surface only). (American Antiquarian Society.)

from merchants in other areas which helped to pay for English textiles sent to Boston. Grant, on the other hand, conducted a small export trade along the Atlantic Coast. His only major commodity for shipment to England was beeswax. Consequently, he was forced to rely on merchant-middlemen in Boston for most of his goods. During the year 1732, he purchased upholstery materials, garlits (a coarse linen), and calicoes valued at £1597 from Charles Apthorp, a leading local importer. He also dealt with James Allen, Fitch's son-in-law and a wealthy merchant, Jacob and John Wendell, two brothers in business together, and Samuel Cary, a ship captain. In repayment for textiles, these men accepted furniture and the services of an upholsterer. Between 1728 and 1740 Grant delivered 141 chairs to the Wendells, 214 to Apthorp, and 400 to Peter Faneuil, another prosperous importer. Most of these chairs were packed into boxes, loaded onto ships owned by the merchants, and sold at distant ports. Some were used to furnish ships' cabins, while others were requested by the merchants for their own homes or those of relatives and friends. In

1732 James Allen ordered a bed, couch, easy chair, and twelve leather chairs for delivery to his brother, Jeremy Allen.[55]

Grant's success as an upholsterer depended on his relationship with local merchants. From 1728 to 1740 his services were constantly in demand and, as a result, he never became a risk to his creditors. He profited by purchasing large quantities of textiles at wholesale prices and reselling them in small lots at higher rates. His charges for labor were minimal when compared to the costs of materials. On July 12, 1731, he billed Jacob and John Wendell for two easy chairs. The frames for each cost £1:17:6; the curled hair, feathers, linen ticking, and webbing for the understructure cost £2:5:8; the outer material and binding was £3:1:6; and the labor was £1:16:0.[56] The labor charge amounted to only one-sixth of the total. The labor charge for a pillow, mattress, or bolster was even less. Grant billed George Rogers £12 for feather bedding which cost only £0:5:0 to make.[57]

Besides describing the business activities of Thomas Fitch and Samuel Grant, the account books provide insights into the popularity, appearance, and style of textiles and furniture. English worsteds were by far the most common textiles used in home furnishings. During a four-year span between 1728 and 1732, Grant used cheyney, a coarse-grained or ribbed worsted, for about ninety percent of his curtains and chair coverings. Ten years later harrateen,[58] another worsted closely related to cheyney, superseded it. From 1738 to 1742 harrateen was employed for sixty percent of his furnishings. Cheyney dropped to about thirty percent during the same period and after 1742 disappeared almost altogether.

55. Samuel Grant, Account Book, February 4, 1732, p. 132 (Massachusetts Historical Society).

56. Ibid., July 12, 1731, p. 106.

57. Ibid., July 19, 1737, p. 590.

58. Harrateen had been in limited use in Boston from at least 1726. Thomas Fitch commented on the new fabric in that year, when he wrote to a patron in New York: "I concluded it would be difficult to get Such a Calliminco as you propos'd to Cover the Ease Chair, and haveing a very Strong thick Harratine which is vastly more fashionable and handsome than a Calliminco I have sent you an Ease Chair Cover'd w[i]th sd Harrateen w[hi]ch I hope will Sute You." Thomas Fitch to Madam Hooglant, Boston, March 9, 1726, Fitch Letterbook (Massachusetts Historical Society).

25. EASY CHAIR. Boston area, c. 1740–1765. Walnut, white pine, and English harrateen or moreen (original); H. 48 inches, W. 35¼ inches, D. 34 inches. (The Brooklyn Museum, Henry L. Batterman, Maria L. Emmons, and Charles Stewart Smith Memorial Funds.)

26. DETAIL OF THE BACK OF AN EASY CHAIR. Boston area, c. 1750–1770. Ma-
hogany, maple, and English harrateen or moreen (original); H. 46 inches, W. 33 inches,
D. 26 inches. (The Bayou Bend Collection of the Museum of Fine Arts, Houston.)
For an overall view of the chair, see *American Art: Furniture, Painting, and Silver in the
Bayou Bend Collection* (Houston, 1974), no. 89.

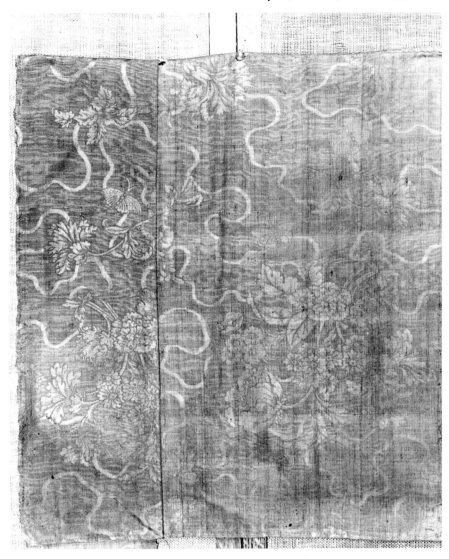

27. FRAGMENT OF A BED CURTAIN. Salem or Boston, c. 1750–1770. English harrateen or moreen. (Essex Institute, Salem, Massachusetts.) *According to family tradition, this curtain was owned by Daniel and Sarah Saunders of Salem who were married in 1770.*

28. ARMCHAIR. Boston area, c. 1710–1725. Maple, red oak, and Russian leather (original); H. 35⅛ inches, W. 24 inches, D. 27½ inches. (The Henry Francis du Pont Winterthur Museum.) *Chairs covered with Russian leather were often sold by Thomas Fitch before 1725.*

Today it is difficult to distinguish between these two fabrics. They are part of a group of heavy worsteds which include camlet and moreen. During the eighteenth century both were often decorated with watering, waving, and figuring (figs. 20 and 25). In watering, the cloth received a special preparation with water and then was passed under a hot press to give a smooth and glossy surface. Waving was done by rolling the cloth under an embossed cylinder to create a rippling design. Figuring was simply the stamping of flowers and figures onto the fabric by means of hot irons.[59] These impressed patterns can easily be seen on the back of an easy chair at Bayou Bend (fig. 26) and on a fragment of a bed curtain at the Essex Institute (fig. 27). Both examples are red or crimson, the most common color named by Grant; blue, green, and yellow followed in popularity.

Boston upholsterers often covered their chairs in leather. Fitch and Grant used Russian and New England leather. The first, imported into this country through England, was common during the early years of the eighteenth century, but by 1725 had become difficult to obtain. On June 26, 1727, Fitch wrote to a Colonel Coddington in Massachusetts that he had "no Rushia leather Chairs nor other, nor Leather to make them of. Russhia Leather is so very high at home that It wont answer, If I had any they would Certainly be att Your Service. I think Mr Downs has New England red Leather, but there's no Rushia in Town."[60]

After 1730 Boston craftsmen turned primarily to New England leather. This material was usually made of seal or goat skins. Grant imported hundreds of seal skins which he sold to Joseph Calef, a local tanner. The skins were dyed black or red, cut into the shape of chair seats, and returned to Grant.

The account books of Thomas Fitch and Samuel Grant are most helpful in describing the styles of chairs made in Boston between 1720 and 1740. On May 4, 1720, Fitch charged Isaac Lopez £16:2:0

---

59. Abbott Lowell Cummings, *Bed Hangings: A Treatise on Fabrics and Styles in the Curtaining of Beds 1650–1850* (Portland, Maine, 1961), p. 18.

60. Thomas Fitch to Colonel Coddington, Boston, June 26, 1727, Fitch Letterbook (Massachusetts Historical Society).

29. PAIR OF SIDE CHAIRS. Boston area, c. 1710–1750. Maple, oak, and leather (original); H. 44⅝ inches, W. 18¾ inches, D. 15 inches. (Private collection, Milwaukee, Wisconsin: photo, Ginsburg and Levy, Inc., New York City.) *Chairs of this type were sold by Thomas Fitch after 1724.*

for "12 carvd Russhia Leather chairs & 1 elbow [chair]."[61] The reference to carving suggests that these were in the William and Mary style. The large elbow chair may have been similar to an armchair in the Winterthur Museum which still retains its Russian leather upholstery (fig. 28). In 1724 Fitch began to sell crooked-back leather chairs without carving. These chairs, probably resembling a pair in a private collection (fig. 29), were often called Boston chairs and remained popular items for export during the following two decades.

61. Thomas Fitch, Account Book, May 4, 1720, p. 84 (Massachusetts Historical Society).

30. ARMCHAIR. New York, c. 1730–1750. Walnut and linen (not original); H. 36 inches, W. 26¼ inches, D. 23 inches. (The Henry Francis du Pont Winterthur Museum.) *This chair descended in the Tibbits family of New York. Chairs with similar round seats were sold by Samuel Grant in 1729.*

Furniture in the Queen Anne style was introduced during the late 1720s. On October 14, 1729, Grant sold an upholstered chair of red cheyney, described as "New fashion round seat."[62] Such a chair was probably related in form to an example attributed to New York (fig. 30). The round seat reflected an increasing emphasis on the curved line, a chief characteristic of the new style. In 1730 Grant recorded the sale of a couch frame with "horsebone feet."[63] Apparently the term referred to a cabriole leg, perhaps with a notch near the bottom of the back of the leg resembling the indentation just above a horse's hoof.[64] On January 22, 1732, Grant charged the mercantile firm of Clark and Kilby £12 for "6 Leath Chairs maple frames hosbone round feet & Cusn Seats."[65] These chairs presumably had cabriole legs, pad feet, and slip seats. It seems likely that they also had straight stiles, curved crest rails, and vase-shaped splats or banisters, as they were often called. Grant, in April, 1732, billed John Breck, a cooper in the North End, for "8 Leathr Chairs horsebone feet & banist[er] backs."[66] Such chairs, no doubt, resembled one illustrated in a portrait of *Mrs. Andrew Oliver and Son* (fig. 31) by John Smibert. This important painting of the daughter of Thomas Fitch was completed only two months after Grant first mentioned the term "banister."

Many examples of these Queen Anne chairs have survived. One with a history of ownership in the Boston area (fig. 32) is related in the shaping of the crest rail to Mrs. Oliver's chair. In later versions of the form, the crest dips in the center to form a yoke (fig. 33).

Between 1732 and 1740 Grant continued to produce leather-backed William and Mary chairs, upholstered armchairs with cheyney and harrateen coverings, and Queen Anne chairs with solid splats. Occa-

62. Samuel Grant, Account Book, October 14, 1729, p. 29 (Massachusetts Historical Society).

63. Ibid., November 21, 1730, p. 65.

64. This notch is often seen on Boston furniture of the Queen Anne style. See, for example, a japanned high chest in the collection of the New Haven Colony Historical Society. Elizabeth Rhoades and Brock Jobe, "Recent Discoveries in Boston Japanned Furniture," *Antiques*, CV (May, 1974), 1082–1091.

65. Samuel Grant, Account Book, January 22, 1732, p. 131 (Massachusetts Historical Society).

66. Ibid., April 29, 1732, p. 146.

31. MRS. ANDREW OLIVER AND SON. Painted by John Smibert, Boston, 1732. Oil on canvas; H. 50½ inches, w. 40½ inches (excluding frame). (Collection of Andrew Oliver, Jr., Daniel Oliver, and Ruth F. O. Evans: photo, Frick Art Reference Library.)

32. SIDE CHAIR. Boston area, c. 1730–1750. Walnut and maple; H. 44½ inches, w. 19¼ inches, D. 21½ inches. (The Bayou Bend Collection of the Museum of Fine Arts, Houston.) *This chair is identical to one in a private collection with a history of ownership in the Boston area.*

33. SIDE CHAIR. Boston, c. 1735–1760. Walnut; H. 40⅜ inches, W. 20⅜ inches, D. 16½ inches. (Museum of Fine Arts, Boston, Gift of Mr. and Mrs. Henry Herbert Edes, 36.21.) *According to family tradition, this chair was owned by John Leach (1724–1799) of Boston.*

34. SIDE CHAIR. Boston area, c. 1735–1760. Walnut and maple; H. 39¾ inches, w. 21½ inches, D. 16¼ inches. (Yale University Art Gallery, Mabel Brady Garvan Collection.) *According to family tradition, this chair was owned by Edward Holyoke, President of Harvard College from 1737 to 1769.*

sionally embellishments were added to these forms. In 1733 Grant sold some chairs with claw feet. A year later he first produced ones with compass-shaped seats (fig. 34). Throughout the later period, however, he presented no radical changes in style, evidence of the continued popularity of earlier forms in Boston.

This survey has focussed on Boston furniture craftsmen of the early eighteenth century and the objects they produced. In an industry with hundreds of workmen, many practiced specialized professions. Japanners, for example, were able to concentrate on the decoration of furniture and looking glasses, a very sophisticated specialty which required a large and wealthy clientele. No other city offered similar opportunities for specialization. Furthermore, as the Holmes accounts reveal, close contacts existed between rural and urban artisans in the Massachusetts Bay area, raising the question of how to discriminate between country and city cabinetwork. When men received materials from Boston, they may also have been given designs or patterns from their employer. Holmes provided sets of veneers to his workmen in Malden. These items, already cut into certain shapes, could easily have been used to build a standard chest or desk which differed little from Boston furniture. Perhaps with the discovery of more documented furniture from Boston and its environs, we may know how these rural examples compared with their urban counterparts.

The papers of Thomas Fitch and Samuel Grant attest to the importance of the upholsterer in colonial Boston. Both men supplied not only expensive and fashionable furnishings to wealthy patrons throughout Massachusetts but also cloth, metalwares, and a wide variety of other dry goods to shopkeepers and country traders. Their careers demonstrate the close connection between the merchant and upholstery trades. The study of eighteenth-century upholsterers, however, is just beginning. Much more data is needed on the less affluent workmen in Boston, Salem, Portsmouth, Newport, and other New England towns, before we can understand how Thomas Fitch and Samuel Grant compared in their craft activities and level of success with others in the upholstery trade.

Most importantly, this study has documented the genesis of the Queen Anne style in Boston. Grant first recorded the production of a chair with a round seat in 1729 and one with horsebone feet in 1732. In the same year, William Randle billed Nathaniel Holmes for japanning a pedimented high chest, the earliest reference to the new style in case furniture. The initial creations of horsebone feet and pedimented high chests were to flower in the following years into the sophisticated Queen Anne furniture for which Boston craftsmanship is famous.

◄● DEAN A. FALES, JR. ●►

Boston Japanned Furniture

T HE exoticism of the East has long whetted the imagination of Western man. In our early decorative arts, the colonies felt shimmers of the Orient through ceramics, textiles, furniture, and books. Whether these were actual productions of the East or not made little difference. Precision was not a requisite to the eighteenth-century mind when sublime remoteness could provide delight through flights of fancy.

In furniture, the true Oriental lacquerwork could not be produced in the West, but simplified imitations became popular in Holland and England by the end of the seventeenth century. In the 1700s, Indian work, or japanning as it became better known, spread to the colonies; Boston and New York became the major centers of this work. First prize goes to Boston, with over a dozen japanners working prior to the Revolution and with an array of varied examples of their works still preserved.[1]

Boston japanners simplified the European process in two ways. The base paints were applied directly over the wood, usually maple in casepieces and pine in clocks, rather than the paint being put over a layer of whiting which was used by the English and New Yorkers to fill in the surfaces of oak or other coarser-grained woods. In English

1. Gertrude Z. Thomas, "Lacquer: Chinese, Indian, 'Right' Japan, and American," *Antiques*, LXXIX (June, 1961), 572–575. For information on Boston japanning, see Joseph Downs, "American Japanned Furniture," *Old-Time New England*, XXVIII (October, 1937), 61–67; Esther Stevens Brazer, "The Early Boston Japanners," *Antiques*, XLIII (May, 1943), 208–211; Richard H. Randall, Jr., *American Furniture in the Museum of Fine Arts, Boston* (Boston, 1965), pp. 66–68; Dean A. Fales, Jr., *American Painted Furniture 1660–1880* (New York, 1972), pp. 58–69; and Sinclair Hitchings, "Thomas Johnston," *Boston Prints and Printmakers 1670–1775*, Colonial Society of Massachusetts, *Publications*, XLVI (1973), 83–131.

japanning the colors were transparent ones, with seed-lac varnish mixed in with the pigments.[2] The Boston japanner used plain oil colors and after raising his figures with whiting, a gesso-like material, gilded them with metallic powders or leaf, painted in details with lampblack, and then varnished the finished product. Interestingly enough, these colonial simplifications were frequently used in English japanned pieces during a later eighteenth-century revival of the art.

The designs themselves were delightful. Chinese buildings, bridges, faceless people, birds, and strange flora of all sorts mingled with griffins, fierce dragons, double-humped camels, unseaworthy boats, plodding wheelbarrows, and pompous horsemen in a scaleless world of make-believe. Many motifs reappear with much variation and little or no duplication on several pieces, but a careful examination of the decorations produces two distinct impressions: that with many qualified japanners working in Boston, it is virtually impossible to separate their work with few exceptions; and that a careful observer will ultimately be struck more by a strabismal myopia than by a pat set of attributions.

At the moment, there are less than half a dozen candidates for known examples by known japanners. The first, and most frustrating, is a tall case clock made by Benjamin Bagnall, formerly in the Philip L. Spalding Collection, bearing the engraved trade card of Thomas Johnston (also spelled Johnson).[3] The fact that the case has been refinished to its naked native pine tearfully removes it as the Rosetta Stone for Johnston's work.

The second example is a William and Mary style high chest of about 1720 at the Adams National Historic Site in Quincy, Massachusetts. The chest is signed by William Randle,[4] a Boston japanner,

2. Ralph Edwards, *The Shorter Dictionary of English Furniture* (London, 1964), pp. 327–331.

3. Illustrated in "Benjamin Bagnall of Boston, Clockmaker," *Old-Time New England*, xxvi (July, 1935), 31; and *Harvard Tercentenary Exhibition* (Cambridge, 1936), no. 257, pl. 46.

4. This high chest was brought to my attention after completion of the article. Richard H. Randall, Jr., discusses and illustrates the chest in "William Randall, Boston Japanner," *Antiques*, cv (May, 1974), 1127–1131.

who advertised in *The Boston News-Letter* of April 25 – May 2, 1715: "Looking-Glasses of all sorts, Glass Sconces, Cabbinetts Escrutoires Chests-of-Drawers, Tables, Beaufetts, Writing Desks, Bookcases with Desks, old Glasses new Silvered, and all sorts of Japan-work, Done and Sold by *William Randle* at the Sign of the Cabbinett, a Looking-Glass Shop in Queen-Street near the Town-House Boston." The Adams high chest has much of its original raised work on the drawers but contains some nineteenth-century overpainting on the moldings and legs. The large, prominent figures are not unlike those on other William and Mary high chests (fig. 44) or the Queen Anne high chest (fig. 35) signed by Robert Davis, another Boston japanner.

The Davis high chest, the third documented example of Boston japanning, is a flat-topped high chest of about 1735 with cabriole legs and pad feet in the collection of the Baltimore Museum of Art.[5] Unfortunately, the ravages of neglect and proximity to a fire have relieved the piece of all of its minor flat decoration, and only parts of its major scenes remain. The three-lobed plants, figures, and animals tie in with the vocabulary of other japanners; their boldness and larger scale are representative of the earlier Boston work before the 1740s. Another high chest that can be linked to Robert Davis, with similar decoration and even cabinetmaking details, was shown in *Antiques*, LXV (February, 1954), 103, and is now in the collection of the Shelburne Museum.

The other candidates are two tall case clocks by Gawen Brown, the japanning of which can be linked to Thomas Johnston by circumstantial evidence. The first, a magnificent example at Winterthur (fig. 36), is in an early style. Brown came to Boston in 1748, and one of his earliest advertisements in *The Boston Evening-Post* (January 16, 1749) stated: "That *Gawen Brown*, Clock and Watch Maker lately from *London*, keeps his Shop at Mr. *Johnson's*, Japanner, in *Brattle-*

---

5. Two signatures appear on one of the drawer dividers in the upper section. The featured one is "Robert Davis" and the other, in smaller script, appears to be "Re. Damini." The initials "W R," possibly those of William Randle, another Boston japanner, also appear on a drawer of the chest. This information was kindly provided by Brock Jobe. See Elizabeth Rhoades and Brock Jobe, "Recent Discoveries in Boston Japanned Furniture," *Antiques*, CV (May, 1974), 1082–1091.

35. HIGH CHEST. Japanned by Robert Davis, Boston, c. 1725–1739. Maple and white pine; H. 68⅞ inches, W. 41¾ inches, D. 22⅞ inches. (The Baltimore Museum of Art.)

36. TALL CLOCK. Works by Gawen Brown, japanning attributed to Thomas Johnston, Boston, c. 1749. White pine; H. 94½ inches, W. 22¼ inches, D. 10¾ inches. (The Henry Francis du Pont Winterthur Museum.)

Street, Boston, near Mr. *Cooper's* Meeting House, where he makes and sells all sorts of plain, repeating and astronomical Clocks, with Cases, plain, black Walnut, Mahogony or Japann'd."[6]

From this, it would appear that Johnston can be considered the japanner of the clock. The buildings, bridge, sultan, and equestrian figure do not appear with any real similarities on any Boston high chests, which have their own formulas for decoration. However, these clock motifs do appear in identical fashion on a rather disheveled case on another Gawen Brown clock at the Henry Ford Museum.[7] These are the only two pieces of Boston japanning I have been able to find with identical decoration throughout. Due to his importance, Johnston has been associated with other japanned pieces. The great high chest at Winterthur (fig. 37) made by the cabinetmaker John Pimm for Commodore Joshua Loring, probably the summit of American japanning, has been linked to Johnston without foundation.[8] It was undoubtedly japanned by the same unidentified person as the fine high chest at the Museum of Fine Arts, Boston, notable for the excellent condition of its decoration (fig. 38).

The 1732 Johnston trade card has also provided overoptimistic opportunities for attributions. The dropped finials of a flat-topped high chest at Winterthur (Downs, *American Furniture,* no. 187) have been likened to those on the trade card. Another group consists of two high chests with broken-arch tops at Bayou Bend (fig. 39) and the Metropolitan Museum of Art (fig. 40), both of which have cherubs in their upper sections. Cherubs also appear on the sign in Johnston's trade card. Unfortunately cherubic and finialistic hopes

6. For more information on Brown and a copy of the advertisement, see David Hansen, "Gawen Brown, Soldier and Clockmaker," *Old-Time New England,* xxx (July, 1939), 1–9.

7. See Helen Comstock, *American Furniture* (New York, 1962), fig. 187. The date 1766 on the Ford example appears to have been added to the nameplate, and the clock is probably earlier than this date—perhaps before 1752 when Brown had moved to King Street.

8. See Esther Stevens Fraser, "A Pedigreed Lacquered Highboy," *Antiques,* xv (May, 1929), 398–401; and Joseph Downs, *American Furniture, Queen Anne and Chippendale Periods in the Henry Francis du Pont Winterthur Museum* (New York, 1952), no. 188.

37. HIGH CHEST. Made by John Pimm, Boston, c. 1740–1750. Maple and white pine; H. 95¾ inches, W. 42 inches, D. 24½ inches. (The Henry Francis du Pont Winterthur Museum.) *According to family tradition, this chest was owned by Joshua Loring (1716–1781) of Jamaica Plain and Boston.*

38. HIGH CHEST. Boston area, c. 1725–1740. Maple and white pine; H. 71¾ inches, W. 42⅞ inches, D. 24¾ inches. (Museum of Fine Arts, Boston, Bequest of Charles Hitchcock Tyler, 32.227.)

do not make firm attributions, and these two high chests, one with a matching dressing table (fig. 41) and all with similar decoration to another matching flat-topped high chest and dressing table (figs. 42 and 43), must remain in the limbo of anonymity until more persuasive testimony is offered.

Other examples of Boston japanning include a six-legged William and Mary high chest with bold figures on a black ground at the Metropolitan Museum (fig. 44) and two similar six-leggers with more intricate decoration, one at Winterthur (much of its decoration gone), and one at Historic Deerfield, Inc. (fig. 45). Most of the earlier examples (to the 1730s) have black backgrounds, while the tortoiseshell grounds (black over red) became more popular in the 1740s and later. The motifs in the decoration tended to become smaller and fussier as time went on.

The sources of the designs in Boston japanning were many. Homage is always paid to Stalker and Parker, whose book *A Treatise of Japanning and Varnishing*, published in Oxford in 1688, was the first work devoted to the subject. Not only were twenty-four plates of chinoiserie motifs included, but the book also served as a basic painter's guide, its prose style being the most lively ever in the field. While it and several other books in the eighteenth century proclaimed the glories of japanning to Englishmen in Europe and America, it was through a vast number of imported pieces that the designs were spread.[9] A handsome japanned English ball-foot desk and bookcase owned by Governor James Bowdoin is at the Detroit Institute of Arts (figs. 46 and 47). English japanned looking glasses have been found locally, and English clocks with japanned cases owned in the Boston area include examples with works by James Atkinson, Edward Faulkner, Richard Motley, and Thomas Wagstaffe.[10] Imported

9. Other works include *The Ladies Amusement, or Whole Art of Japanning Made Easy* (London, n.d., c. 1760); and George Edwards and Mathias Darly, *New Book of Chinese Designs* (London, 1754).

10. For japanned English clocks with Boston-area histories, see *Antiques*, XLIII (May, 1943), 209; Martha Gandy Fales, "Thomas Wagstaffe, London Quaker Clockmaker," *The Connoisseur*, CLI (November, 1962), 198–201; and Wallace Nutting, *The Clock Book* (Framingham, Massachusetts, 1924), fig. 80.

39. HIGH CHEST. Boston area, c. 1730–1750. Maple and white pine; H. 92½ inches, W. 41 inches, D. 23 inches. (The Bayou Bend Collection of the Museum of Fine Arts, Houston.)

40. HIGH CHEST. Boston area, c. 1740–1750. Maple and white pine; H. 86¾ inches, W. 41 inches, D. 22 inches. (The Metropolitan Museum of Art, Pulitzer Fund, 1940.) *According to family tradition, this chest and matching dressing table (fig. 41) were owned by Benjamin Pickman (1708–1773) of Salem.*

japanned examples were advertised from 1716 on with some frequency.

The number of forms bearing japanned decoration and made in Boston exceed those of any other area in America. While only looking glass frames and clock cases are known in New York, Boston examples include these forms plus chests, high chests of drawers, dressing tables, and picture frames. The often cited advertisement of William Price in the April 4–11, 1726, *Boston Gazette* listed japanned chests of drawers, corner cupboards, large and small tea tables, etc., "*done after the best manner by one late from London.*" Thomas Johnston's 1732 trade card also lists japanned chests of drawers,

41. DRESSING TABLE. Boston area, c. 1740–1750. Maple and white pine; H. 30 inches, W. 33 ½ inches, D. 20¾ inches. (The Metropolitan Museum of Art, Pulitzer Fund, 1940.) *This table is a mate to the chest illustrated in fig. 40.*

42. HIGH CHEST. Boston area, c. 1730–1750. Maple and white pine; H. 70¼ inches, W. 40 inches, D. 21¾ inches. (The Metropolitan Museum of Art, Gift of Mrs. Russell Sage, 1910.)

43. DRESSING TABLE. Boston area, c. 1730–1750. Maple and white pine; H. 30½ inches, W. 34 inches, D. 21 inches. (The Metropolitan Museum of Art, Gift of Mrs. Russell Sage, 1910.)

chamber tables, tea tables, writing desks, and bookcases.[11] Japanned tea tables are listed in several Boston inventories and other advertisements, and surely a good maple example must yet lurk somewhere with its decoration largely intact.

Later japanning was done in Boston after the Revolution and into the nineteenth century, the figures not being raised and the decoration limpidly differing from the earlier work.[12] A single example to illustrate a revival of the earlier motifs is seen in a Queen Anne side

11. Thomas Johnston's trade card is reproduced in Hitchings, "Thomas Johnston," p. 87.

12. A good description of the earlier and later methods of japanning is found in [Thomas Dobson, comp.], *Encyclopaedia; Or A Dictionary of Arts, Sciences, and Miscellaneous Literature* (Philadelphia, 1798), IX, 72–76. For a later example with a Boston history, see *Antiques*, LXXXI (April, 1962), 346.

44. HIGH CHEST. Boston area, c. 1710–1725. Maple and white pine; H. 62½ inches, W. 39½ inches, D. 21¼ inches. (The Metropolitan Museum of Art, Pulitzer Fund, 1940.) *This chest descended in the Pickman family of Salem.*

45. HIGH CHEST. Boston area, c. 1710–1725. Maple and white pine; H. 67 inches, W. 40 inches, D. 22 inches. (Historic Deerfield, Inc., Deerfield, Massachusetts.)

chair in the Bayou Bend Collection (fig. 48). One of six (two at
Bayou Bend, two at Historic Deerfield, and two in the collection of
Mrs. Charles L. Bybee and the late Charles L. Bybee), this chair has
long been listed as being decorated later in China and owned in the
Winthrop-Blanchard families of Boston.[13] A study of the coat of
arms on the front seat rail shows that it is identical to that used by the
Boston merchant Samuel Pickering Gardner (1767–1843) on his
bookplate. Gardner was guardian to his grandniece, Eliza Blanchard,
after her parents died, and on March 12, 1832, she married Robert C.
Winthrop.[14] Thus, the family history works out; the watermark date
of 1809 on Gardner's bookplate, together with the wedding date,
provides a clue to the date of the decoration. The scenes on the splat
have the lustreless, stylized appearance of later decoration, and the
scrolls on the stiles and legs have much in common with borders of
early nineteenth-century Chinese porcelain made for the American
market. The decoration was done locally, however, and the chairs
did not enjoy the salt air of a trans-Pacific crossing. Other furniture
was frequently redecorated in the nineteenth century by coach painters, who became the later inheritors of the japanning tradition.

Boston japanning, then, continued for a century. Its heyday oc-
curred during a fifty-year period preceding the Revolution. Much
remains to be discovered about it. We should be on the lookout for
tea tables and regard looking glasses with caution, since most frames
were imported. They were made here, though, and japanner Stephen
Whiting's modest advertisement in the November 12, 1767, *Boston
News-Letter* states that he "*does more at present towards manufacturing
Looking-Glasses than any one in the Province, or perhaps on the Continent.*"

The japanning itself should be examined carefully, since it and the
flat gilt decoration have frequently undergone overhelpful meta-
morphoses at the hands of later restorers and improvers. When working with documents, we should remember that furniture japanning

13. Comstock, *American Furniture*, fig. 174.
14. See Lawrence Shaw Mayo, *The Winthrop Family in America* (Boston, 1948);
Frank Augustine Gardner, *Gardner Memorial* (Salem, 1933).

46. DESK AND BOOKCASE. England, c. 1700–1725. H. 90 inches, W. 39 inches, D. 23 ¾ inches. (The Detroit Institute of Arts, Gift of Mrs. Lendall Pitts.) See also fig. 47. *According to family tradition, Governor James Bowdoin (1726–1790) of Boston presented this desk and bookcase to his niece Elizabeth Pitts when she married Jonathan Warner of Portsmouth, New Hampshire, in 1781.*

was only a part of a japanner's output, and that iron, tinware, and clock faces were japanned by most of them frequently. Also, in inventory listings of craftsmen's possessions, when a japanned something is listed, that does not mean everything in the listing is japanned!

47. INTERIOR OF DESK AND BOOKCASE. England. (The Detroit Institute of Arts, Gift of Mrs. Lendall Pitts.) See also fig. 46.

48. SIDE CHAIR. Boston, c. 1730–1760, japanning added c. 1800–1820. Walnut and maple; H. 39¾ inches, W. 20½ inches, D. 20½ inches. (The Bayou Bend Collection of the Museum of Fine Arts, Houston.) *This chair was owned by Samuel Pickering Gardner (1767–1843) of Boston and later by his grandniece Eliza Blanchard.*

While this article has dealt with japanning in its strictest sense, we should not forget the early simpler painted furniture influenced by it. The so-called "Harvard" chests of eastern Massachusetts and the painted casepieces from the Windsor, Connecticut, area owe much to the japanner's art, which truly spiced many colonial homes with delicious whiffs of the distant East.[15]

15. See Fales, *American Painted Furniture*, pp. 36–38; 62.

SINCLAIR H. HITCHINGS

Boston's Colonial Japanners: The Documentary Record

FOR decades, scholars have been looking with fascination at co-lonial japanned furniture made in Boston. They have lavished attention on these pieces, elegant or gaudy, according to your eye, and their writings have expressed a deep yearning to know who decorated them. As so often happens, history has not been co-opera-tive. No one, in the past, has been able to combine documentary evidence and decorative detail to form vocabularies of ornament and technique attributable to individual japanners. Because the yearning for identification was very great, and because much is known about one Boston japanner, Thomas Johnston,[1] a number of examples of japanning were attributed to him, often with the wistful suggestion that a detail of his engraved trade card of 1732, showing a shop sign and lettering listing his skills and wares, might be identified with a detail of a particular piece of furniture. There might have been at least a shred of plausibility to these identifications if Johnston had been a carver or joiner who might, at one time, have fashioned an elaborate shop sign with his own hands. He is first identified in Bos-ton records, however, as a painter-stainer and later, almost invari-ably, as a japanner. He was also a printmaker, painter of coats of arms, and organ-builder. During the past four decades, discussions of Bos-ton japanning in books and articles have been peppered with "pos-siblys" and "probablys": "probably by Thomas Johnston"; "a pos-

1. For more information on Johnston, see Sinclair Hitchings, "Thomas Johnston," *Boston Prints and Printmakers 1670–1775*, Colonial Society of Massachusetts, *Publications*, XLVI (1973), 83–131.

sible William Randle piece"; "perhaps japanned by Robert Davis"; "perhaps by Nehemiah Partridge." Refreshingly, Dean Fales has reined in the adverbs. He is less interested in attributions than in telling what really is known.

Documentary information, meanwhile, continues to surface. In the light of our inability to identify most pieces of colonial japanning as the work of a particular man, we need this information badly; and I suspect we will soon go beyond quoting it and will try to bring together and print a substantial amount of it in one place.

Our list of Boston's colonial japanners is still primarily the list painstakingly put together and published by Esther Stevens Brazer in her May, 1943, article in *Antiques*: Nehemiah Partridge, active in Boston between 1712 and 1714 and later living in Portsmouth, New Hampshire; William Randle, active in Boston beginning in 1714 and apparently for more than four decades following; Joshua Roberts, who died in Boston in 1719; Robert Davis, who died in Boston in 1739; Thomas Johnston, active from the late 1720s to his death in 1767, and his son-in-law, Daniel Rea, Jr., who bought out the business and continued it into the nineteenth century; Johnston's sons, Thomas, Jr., John, and Benjamin, who for a time worked in the family business and were described as japanners by occupation; two people who advertised that they taught japanning, John Waghorne in 1740 and Mrs. Heller in 1755; David Mason, who opened his shop in Boston in 1758; and both Stephen Whiting, Sr., active between 1743 and 1773, and his son Stephen, Jr., active between 1767 and 1773. Three additional names discovered after the appearance of Esther Brazer's article are Roger Pendleton, who died in 1712; Robert Hughes, active in 1726; and John Gore, who worked as a japanner, painter, and "colour merchant" from about 1740 to 1796.[2] The list

2. For information on Pendleton, see Suffolk County Registry of Probate, Boston, Massachusetts, docket 3380; *The Diary of Samuel Sewall*, Massachusetts Historical Society, *Collections*, 5th ser., VI (1879), 333. For Hughes, see the 1726 volume of the records of the Suffolk County Inferior Court of Common Pleas, Boston, Massachusetts, pp. 45, 171. For references to Gore as a japanner, see Suffolk County Registry of Deeds, Boston, Massachusetts, LXXIV, 173–174, 200. See also George Francis Dow, *The Arts and Crafts in New England 1704–1775* (1927; rpt. New York,

also includes William Price, who from my own study of his career did not himself practice japanning but had associations with two japanners, Robert Davis and Thomas Johnston. Price, who sold japanned furniture along with maps, views, looking glasses, spy glasses, toys, and musical instruments, is one of the key figures in the study of the arts and crafts of Boston after 1720.

We know a good deal about Price and a great deal about Johnston, and more information about them comes to light every year. We know remarkably little about the others.

Pursuing the possibilities of documentary evidence, let me suggest five kinds of documents which yield, or might yield, valuable facts about japanned furniture made in colonial Boston.

First, in terms of abundance of detail, are the inventories of the japanners. "The Boston probate records," wrote Esther Brazer in a sentence which some scholars probably can quote from memory, "are a fertile field for information concerning the early japanners, since virtually all of them died insolvent or intestate." We have the inventories of Joshua Roberts, who died in 1719; of Robert Davis, who died in 1739; and of Thomas Johnston, who died in 1767. All contain detailed listings of tools and materials. The Roberts and Davis inventories are quoted in Brazer's *Antiques* article of 1943; the Johnston inventory is printed in full in the Colonial Society of Massachusetts' volume, *Boston Prints and Printmakers 1670–1775*, pages 126–128.

A second major source are account books, the ones with which I am familiar being the accounts of the Johnston & Rea decorating business. There are ten volumes of these, from 1764 to 1802, in the Baker Library at Harvard Business School. They have been extensively mined,[3] and it would be surprising if, in the next few years, at long last, they were not transcribed and printed to join the easily available sources in all major libraries. In the accounts, I have found

---

1967), pp. 239–243; William Whitmore, *A Brief Genealogy of the Gore Family Especially in the Line of Gov. Christopher Gore* (Boston, 1875), pp. 5–6.

3. Various details are quoted, for instance, in Mabel M. Swan's article, "The Johnstons and the Reas—Japanners," *Antiques*, XLIII (May, 1943), 211–213.

no references to the japanning of chests, clocks, or other pieces, but frequent entries in several volumes refer to the japanning of compass boxes. At first I thought of these as boxes with japanned decorations, but Martha Gandy Fales suggests that they were simply painted black or dark green, the base colors of japanning. They would then have been varnished, making them waterproof and more durable. She owns a ship's compass in a wooden box painted blackish-green, along with a large triangular sextant-box painted black. The varnish on both boxes has long since disappeared, and the paint, as on other such boxes she has seen, has come to look as if it had been through a fire. She points out that this description of the japanning of the boxes would fit what is known of japanned metal work. A number of metal workers advertised japanning, and their surviving products are painted black, dark green, and occasionally red or blue, without decorations. An example is the japanning of clock dials.

Third, among documentary sources, are bills and receipts. Four splendidly detailed bills from Thomas Johnston to several customers are in the Massachusetts Historical Society. Two of them, one dated in 1746 and 1747, the other covering work done in 1754–1756, mention japanning: of compass boxes by the dozens, of a spy glass in one entry, and of two large prospect glasses in another. In addition, the making of a new foot for a clock case is listed, as is the "Japaning Cleaning & pollishing" of it.

My fourth category of documentary evidence is the voluminous surviving record of court cases. We might hear of japanning—in fact, we do, briefly—in these records. The Johnstons of Boston were litigious Yankees, sometimes suing, more often being sued; there are records of no fewer than eleven suits involving Thomas Johnston, Sr., and his sons Thomas, Jr., and Benjamin. The elder Johnston in various cases is described as "Japanner"; Benjamin is called "Painter-stainer" and "Japanner"; Thomas, Jr., is called "Gentleman" and "Japanner." There are no other references to japanning. Benjamin, incidentally, was living in Salem in 1763–1764 at the time of two of the suits concerning him. The records of these cases are in the offices of the Clerk of the Superior Court in the Suffolk County Courthouse.

Fifth and finally, there is a "possible." We might have mention of japanning in letters, though not in my personal knowledge. We come close in a long letter of May 4, 1770 (owned by the Massachusetts Historical Society), from William Johnston in Barbados to John Singleton Copley in Boston. Johnston included a recipe for boiling oil. As one of the sons of Thomas Johnston, and a graduate of the family business (he went on to become a limner and organist), he knew what he was talking about.

To turn very briefly from manuscript evidence to the printed word, familiar and easily available newspaper advertisements suggest to me the picture of shops in which ready-made japanned furniture was an eye-catching feature. No record of a bill or receipt for major pieces of japanned furniture, either ready-made or made to order, has come to my attention. To have such a bill, coupled with the piece itself, would be ideal; but perhaps we should be grateful for a documentary record more extensive than the record available to past generations. The record as we know it suggests to me that the application of decoration to japanned furniture was, like the making of other decorative details, a secondary craft which would seldom be occasion for signed work. Cabinetmakers were the real builders of furniture, after all. They often signed their handiwork, and their individual craftsmanship will continue to be identified. In contrast, I doubt if we shall ever be able to point to more than a few examples of japanning and say, this is by Johnston or Davis or Partridge or Randle or Roberts. We haven't even reached that level of variety and certainty, yet. As more pieces of the puzzle are found and fitted, from study of the furniture itself and of surviving documents and printed advertisements, we should be able to establish that sound, though still modest, working knowledge.

◆ MARGARETTA MARKLE LOVELL ◆

Boston Blockfront Furniture

The arts are undeniably forwarder in Massachusetts-Bay, than either in Pensylvania or New York. The public buildings are more elegant; and there is a more general turn for music, painting, and the belles lettres.[1]

THUS Andrew Burnaby, Vicar of Greenwich, England, described Boston in 1760. He was impressed by the gentle elegance and artistic temper of the inhabitants. Among these was a group of wealthy merchants whose impressive fortunes were often reflected in a fine domestic display. The home of such a merchant, obviously a composite of native craftsmanship and imported wares, is described by John Adams in 1766: "Dined at Mr. Nick Boylstones. . . . Went over the House to view the Furniture, which alone cost a thousand Pounds sterling. A Seat it is for a noble Man, a Prince. The Turkey Carpets, the painted Hangings, the Marble Tables, the rich Beds with crimson Damask Curtains and Counterpins, the beautiful Chimny Clock, the Spacious Garden, are the most magnificent of any Thing I have ever seen."[2]

Mr. Boylston and his peers surrounded themselves with articles in the latest fashion, and the ruling fashion in Boston, from about 1730 until 1765, was the style known today as Queen Anne. This style is best described by its noted proponent, William Hogarth: "There is scarce a room in any house whatever, where one does not see the waving-line employ'd in some way or other. How inelegant would the shapes of all our moveables be without it? how very plain and

1. Andrew Burnaby, *Travels Through the Middle Settlements in North-America in the Years 1759 and 1760*, 2nd ed. (1775: rpt. Ithaca, New York, 1960), p. 101.
2. *Diary and Autobiography of John Adams*, ed. L. H. Butterfield, 4 vols. (Cambridge, 1961), I, 294.

unornamental the mouldings of cornices, and chimney-pieces, without the variety introduced by the *ogee* member, which is entirely composed of waving-lines."[3]

The elegance and variety Hogarth associates with the "waving-line" in *The Analysis of Beauty* is introduced by the curve and reverse curve of the vertical façade blocks in blockfront case furniture. It is possible, moreover, that ogee[4] or "OG" was one term used in the eighteenth century to refer to this design.[5]

In origin and feeling, the Queen Anne style might be called "bourgeois baroque." It is the Basilica of St. Peter at Rome domesticated, diminished, yet retaining a basic reliance upon sweeping curves, focussed and symmetrical movement. Blockfront furniture is characterized by richness, rationality, classic proportions, and an uncompromising symmetry. Spiritually antithetical as this style might appear, the Bostonians adopted and metamorphosed it into something

3. William Hogarth, *The Analysis of Beauty*, ed. Joseph Burke (Oxford, 1955), p. 65. First published in 1753.

4. "Ogee" (or "OG"), according to the *Oxford English Dictionary*, is a term of obscure derivation which was defined in eighteenth-century England as "a Moulding, somewhat resembling an S" (T.N. *City and C. Purchaser*), or more generally "Any curve or line having this form."

5. In Newport cabinetmaker John Cahoone's account book (Newport Historical Society), it appears from the prices paid for such items as "a mahogany OG Case of Draws" (mentioned on p. 38, 1754, and on p. 83, 1759)—being as much as half again as much as items listed as "a mahogany case of drawers"—they must have been singular in more than the moldings used. An oxbow or breasted front might be equally described by the general term "OG" but the blockfront, being by far the most common at that time, is more likely. No labelled furniture is known from the workshop of Cahoone or from those of the cabinetmakers employed by him. Another term which may have been used to describe the blockfront is "swell'd." In a letter of 1763 (quoted by R. Peter Mooz, in "The Origins of Newport Block-Front Furniture Design," *Antiques*, xcix [June, 1971], 882), John Goddard of Newport writes to a patron: "there is a sort which is called a Chest on Chest of Drawers & Sweld. front which are Costly as well as ornamental. . . ." Similarly, Thomas Wood of Charlestown, Massachusetts, used this term in his 1776 claim for restitution of property damaged by the British: "Three swell front Desks" (Mabel M. Swan, "Furnituremakers of Charlestown," *Antiques*, xlvi [October, 1944], 204). Although "blocked" is the usual modern term applied to these façades, other terms have been applied. For instance, Percy Macquoid in his *History of English Furniture*, 4 vols. (London, 1906), iii, 49–52, figs. 39, 40, speaks of a (probably Boston) desk with "tubbed and recessed surfaces."

native, comfortable, and harmonious with their lives. This style of furniture captured the imagination of New England cabinetmakers and their wealthier patrons for almost a hundred years. And judging from the number of surviving examples, blockfronts seem to have been made in great numbers.

Massachusetts blockfront furniture was made both in the urban center—Boston proper and Charlestown—and in the outlying regions of Salem, Beverly, and Concord. Its period of popularity almost spanned the century—from the 1730s until 1800, long outliving the period of Queen Anne dominance in high-style design. The blockfront appears not to have been the invention and hallmark of a single shop or cabinetmaker; it was a form which was known and imitated by many workmen. Given the number of blockfronts made, the paucity of documented examples is surprising. Their makers have remained in most cases anonymous, but half a dozen important examples are signed, or bear histories of family ownership.

The several hundred extant examples of Boston blockfronts exhibit a wide variety of forms and a healthy tendency toward experimentation on the part of the makers, yet there are certain features which are constant and which justify furniture historians in calling the Boston-area cabinetmakers a unified "school." Materials, methods of case construction, methods of drawer construction, types of carving, varieties of feet, and decorative and design motifs are all fairly predictable within a wide range of design possibilities.

The alternate raising and depressing of vertical façade panels, which has come to be called "blocking," serves no functional purpose. Since such a façade is time-consuming and difficult to construct, as well as wasteful of expensive mahogany, it may be assumed that these desks, chests of drawers, and dressing tables were destined for the homes of the style-conscious upper sort—the prosperous merchants and men of affairs. As little documentary evidence pertaining to the sale of blockfront furniture is known, it is difficult to assess how much more costly these items were than ordinary flat-façaded pieces; however, it is not unreasonable to assume that this large-scale decorative device cost the patron half or two-thirds again the price of the plain item (see fn. 5). That these showpieces were made for the Boston area's most prominent citizens is attested by two documented examples—a desk bought by the wealthy merchant Josiah Quincy (fig. 91), and a high chest bought as a bridal gift for William Emerson, the prestigious clergyman of Concord and grandfather of Ralph Waldo Emerson (fig. 90).

Boston blockfronts have been largely ignored by furniture historians, partly because of a lack of such documents as account books and signed examples, but principally because they have been overshadowed by the more aesthetically impressive, better documented,

49. CHEST OF DRAWERS. Made by John Townsend, Newport, Rhode Island, 1765. Mahogany and tulipwood; H. 34½ inches, W. 36¾ inches, D. 19 inches. (The Metropolitan Museum of Art, Rogers Fund, 1927.) *A typical Newport chest.*

more sought-after examples of the Newport school. Blockfronts appear to have been made in limited numbers as far afield as Delaware and Virginia but their principal centers of production were Boston and Newport, Rhode Island (and its stylistic satellite, Connecticut). A concerted effort has not heretofore been made to identify the characteristics of these two major regional styles, and to differentiate between them.

The blockfronts of Boston differ from those of Newport not only in exterior decorative elements and design features but also in standard methods of internal construction. It has long been recognized that the hallmark of Newport façades—the shell which terminates the blocking—is not found in Boston workmanship. Similarly, the rococo decorative carving used on such Boston blockfronts as the

50. CHEST OF DRAWERS. Boston area, c. 1750–1790. Mahogany and white pine; H. 35¼ inches, w. 40 inches, D. 22½ inches. (The Henry Francis du Pont Winterthur Museum.) *A typical Boston chest.*

51. DETAIL OF A NEWPORT CHEST OF DRAWERS.
This drawing shows the typical top molding, visible dovetail joint between drawer divider and side, and carved shell.

52. DETAIL OF A BOSTON CHEST OF DRAWERS
This drawing shows the typical top molding, the strip covering the joint between drawer divider and side, and more unusual feature—a run-through drawer divide (found on the Job Coit desk and bookcase [fig. 62] and the Joseph Hosmer high chest [fig. 90]).

Quincy desk and bookcase does not appear in Newport design. Scholars have also recognized that the two-tiered organization of Boston desk interiors is radically different from the Newport variety. The more elusive internal habits of construction have been little explored, however, and have not been considered in conjunction with design motifs.

In composition the Boston façades are much more linear and vertical than the curving modulations of the self-contained Newport blockfronts (figs. 49 and 50). The complicated top molding which frames the Newport composition and refers the eye back to the base molding has no counterpart in the light, perfunctory, terminating horizontal of Boston chests of drawers (figs. 51 and 52). As dissimilar in structure as in design, the two tops are secured in place by radically different methods. The Boston top is rather summarily jointed to the side, occasionally accompanied by an external supporting fillet. In the Newport design this fillet grows into a well-articulated molding which bands the front as well as the sides of the chest. The added height of this cove permits the Newport cabinetmaker to add two internal supporting horizontals (fig. 53) which anchor the top by means of neat dovetailed "keys," the rear one visible from the back (fig. 54). This arrangement has no counterpart in Boston construction, where the top is usually grooved from front to back to accept the side pieces (fig. 55).

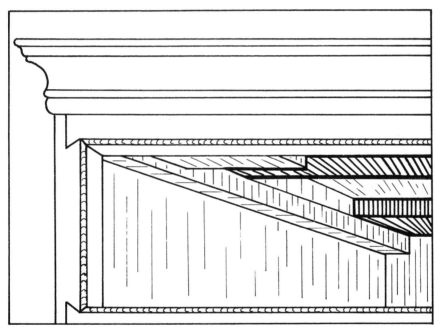

53. DETAIL OF A NEWPORT CHEST. *This drawing shows the two interior horizontal pieces of secondary wood running from side to side which secure the top.*

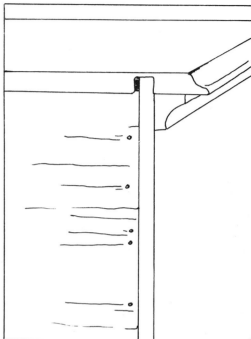

54. DETAIL OF THE BACK OF A NEWPORT CHEST. *This drawing shows the distinctive "key" which secures the top in place, joining it to the back and to the secondary elements.*

55. DETAIL OF THE BACK OF A BOSTON CHEST. *This drawing shows the usual means of fastening the top to the side and a more uncommon feature—an external fillet below the top.*

The case bottoms are constructed with an equally marked difference (figs. 56 and 57). In Boston blockfronts the strip of mahogany from which the bottom molding is carved is secured to the secondary piece of wood on a flush plane by means of a large central dovetail behind the central concavity. In Newport, on the other hand, the piece of mahogany from which the wide base molding is carved is quite straight. Although it may have a thin supporting bar of secondary wood behind, the piece which forms the actual bottom is found at least two inches below the top of the mahogany molding, and lacks the distinctive Boston giant dovetail.

One curious feature in the otherwise meticulous design and con-

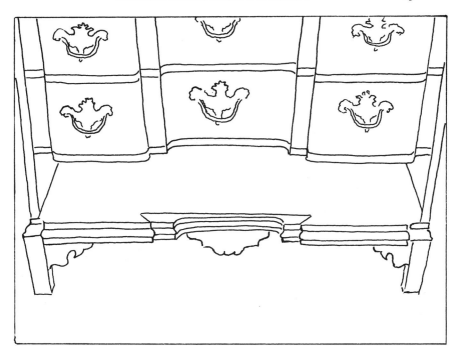

56. DETAIL OF A NEWPORT CHEST WITH BOTTOM DRAWER REMOVED.
This drawing shows the typical form of case construction (horizontal mahogany strip behind the molding is flat in back and occasionally is supported by a small strip of secondary wood; case bottom is about two inches below the top edge of the molding).

struction practices of Newport cabinetmakers is their use of visible dovetails to fasten the drawer dividers to the sides of the case (fig. 58). Perhaps it was precisely a matter of pride in their tightness of construction which prompted this practice. It is, however, a motif which appears too often and under too many names to be the idiosyncrasy of one man or one shop.[6] Boston cabinetmakers, on the

6. The labelled John Townsend desk (Israel Sack, Inc., New York), the labelled Edmund Townsend kneehole bureau (Museum of Fine Arts, Boston), and flat-façaded chests of drawers signed by Constant Bailey (in a private collection, North Carolina) and Benjamin Baker (Newport Restoration Foundation) all display this characteristic.

other hand, follow the usual British procedure of tacking a thin strip of mahogany the length of the side piece covering the joints (fig. 59). Occasionally, as in the Job Coit desk and bookcase (fig. 62) and in less distinguished pieces of Boston furniture, the drawer dividers run clear through the front edge of the side boards and are visible from the sides of the case whether or not the façade strip is present.

Drawer construction also differs. In Newport the dovetails often have very thin necks, and the drawer bottoms run through the side, sandwiched in place by applied runners (fig. 58). In Boston, however, the dovetails present a much less military aspect and the drawer runs on the edge of the drawer side or on an applied runner; the drawer bottom is usually contained by the drawer side (fig. 59).

The feet found on Boston casepieces are much more varied than those found on Newport designs. The typical Boston foot, a sturdy vertical bracket (fig. 61), complements the design above, just as the swelling, involuted Newport ogee foot does its composition (fig.

57. Detail of a Boston Chest with Bottom Drawer Removed. *This drawing shows the typical form of case construction (mahogany molding joins flush with case bottom in a "giant dovetail" pattern).*

ERRATUM

The illustration accompanying caption
number 56 should be reversed with
that accompanying caption number 57.

58. DETAIL OF NEWPORT CASE AND DRAWER CONSTRUCTION. *This drawing shows the typical form of drawer construction (the end of the drawer bottom is often visible from the side, with a runner applied beneath), and visible joint between drawer divider and case side.*

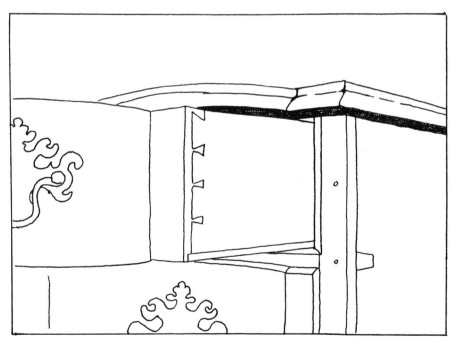

59. DETAIL OF BOSTON CASE AND DRAWER CONSTRUCTION. *This drawing shows the typical form of drawer construction (the end of the drawer bottom is not visible from the side; a runner is often applied beneath), and strip covering joint between drawer divider and case side.*

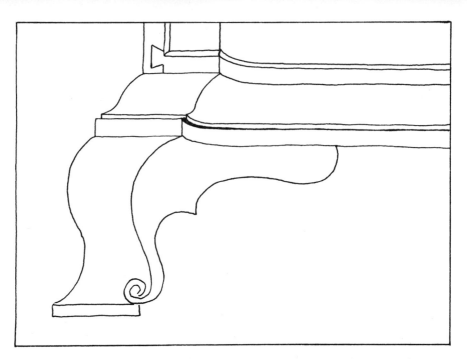

60. DETAIL OF THE TYPICAL NEWPORT FOOT. *Ogee curved feet are seen in the Boston area only on occasional pieces of Salem origin (fig. 89) which show a considerable Newport influence in several other features of design and construction.*

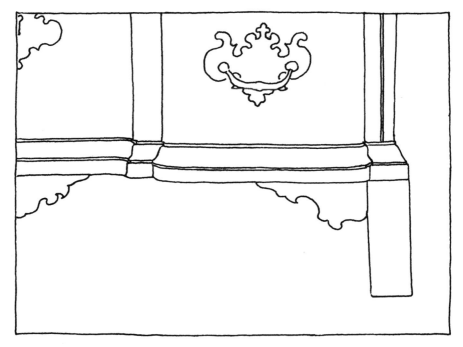

61. DETAIL OF THE BOSTON FOOT OF THE STRAIGHT BRACKET TYPE. *Very common, this type of foot is almost as popular in Boston blockfronts as the ornamental claw and ball foot. A central drop is also a Boston feature.*

60). Often, however, Boston cabinetmakers indulged in ornately carved feet, usually claw and ball, calling attention to this member in a way that would be inconsistent with Newport principles of design. Midway between the feet an ornate decorative drop often punctuates the lower outline of Boston desks and chests of drawers.

The intention of these observations is to clarify some regional characteristics and to point to earmarks by which one may ascertain the origin of specific blockfronts. Those made in Marblehead, Concord, Charlestown, and other towns in the Boston district follow the pattern of that city's construction and design. Those made in rural Rhode Island and Connecticut (and, incidentally, Delaware) follow the pattern of Newport design.[7] Curiously, there is a group of desks from Salem which has as much in common in terms of design and construction with Newport as with Boston. (They will be discussed in detail below.) This unexpected fact brings up the question of regional characteristics—their adoption by whole schools of cabinetmakers and their distribution in that city's shopping sphere. The phenomenon of regional characteristics is as yet little understood. Starting with signed and documented examples, however, one may at first determine and later check the structural rules and common secondary woods of a given district,[8] and then trace the migration of craft practices and design motifs. The consistency with which Boston cabinetmakers used such visible motifs as the thin flat top piece on chests, dark mahogany, and such structural elements as the oversize dovetail for the bottom of the case points to a high degree of communication and exchange between competitors, or perhaps to the

7. A blockfront desk with a history of ownership in Delaware, and probable manufacture in that state, is at Colonial Williamsburg. Although unorthodox in many of its details, the case construction is similar to that used in Newport.

8. Secondary woods are typically white pine for Boston, and chestnut or tulipwood for Newport. Newporters also generally favored a lighter tone to the mahogany in their façades. James Birket in *Some Cursory Remarks Made . . . in his Voyage to North America 1750–1751*, ed. Charles M. Andrews (New Haven, 1916), p. 24, noted of Boston in 1750, "but now their woods are very much Cut down and destroy'd and what they have is brought along way by land Carriage." It seems reasonable to assume that the omnipresent white pine in Boston is a matter of choice as much as of convenience.

importance of apprenticeship training in forming both design and habits of construction. This predictability of motifs is particularly remarkable in Boston where extensive experimentation with the possibilities of the blockfront form produced more than a dozen distinct types. Apparently, the artificer's imagination worked within a distinct and predictable set of habits.

While the Newport form of blockfront tends toward repetition of an established formula, the Boston type shows a wide spectrum of variants. Perhaps this fertile experimentation is the greatest virtue of Boston's blockfront designs. Of the hundreds of cabinetmakers who worked in Boston during the eighteenth century, many probably made blockfronts, although only seven are known by signed or documented examples.

The earliest dated example of American blockfront furniture is the desk and bookcase signed by Job Coit and by Job Coit, Jr., and dated 1738 (fig. 62).[9] It is of black walnut with secondary woods of northeastern white pine and sugar pine, executed in a polished but not extraordinary manner. Its ambitious monumental design is composed of a blocked lower façade with unusual rounded elements terminating the blocking, and an upper section with mirrored doors. The arching pediment and the cupped inlaid fans on the interior of the bookcase complement the rounded blocking below and unify the composition (fig. 63).

Not a great deal is known about the important Coit family of cabinetmakers. Their marriage and apprenticeship connections link them to several cabinetmakers whose blockfront work is known by signed examples. Yet the records are fragmentary.[10] Job's son, Captain Job Coit (1717–1745), who worked on this desk with his father, is a significant figure in the family. He married Rebecca Parkman (1696–1788), first cousin to the wealthy and influential cabinetmaker and merchant William Parkman. Young Coit was engaged in the

9. See Nancy Goyne Evans, "The Genealogy of a Bookcase Desk," *Winterthur Portfolio 9* (Charlottesville, Virginia, 1974), pp. 213–222.

10. Job Coit, Sr., was born in 1692, and is known to have been working in Boston by 1718. His business was located on Ann Street in 1731, and he died in 1742.

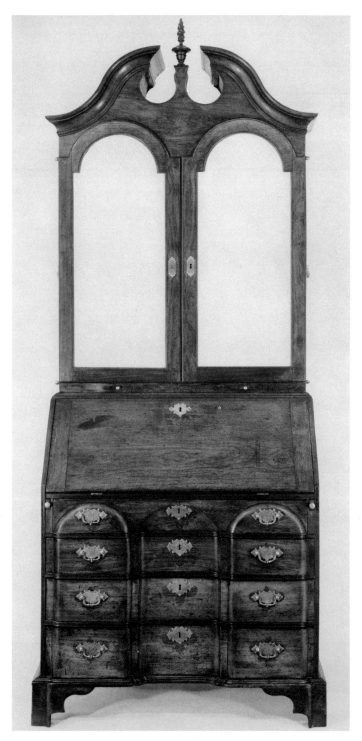

62. DESK AND BOOKCASE. Made by Job Coit and Job Coit, Jr.,
Boston, 1738. Walnut, white pine, and sugar pine; H. 99½ inches,
W. 39⅝ inches, D. 24⅜ inches. (The Henry Francis du Pont Winterthur Museum.) See also figs. 63 and 64. *This desk and bookcase was
probably constructed for Daniel Henchman (1689–1761), a stationer and
merchant of Boston. One of the few blockfronts with rounded elements capping the blocking, this example is the earliest known blockfront.*

63. INTERIOR OF DESK AND BOOKCASE. Made by Job Coit and Job Coit, Jr.
(The Henry Francis du Pont Winterthur Museum.) See also figs. 62 and 64.
The bookcase section displays inlaid fans.

West Indian trade and may well have seen Spanish or French architecture or furniture ornamented with undulating façades in his travels.[11] He was lost at sea returning from the West Indies in 1745,[12] and
his widow married Jeremiah Townsend, perukemaker of Boston and
New Haven.[13] Jeremiah was not related to the Newport cabinetmaking Townsends,[14] but his family had intermarried with the
Charlestown cabinetmaking Frothinghams. Three years later, Rebecca Parkman Coit Townsend's sister-in-law, Elizabeth Coit (youn-
gest daughter of Job Coit), married John Ingraham of New Haven.[15]
Two pieces of furniture, a mahogany table and a blockfront desk,
are branded "J. S. INGRAHAM" and may have been made by this
John Ingraham.[16] He may have been a cabinetmaker apprenticed to
or associated with the Coits as this marriage suggests. These marriage
connections with Parkmans, Frothinghams, and Ingrahams demonstrate wide-ranging alliances within the cabinetmaking trade which
Brock Jobe sees as a prerequisite to success in eighteenth-century
Boston (see pp. 11–12). They also suggest connections through which
design ideas were transmitted from shop to shop.

The Coit desk and bookcase is the earliest landmark, yet known, in
American blockfront history. Before the recent discovery of this desk
and its signature, credit for the formulation and development of the

11. It has been thought that the West Indies in general, and Havana in particular,
were a source for baroque-inspired blockfronted pieces in North America. Wendell
Garrett, "Speculations on the Rhode Island Block-Front in 1928," *Antiques*, XCIX
(June, 1971), 887–891. There are other closer and earlier precedents than the Havana
cathedral furniture, but the idea might well have migrated from Europe via the West
Indies as easily as via Great Britain.

12. Charles Townsend, *1375 to 1897: The Direct Ancestry and Posterity of Judge
Charles Townsend, A Pioneer of Buffalo, New York* (Orange, New Jersey, 1897), p.
29; Charles Townsend Rich, *Genealogy of the Townsend Family* (Buffalo, 1877), p. 17.

13. Jeremiah must have known Rebecca before she was widowed, as he removed
from Boston to New Haven in 1739 and she was not widowed until 1745.

14. The Newport Townsends spring from a triumvirate of brothers, John, Henry,
and Richard, of Norfolk, England; the Boston Townsends trace their lineage to
Thomas of Gedding, Suffolk.

15. Ingraham still owned property in Boston until 1752. See the settlement of the
estate of Lydia Coit, Suffolk County Registry of Probate, Boston, Massachusetts,
docket 9797 (hereafter Suffolk Probate Records).

16. The former is on loan to the Museum of Fine Arts, Boston; the latter is at
Historic Deerfield.

blockfront style was given to Newport—a center which was not to become important in blockfront history until thirty years after the date of this desk.[17] That this is indeed not only the earliest example known but also is probably one of the earliest examples made is indicated by internal evidence. There are elements of both design and cabinetwork that point to a struggle on the part of the maker with a new idea. It is difficult to say whether the artificer is paraphrasing a design idea which he has seen in passing or formulating his own design, but it seems likely, from some awkwardness in execution, that the former is the case.

Although the design is quite harmonious and successfully complex, the general level of finesse in the construction of this desk is rather mediocre. There are, for example, protruding drawer dividers, visible from the sides, very abbreviated columns on the document drawers, and rather perfunctory drawer construction throughout. Most significantly there seems to have been an on-the-job struggle between the cabinetmaker and his material in the crucial matter of the blocking. The line of the blocking along the bottom molding where the walnut meets the secondary wood behind has been changed and adjusted to accommodate a change in design or a faulty initial cutting (fig. 64). In either case, the craftsman is evidently not working from a familiar template, but struggling with the blocking as he works. This construction of the case bottom is not seen in other examples.

No other signed examples of Job Coit or Job Coit, Jr.'s work are known although there are several idiosyncratic earmarks both of design and construction which may point to reasonable attributions. Principally the rounded elements capping the blocks and the unusual

17. See the frontispiece of *Antiques*, LXXXVI (October, 1964), 430–431; also Mooz, "Origins of Newport Block-Front Furniture Design," pp. 882–886. The men who are known to have made blockfronts, John Townsend, Edmund Townsend, and probably John Goddard, were not born until 1733, 1736, and 1724, respectively. There is no evidence that the older generation, Christopher and Job Townsend, made blockfronts.

64. Detail of Desk and Bookcase Showing Unusual Case Construction. Made by Job Coit and Job Coit, Jr. (The Henry Francis du Pont Winterthur Museum.) See also figs. 62 and 63. *This case lacks the typical Boston "giant dovetail" seen in fig. 57. The shaping of the bottom contour has been recut and the design adjusted for a smaller central concavity.*

lack of the Boston giant dovetail on the bottom of the case separate this desk from other known blockfronts.[18]

One piece of furniture which might be very tenuously connected with the shop of Job Coit is a small dressing table at Winterthur (fig. 65). On the back panel of this dressing table is a bold inscription, "Cushing" (fig. 66). The Cushings were an influential mercantile family in eighteenth-century Boston, and Thomas Cushing, Jr., is known to have bought furniture from Job Coit, cabinetmaker, in 1739, the approximate date of this dressing table.[19] Although this speculation is very tenuous indeed (Cushing also patronized Thomas Sherburne, cabinetmaker, and Nathaniel Holmes, joiner), it is not altogether impossible. This dressing table belongs to a small group of related examples which evidently spring from the same source, all demonstrating a high quality of design.

18. The drawer construction and protruding drawer dividers are unusual but not unknown in Boston. The distinctive solution to the problem of joining the walnut frame to the secondary wood on the case bottom is not used in other examples known to the author.

19. Thomas Cushing, Jr., Waste Book, September 8, 1739 (Baker Library, Harvard University).

The Cushing family dressing table is one of the most successful blockfront designs. The interplay and repetition of curves, so characteristic of the Queen Anne period, are calculated to give stature and cohesion to this rather diminutive dressing table. Each curve is scribed in one plane, and then another, and then in three dimensions. It is a very sophisticated piece of furniture, and it is astonishing to find such a fully developed design in what appears to be a very early example.

A related example at Winterthur utilizes a flattened form of blocking (fig. 67). As this and the above example have almost identical dovetailing on the drawers, and are constructed in the same peculiar manner (i.e., with the use of wooden pegs), it is probable that they

65. DRESSING TABLE. Boston area, c. 1730–1750. Walnut and white pine; H. 31⅛ inches, W. 33⅝ inches, D. 21¾ inches. (The Henry Francis du Pont Winterthur Museum.) See also fig. 66. *One of a group of handsomely designed tables, this may be from the Coit workshop.*

66. Detail of the Inscription "Cushing" Appearing on the Back of the Dressing Table in fig. 65. Boston area. (The Henry Francis du Pont Winterthur Museum.) *Thomas Cushing, Jr., is known to have been a patron of Job Coit.*

67. Dressing Table. Boston area, c. 1730–1750. Walnut and white pine; H. 32¼ inches, W. 36¼ inches, D. 21¼ inches. (The Henry Francis du Pont Winterthur Museum.)

68. DRESSING TABLE. Made by Joseph Davis, Boston area, c. 1730–1750. Walnut and white pine; H. 30 inches, W. 35¾ inches, D. 22¾ inches. (Dietrich Brothers Americana Corporation: photo, Israel Sack, Inc., New York City.) *This boldly ornamented blockfront was made by an apprentice of Job Coit.*

were made in the same shop or by close associates.[20] This close similarity is important to point out as it has been suggested that there is a regional, qualitative, or chronological difference between examples employing "rounded" and "flat" blocking. Obviously these two types were coexistent variants.

A dressing table which is related to figure 67 is illustrated in figure 68. It is an unusual and ambitious although disjointed design, and bears the signature of Joseph Davis in chalk on the bottom of a

20. Pegs anchoring a mortise and tenon joint are uncommon at this date (c. 1740) in an urban area and a Queen Anne design.

69. RECEIPT SIGNED BY JOSEPH DAVIS INDICATING HIS APPRENTICESHIP
TO JOB COIT. Boston, 1726. (The Henry Francis du Pont Winterthur Museum
Libraries.)

drawer. A Joseph Davis served as an apprentice to Job Coit as is
attested by a signed receipt:

Received of Joseph Baxter of Medfield for my Master Mr Job Coit eight
pounds, and Fifteen shillings for work done by my Master, and is in full
of all accounts. I say received

By me
[signed]
Joseph Davis

Boston Febr: 3 d. 1725/6[21]

The signature on the receipt (see fig. 69) and the signature on the
drawer bottom are alike, establishing this piece as the work of Job

21. 63 × 69 (Henry Francis du Pont Winterthur Museum Libraries, Joseph Downs
Manuscript Collection).

Coit's apprentice. Although its overall effect is distinctly different, certain decorative motifs on this walnut dressing table point to a relationship with the Coit desk and bookcase. The rudimentary columnar motifs, used on the document drawers of the Coit desk, here assume a major role on the façade. Still lacking the footing and capitals which seem to be required by the fluted shaft, their rather embarrassed interpretation of classicism dominates the façade. The top of the dressing table is inlaid with a central star and corner darts which recall the inlaid fans on the interior of the Coit bookcase.[22]

Joseph Davis must have been nearing the termination of his apprenticeship when he received the payment in 1726 for Coit's work, for he was married on January 1, 1728, to Sarah Parsons of Gloucester. He was working on his own as a cabinetmaker in Boston in March of 1733, but there is no further record of his residence in Suffolk County after this date.[23]

The Coit-Davis relationship is the only known case in this period in which the work of a master craftsman and his apprentice are known by signed examples. That they were pioneers in the long-lived tradition of blockfront design cannot be doubted, although there were probably quite a few other Boston-area cabinetmakers experimenting with the form concurrently. The shortcomings in their cabinetwork and their difficulties with design may perhaps be excused in consideration of the early date of their work. However, there are contemporary Boston examples which achieve technical and aesthetic excellence (figs. 70 and 71).[24] What other cabinetmak-

22. There is a small group of related examples. See Frances Clary Morse, *Furniture of the Olden Times*, 2nd ed. (New York, 1917), p. 34. A high chest illustrated in *Antiques*, C (July, 1971), 13, has similar decorative motifs.

23. There is, however, one reference to a Joseph Davis in 1742 who is paid five shillings by Katherine Davis, widow and executrix of James Davis, a blockmaker of Boston. This list of disbursements also includes three pounds paid to Job Coit for a coffin. Suffolk Probate Records, docket 6911.

24. There is an unblocked Boston desk and bookcase at the Museum of Fine Arts, Boston (figs. 70 and 71), roughly contemporary with the Coit-Davis products, which possibly shows the very finest of contemporary cabinetwork—that which served as their model. Several design motifs which are executed here are abbreviated by Coit

ers Coit could have trained remains a matter of speculation, but it might be inferred that the movement toward stylistic and technical excellence in blockfront design is not to be looked for in the work of Joseph Davis. His work exhibits the tendency toward abbreviation and strange invention which is the mark of country and simple city furniture. The products of succeeding generations of Boston cabinet-makers show a conscious stylishness, a studied use of "correct" classi-cism, curves and proportion which indicate an antecedent more sophisticated than Davis.

Unfortunately, most of the makers of Boston blockfronts did not sign their products. Nor did they leave such notations on appropriate case parts as "bottom," "left side," "center front," which enable the patient student of calligraphy to sort out the makers of Newport blockfronts. Perhaps the lack of these notations (omnipresent in Newport work) indicates a smaller shop unit in Boston where such communication with fellow-workmen was unnecessary.

Despite the paucity of dated examples of Boston blockfronts after the 1738 Coit desk and bookcase, the many types fall into distinct groups which can be arranged—on the basis of stylistic features—into a roughly chronological sequence. Some—like the above—can be connected to a single shop or area. Others were made by many different known craftsmen, and still other groups are completely anonymous.

One of the most unusual of the anonymous groups of Boston blockfronts is the chest-on-chest illustrated in figure 72. Its distin-guishing features are a curious pediment, old-fashioned chest of drawers-with-doors upper section, and uncommon secondary woods

---

and Davis: the inlaid stars (in the M.F.A. desk, in tricolor and two parts; in the Davis, simplified), the fans above the bookcase section (in the M.F.A. desk, carved in undu-lating three dimensions; in the Coit, flattened in inlay), the scribe line around the bonnet (in the M.F.A. desk, in two-color inlay; in the Coit, a simple incised line), the amphitheater desk interior (greatly simplified in the Coit), and the round-capped recessed interior blocking (in the M.F.A. desk, a minor feature; in the Coit, the central feature).

70. DESK AND BOOKCASE. Boston, c. 1720–1740. Walnut, white pine, and maple; H. 88½ inches, W. 29⅝ inches, D. 20½ inches. (Museum of Fine Arts, Boston, M. and M. Karolik Collection, 39.176.) See also fig. 71. *This desk and bookcase descended in the Avery, Greenough, and Townsend families of Boston. It exhibits motifs such as the inlaid "compasses" which are found in abbreviated form on the top of the contemporary Joseph Davis dressing table.*

71. INTERIOR OF DESK AND BOOKCASE. Boston. (Museum of Fine Arts, Boston, M. and M. Karolik Collection, 39.176.) See also fig. 70. *Such motifs as the shells above the bookcase section and the fluted pilasters in the desk interior are found in abbreviated form in the contemporary Coit desk and bookcase.*

72. CHEST-ON-CHEST. Boston area, c. 1730–1750. Mahogany and red cedar; H. 87 inches, w. 42½ inches, D. 21½ inches. (Ginsburg and Levy, Inc., New York City.) *The sweeping bonnet and the doors in front of drawers in the upper section mark this group of chests as unusual and early.*

73. DESK AND BOOKCASE. England, c. 1710. H. 104 inches, W. 42 inches, D. 25 inches. (City Art Gallery, Bristol, England.) *This English desk with its curving pediment and recessed indentation in the lower section may be related to such American blockfronts as that illustrated in fig. 72.*

74. Chest-on-Chest. Attributed to Nathaniel Treadwell, Beverly, Massachusetts,
c. 1780–1800. Mahogany and white pine; H. 92 inches, W. 42½ inches, D. 24 inches.
(Yale University Art Gallery, Mabel Brady Garvan Collection.) See also fig. 75. *This
popular design was produced throughout the Boston area.*

75. DETAIL OF TREADWELL STAMP ON CHEST-ON-CHEST. Attributed to Nathaniel Treadwell. (Yale University Art Gallery, Mabel Brady Garvan Collection.) See also fig. 74.

(figs. 72 and 96). There are three known examples of this type.[25] The use of doors in front of the upper set of drawers and the presence of a very baroque pediment imply an early date—probably the 1740s.

One might doubt the American origin of a chest with such a pediment, or the Boston provenance with cedar and oak substituted for the more habitual white pine secondary wood, but there is good evidence that this group of chests is indeed a Boston product. The construction is that of Boston, with the giant lower-frame dovetail and the run-through drawer dividers. And the design elements, including stiff bracket feet and central ornamental drop, are certainly Boston characteristics. Although two of the chests have lost their pre-twentieth-century history, the one at John S. Walton, Inc., New York, is said to have descended in the Green family of Boston.[26]

25. They are owned by Yale, Ginsburg and Levy, Inc., New York, and John S. Walton, Inc., New York. They are made of mahogany or walnut with unusual secondary woods: the Ginsburg and Levy interior is red cedar, Yale's is white oak and chestnut. Walton's has the usual white pine, but lacks the doors over the upper set of drawers. The Ginsburg and Levy chest has mirrored doors, a drop below the bottom front, and a molding between the top and bottom halves; the other two lack these additions. A similar example with inlaid stars, side columns, and a bonnet top is owned by the Henry Ford Museum.

26. "It is thought by the family that this piece was made for Dr. John Sprague of Dedham, and it is known to have descended in the Swett and Green families. Samuel Swett, of Boston, married Elizabeth Sprague in 1800." Letter to the author from Hazel Kimball of John Walton, Inc., March 2, 1973.

One might be led to suspect that the heavy baroque pediment with its rich curves is Continental in inspiration, perhaps Dutch. However, the closest parallel to this form is found in England. A desk at the Bristol City Art Gallery, said to be English, c. 1710, shows a rudimentary form of blocking in the bottom section and a rich undulating pediment above the doors (fig. 73). It is not unlike the three Boston "baroque" pedimented chests, although not an exact prototype.

In this unusual form may be seen a principle of Boston design which distinctly separates it from Newport work. The bottom section is blocked in a tripartite three-dimensional façade, while the top section is quite flat and linear (except in the capping elements), and follows a design pattern independent of the bottom section. This division between halves does not occur in Newport; there the design motifs echo and refer back to one another throughout the composition. In Boston there is a seemingly determined juxtaposition of linear with plastic elements, of top with bottom section.

There is another, later, distinctive group of chest-on-chests in which the blocked lower chest supports a flat-fronted series of drawers above (figs. 74–77). These upper drawers are flanked by fluted pilasters and are capped by three smaller drawers whose line echoes the curving pediment. Quite a few examples of this design survive; it seems to have been a popular solution to the problem of elegant storage. Although one might at first assume that this design type was characteristic of a single craftsman, examples do not derive from a single shop or even a single town. They represent the efforts of at least four cabinetmakers working north of Boston in such disparate areas as Charlestown, Marblehead, Salem, and Beverly. This fact is significant in view of the standard method of furniture attribution which tends to see similarities or identities of design as an indication of the work of one workman. This is a more appropriate procedure in rural areas where individual idiosyncrasies in detail, proportion, and design are fostered by isolation. But in the urban environment such similarities are no sure guide to a single source. A good businessman evidently kept his eye on his neighbor's successful wares and adopted them when the public showed enthusiasm.[27]

One of the chest-on-chests of this type is in a private collection and bears the label of Benjamin Frothingham whose shop was in Charlestown (fig. 1).[28] Frothingham descended from a prosperous family of chaise- and coachmakers. The products of his cabinetshop are well known today because quite a few pieces of furniture—tables, desks, high chests, both flat and blocked—bear his label. The practice of labelling furniture was not common in Boston. A label was apparently both a guarantee of quality and an advertising device, especially for furniture shipped as venture cargo. As his work is identifiable, Frothingham's name is well known and anonymous products are often attributed to his workshop.

As close as the privately owned Frothingham chest-on-chest is to the similar example in the Garvan Collection (fig. 74), however, it is likely that the latter is the work of Nathaniel Treadwell of Beverly.[29] It is stamped "TREADWELL" five times on the interior structural members (fig. 75).[30] The Treadwell name is considerably more obscure in American cabinetmaking history than that of Frothingham. Treadwell's interpretation of the typical Boston-area chest-on-chest appears somewhat narrower in the top section than the other two examples illustrated here: he has widened the pilasters and emphasized the upsweeping line of the cornice. It is, however, a well-proportioned interpretation of this familiar design.

Another little-known maker of a chest in this style is Abraham

27. As the chest-on-chests in this form are approximately of the same vintage, the link between the makers is more likely to be a matter of style distribution than of apprenticeship.

28. There were three cabinetmakers of this name, living respectively 1708–1765, 1734–1809, and 1774–1832. The label on this chest is that of the second of the name. See Thomas B. Wyman, *The Genealogies and Estates of Charlestown*, 2 vols. (Boston, 1879), I, 381–395.

29. According to a checklist of cabinetmakers in the American Decorative Arts Department, Museum of Fine Arts, Boston, Treadwell was working in Beverly in 1799.

30. Stamping, although known in France, is uncommon in America until the late eighteenth century when it was used by French emigré cabinetmakers and Windsor chairmakers to identify their widely distributed wares.

76. CHEST-ON-CHEST. Attributed to Abraham Watson, Salem, c. 1770–1780.
Mahogany and white pine; H. 84 inches, W. 42 inches, D. 15½ inches. (Private
collection: photo, Samuel Chamberlain.) *This chest descended in the family of Abraham Watson. One of two surviving pieces by this maker, the chest shows a classic formula
with inventive detail.*

Watson of Salem (fig. 76).[31] Although the chest-on-chest presently in a private collection in Salem is not signed by Watson, its history of descent in the Watson family and its fabrication for the cabinetmaker's own use support this attribution.[32] It deviates from the archetypal model of this form in small irregularities in the pediment area, but its overall design is the same.

One of the handsomest examples of this form is that in the Museum of Fine Arts, Boston (fig. 77). It is unsigned and may be the product of a cabinetmaker as yet unknown. However, its striking resemblance and nearly identical measurements in the upper chest to the doubly signed Ebenezer Martin and Nathan Bowen oxbow chest-on-chest (fig. 95) indicate that its source may well have been the Marblehead workshop of Bowen and Martin.[33]

The form of chest-on-chest seen in the previous four examples is particularly Boston in flavor. It combines a blocked lower chest with a flat-façaded upper chest of drawers yoked across the top by a beaded drawer outline and contained within pilasters. A stiffly carved fan and swan's neck pediment complete the decoration of the upper case. Such a composition harmoniously unites diverse, almost antithetical elements. When the form first appeared is not known, but Watson is said to have made his chest for his new house in 1770. Frothingham worked until 1809, and Treadwell's only known date is 1799. Thus the style spans the last quarter of the eighteenth century and probably intrudes into the nineteenth.[34] This extreme conservatism—the clinging to a vital high-style aesthetic formula considerably beyond its

31. Watson was working between 1737 and 1762 and possibly to 1790. See Dean A. Fales, Jr., *Essex County Furniture: Documented Treasures from Local Collections 1660–1860* (Salem, Massachusetts, 1965), fig. 44; Benno M. Forman, "Salem Tradesmen and Craftsmen Circa 1762: A Contemporary Document," *Essex Institute Historical Collections*, CVII (January, 1971), 65, 73.

32. Samuel Chamberlain, *Salem Interiors: Two Centuries of New England Taste and Decoration* (New York, 1950), p. 85; Fales, *Essex County Furniture*, fig. 44.

33. Richard H. Randall, Jr., *American Furniture in the Museum of Fine Arts, Boston* (Boston, 1965), fig. 41.

34. A blockfront chest-on-chest signed by Nathan Bowen of Marblehead and dated 1774 fits into this period as well. See Richard H. Randall, Jr., "An Eighteenth Century Partnership," *The Art Quarterly*, XXIII (Summer, 1960), 153–161.

ostensible period—is perhaps indicative of the gradual waning of Boston as a commercial giant and generative style center in favor of the newly wealthy towns of New York and Baltimore. However, the documentation of these four chests is most important as a testament of the multiplicity of producers and widespread popularity of a single form throughout the Boston area.[35]

Boston was a foremost mercantile city during the long era of blockfront popularity, so it is not surprising that some of the finest blockfront casepieces are desks. These richly grained mahogany sculpturesque desks often stand on bold claw and ball feet, and imply by their grand scale of design the worldly competence and solidity of Boston's successful citizenry. This class of blockfront, the Boston slant-lid desk, was apparently made in large numbers and many survive. Most have been found in the vicinity of Boston, but it is evident that they were also shipped outside the immediate area. A walnut desk of this type on cyma bracket feet was located in Maine before the close of the eighteenth century—as the inscriptions by members of the Wasgatt family of Mount Desert attest.[36] But both the histories and the makers of most of the Boston desks exemplified by figures 80 and 81 are obscure.

One prominent exception to the general anonymity of this form is a large, handsomely figured mahogany desk on hairy paw feet in the Historic Deerfield Collection (figs. 78, 168, and 169). It is labelled by the celebrated Benjamin Frothingham (fig. 79). Although the desk has been restored,[37] it is essentially in its eighteenth-century guise and may serve as an introduction to the others of its type. All of these desks are very well made with neat, tight dovetails, boldly

35. Another of the many examples of this form is to be found in the Bennington Museum, Bennington, Vermont.

36. It bears the names "E. Wasgatt," "Sarah Hayes Wasgatt," and "Mary Wasgatt." They were the daughters of Thomas Wasgatt of Maine; "E. Wasgatt," Eunice, married David Bradstreet of Mount Desert in 1792, so this desk must predate that marriage. It is now in the Garvan Collection at Yale.

37. The fall front and central interior fan-carved door are new, the bottom of the case has been replaced in part (the front four inches are new). The brasses have been changed twice.

77. CHEST-ON-CHEST. Marblehead, Massachusetts, area, c. 1760–1790. Mahogany
and white pine; H. 91½ inches, W. 41½ inches, D. 24⅞ inches. (Museum of Fine Arts,
Boston, Bequest of Mrs. Sarah W. Whitman, 04.1727.) *The visual discontinuity between
the upper and lower sections of this chest is typical of Boston-area design.*

78. DESK. Made by Benjamin Frothingham (paper label), Charlestown, c. 1755–1790. Mahogany and white pine; H. 49½ inches, W. 45½ inches, D. 25½ inches. (Historic Deerfield, Inc., Deerfield, Massachusetts.) See also figs. 79, 168, and 169. *One of the most successful of Boston-area blockfront designs, this example stands on elegant hairy paw feet.*

carved details, and precise stately proportions.[38] In terms of design and elegance, these and the desks and bookcases form the grandest group of Boston blockfronts.

A desk in the Garvan Collection of this type (fig. 80), traditionally

38. This desk differs in construction with a high chest signed by Frothingham in the Winterthur Museum. See, in particular, the dovetails and drawer runners—the latter in the Deerfield desk have vertical insets, a very unusual feature.

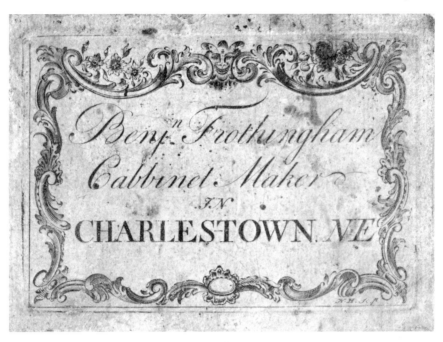

79. DETAIL OF PAPER LABEL ON DESK: "Benjn. Frothingham / Cabinet Maker / IN / CHARLESTOWN. NE." (Historic Deerfield, Inc., Deerfield, Massachusetts.) See also figs. 78, 168, and 169.

said to have descended in the Winthrop family of Boston, is very much like the Deerfield desk. It differs principally in the arrangement of the interior. The Garvan desk exhibits the classic formula for Boston blockfront interiors: the bottom tier is flat, plain-fronted, and on an advanced plane. The central fan-carved door is flanked by unfluted colonnettes, paired pigeonholes above notched single drawers, and finally by fan-capped pairs of shallowly blocked drawers.[39] This formula changed, however, as the century progressed. By the 1760s Newport was making extremely fine furniture and one finds, curiously enough, in such an example as the Boston desk illustrated in

39. In the Museum of Fine Arts, Boston, is a desk almost identical in form and construction.

figure 81 an echo of the standard Newport formula for desk interiors (fig. 82). Still evincing the Boston preference for the advanced lower tier and the stiffly carved fans, the example illustrated in figure 81 adopts the Newport concave arched drawers above the pigeonholes. That the influence is that of Newport on Boston is more definitely established by a handsome but hybrid Massachusetts desk and bookcase at the Museum of Fine Arts, Boston (fig. 83). Its interior is wholly after the pattern of Newport except in the retention of the colonnettes on the document drawers. The adoption of the Newport style, however, is strictly confined to this interior section—the gen-

80. DESK. Boston area, c. 1750–1770. Mahogany and white pine; H. 44½ inches, W. 46½ inches, D. 23½ inches. (Yale University Art Gallery, Mabel Brady Garvan Collection.) *This two-tiered desk interior was much favored in Boston.*

eral construction of this desk and bookcase and its decorative details
are distinctly Boston.

The autonomy of regional styles was based upon isolation of one
style center from another, and other more complex factors. The
preferences of patrons, the apprentice system, and the independent
specialist suppliers were major factors in the codification of a style,
and may have done much to produce the local unity of a "school."
But intercity trade and communication in eighteenth-century New
England was lively and the craftsmen in Newport and Boston were
certainly aware of each other's products.

81. DESK. Boston area, c. 1760–1780. Mahogany and white pine; H. 44¾ inches, W. 41
inches, D. 22⅜ inches. (Museum of Fine Arts, Boston, M. and M. Karolik Collection,
39.87.) *The influence of Newport is evident in the cusped pencil drawers.*

82. INTERIOR OF DESK. Made by John Townsend, Newport, 1765. Mahogany, cedar, and tulipwood; H. 42 inches, W. 42 inches, D. 23 inches. (Israel Sack, Inc., New York City.) For an overall view of the desk, see *Antiques*, CI (January, 1972), inside cover. *The archetypal Newport desk interior in a signed and dated example.*

The movement of craftsmen from Boston to Newport may be documented from early in the century.[40] But perhaps more important for the migration of furniture styles were the close commercial ties between merchants in both cities.[41] Stephen Greenleaf, a wealthy merchant of Boston, supplied his friends in Newport with furnishings and paintings commissioned in Boston. In a letter of May 26, 1749, to Abraham Redwood, in Newport, Greenleaf records: "I receiv'd yours p[er] Friend Proud and have ordered the Chairs and two roundabouts to be made which will be strong and neet and not high pris'd—have searched ye town for a [Looking] Glass and can have some of ye Size you want @ £75, but there is some Guilding about them which you wont like; I design to get one made for you that will be plain & hope will please—& shall have it ready in a fortnight, and possibly ye chairs may be done to go with

40. William Claggett, clockmaker, moved from Boston to Newport in 1726. James Franklin, the brother of Benjamin Franklin, moved his printing business to Newport in 1727. Samuel Casey, a silversmith of Rhode Island, served his apprenticeship in Boston and set up shop outside Newport about 1750, to mention a few examples.

41. Godfrey Malbone and the Deblois family maintained large commercial establishments in both cities.

83. DESK AND BOOKCASE. Boston area, c. 1770–1800. Mahogany, chestnut, white pine, and tulipwood; H. 95⅝ inches, W. 42⅜ inches, D. 22 inches. (Museum of Fine Arts, Boston, M. and M. Karolik Collection, 39.156.) *According to family tradition, this desk and bookcase descended in the Cooke family of Rhode Island. The influence of Newport is pronounced in the desk interior, but the exterior appearance, case construction, and interior colonnettes are typical of Boston.*

it."[42] Such Massachusetts-made furnishings sent to Rhode Island might well have included blockfront casepieces which were seen, imitated, and adapted by local craftsmen.

The adoption of the blockfront façade by Newport craftsmen around the middle of the century is more easily understood than the apparent countercurrent of influence which occurs a decade or two later. The use of Newport-type desk interiors in Boston has been discussed above. By far the most significant influence on Boston-area blockfronts by Newport is seen in the products of Salem. In that area, Newport construction techniques as well as design principles fuse with the native product to produce a wholly distinctive style. The use of a blocked desk lid, of squared (rather than slightly rounded) corners on the blocking of the top drawer and the use of the flat mahogany strip instead of the giant Boston dovetail at the bottom of the case are Newport elements found in Salem blockfronts of the 1770 to 1790 period.

The source of the Newport influence in Salem work is not clear, but it may be a result of the close connections maintained among Quakers in eighteenth-century New England. Ezra Stiles, a curious and faithful observer of civil and religious matters, records: "Quakers In New England are resolved into 3 Quarterly Meetings of Business & One Yearly Meeting of Business. The three Quarterly Meetings are *Salem, Sandwich,* and *Newport.* . . . Delegates or messangers from the two Quarterly Meetings of *Salem* and *Sandwich* assemble at the Yearly Meeting of Business in Newport. . . . The whole state of the Quaker Interest in New England is from year to year transmitted by the yearly meeting from Newport to the General Meeting in London."[43] The Townsend family—well-known

42. Abraham Redwood, Letterbook, III, 7 (Newport Historical Society). See also William Ellery, Daybook, 1737, folio 72 (Newport Historical Society): "Father Almy [kin to Townsend cabinetmakers] to 1 barrell of Loaf sugar bought for you in Boston by Greenleaf £28:3:8; to a Tryton painting & carting £13:15:6."

43. Ezra Stiles, Miscellany, 1758–1762, p. 339, undated entry probably 1762 (Beinecke Library, Yale University). Several accounts, such as those found in the Jonathan (?) Marsh Account Book (Newport Historical Society)—where notations for 1754, 1755, and 1764 suggest that the scope of the Newport meeting was enlarged to include delegates from the Jerseys, Philadelphia, and England—attest to the accuracy of Stiles's report.

makers of the Newport blockfronts—were staunch Quakers as were other lesser-known Newport craftsmen. Perhaps the Yearly Meetings facilitated friendships and exchanges which introduced Newport design and construction techniques into Salem work.

Whatever their source, the Salem blockfront desks are distinctive.

84. DESK. Made by Henry Rust, Salem, c. 1762–1800. Mahogany and white pine; H. 44 inches, W. 41½ inches, D. 22 inches. (Ginsburg and Levy, Inc., New York City.) See also fig. 85. *Features of this desk—square-cornered blocking, realistic ornamental scallop shell, blocked desk lid, and Newport-type case construction—are distinctive of Salem.*

85. DETAIL OF CARVED INSCRIPTION ON BOTTOM OF DESK: "H x Rust."
(Ginsburg and Levy, Inc., New York City.) See also fig. 84.

The only signed example was made by Henry Rust, a little-known cabinetmaker who worked in Salem, c. 1762 to 1800 (figs. 84 and 85).[44] The Rust desk stands on dwarf cabriole legs with claw and ball feet and undulating brackets of a type well known in the Boston area. The use of a central drop is also a Boston-area characteristic, but here ornamented with an unusually three-dimensional, realistic scallop shell. This three-dimensional shell is a recurring motif in the desks of this group. The blocked desk lid is also peculiar to this group—echoing the use of the blocked lids in Newport work and here producing the same effect—a unified façade, the parts of which refer to and echo one another. However, in the examples of this type which include a bookcase the Boston custom of a clear delineation between the decorative pattern of the top and bottom halves prevails.

A related monumental desk and bookcase was purchased by Joseph Waters of Salem about 1780 and descended in the Waters family. It is an archetypal example of this Salem form (fig. 86),[45] incorporating

44. The signature on this piece is a gouged "H x Rust" on the bottom of the case—an unusual but not implausible means of identification (fig. 85).

45. In the registrar's files at the Winterthur Museum there is a photograph of this desk (c. 1870) with the captions: "Great Grandfather Joseph Waters's Desk: sold by Sarah W." and "From Cousin Fitz. Photo of Great Grandfather Waters's Desk and Bookcase. Molly Mott leaning against it, Waters' House, Washington Square [Salem]." See Joseph Downs, *American Furniture, Queen Anne and Chippendale Periods in the Henry Francis du Pont Winterthur Museum* (New York, 1952), no. 225.

86. DESK AND BOOKCASE. Salem, c. 1770–1790. Mahogany, white pine, and white oak; H. 90 inches, W. 41 inches, D. 23 inches. (The Henry Francis du Pont Winterthur Museum.) *Bought by Joseph Waters (1756–1833) of Salem, this desk and bookcase descended in his family.*

87. DESK AND BOOKCASE. Salem area, c. 1770–1800. Mahogany and white pine; H. 101 inches, W. 42 inches, D. 23 inches. (The Metropolitan Museum of Art, Gift of Mrs. Russell Sage, 1909.) *The figures on this desk and bookcase were carved by the Skillin family.*

the blocked desk lid, three-dimensional scallop shell, and Newport case construction seen in the Rust desk. A similar desk and bookcase with Skillin-family carved allegorical figures on the pediment is in the Metropolitan Museum of Art (fig. 87). Another example of this type is in the Garvan Collection at Yale (fig. 88),[46] and a fourth is owned by Ginsburg and Levy, Inc., New York (fig. 89). With slight differences these desks all conform to the same general design and construction principles, and were probably all made in the Salem area. Their significance lies not only in their handsomely rational design but also in their testament to the communication and exchange of ideas between Newport and Boston-area cabinetmakers.

The movement of design ideas between communities was not confined to the stylish urban centers and the prosperous North Shore communities. Joseph Hosmer of Concord (1736–1821), although trained by an immigrant Frenchman (Robert Rosier), appropriated the Boston sytles.[47] He was, according to contemporary accounts, "a farmer and a cabinetmaker," a yoking of vocations not unusual in rural communities.[48] When called upon to make a distinguished piece of furniture for the new house (built in 1769 and now known as "the Old Manse") of Concord's eminent clergyman William Emerson, Hosmer employed fashionable blocking to update and refine an old form—the high chest (fig. 90). Blockfront high chests are rare—perhaps because of the fundamental visual disharmony of "animal" legs supporting an architectonic shape. It is significant that the blockfront motif was so well known and widely understood as an index of status that it is borrowed and misapplied even when it contradicts the integrity of the basic form.

In another sense, the importance of this blockfront is considerable

46. It bears the inscription "William H. Allen," probably a nineteenth-century owner of the desk.

47. According to *The Centennial of the Social Circle in Concord* (Cambridge, 1882), p. 114, Joseph Hosmer's father, James, "purchased . . . the farm belonging to Joseph Shevally, a Frenchman, who married his cousin Sarah Hosmer. . . . Robert Rosier, a Frenchman, married Mary Chevally, and lived near the bridge. . . . He was a very excellent cabinetmaker, and Major Hosmer learned his trade from him."

48. Cited (no source given) in a letter to the author from Amelia F. Emerson, March, 1972.

because it is the only instance in which the maker (and the maker's teacher), the date of manufacture, the patron, and the house for which a blockfront was made are all known. Although there are no inscriptions on the highboy itself, the static nature of Concord reinforces the probable accuracy of this tradition of fabrication, ownership, and residence.[49] The imposing height of the high chest and the use of high-style decorative motifs imply a social statement consistent with the status of an important clergyman. The blocked façade is a nod toward the refinement and elegance of contemporary urban establishments of distinction.

Perhaps the masterpiece of the Boston blockfront tradition is the handsomely proportioned and exquisitely detailed desk and bookcase illustrated in figure 91. The patron who commissioned this work was Colonel Josiah Quincy (1710–1784), an extremely wealthy gentleman. He had retired from commerce in 1748 when a single venture of his ship *Bethell*, a privateer, netted him one hundred sixty-one chests of Spanish silver and two chests of gold.[50] The desk is inscribed: "This desk was / purchased by / Josiah Quincy / Braintree 1778." In 1770 Colonel Quincy had rebuilt his house in the latest taste. "At that time," records Eliza Susan Quincy in the mid-nineteenth century, speaking of the 1770s, "it was considered as a spacious and elegant mansion."[51] The house still stands in Quincy, overlooking the harbor. The purchase of this desk may have been necessitated by the loss of furniture in the fire of 1769 which destroyed the original house. However, it is probable that it was inspired by a wish to acquire elegant furnishings worthy of the fashionable new interior, as several considerably older pieces of furniture evidently survived the fire.[52]

49. See Kenneth Scott and Russell H. Kettell, "Joseph Hosmer, Cabinetmaker," *Antiques*, LXXIII (April, 1958), 356–359.

50. *The Memorial History of Boston*, ed. Justin Winsor, 4 vols. (Boston, 1881), II, 121–122 fn.

51. Eliza Susan Quincy, "Memoir," I, 54 (Massachusetts Historical Society).

52. Josiah Quincy's inventory of 1784 includes "1 Chest of old fineered Draws 24 [shillings]," and "1 Japan Chest Draws 36 [shillings]." The japanned chest is still in the house. Suffolk Probate Records, docket 18158.

88. DESK AND BOOKCASE. Salem area, c. 1770–1800. Mahogany and white pine; H. 100 inches, W. 43 ¼ inches, D. 24 ¾ inches. (Yale University Art Gallery, Mabel Brady Garvan Collection.)

According to the inventory taken at Colonel Quincy's death in 1784, a desk and bookcase, valued at a considerable £7:4:0 (the only desk and bookcase in the house), was located in the east lower room. This room was evidently the best parlor for there are found also "1 Marble Slab Mohogany Frame [pier table] 96 [shillings]" and such accoutrements of the elegant life as a "Glass Pyramid," a hamper of Queensware, and "12 Fruit Knives & 12 Forks Silver handled." Such a place was suitable to the proper rococo dignity of the Quincy blockfront. But unfortunately it was made toward the end of the Chippendale style period, and the thin tight rectilinear Federal style soon eclipsed its artistic virtues and status value. According to Eliza Susan Quincy, a "carved desk and bookcase"—almost certainly this one—was "bought by a farmer in the neighborhood [but] was bought back in 1840 and is now in the possession of the family."[53]

The maker of this blockfront is unfortunately unknown. Its details of construction and design are unusual in some respects (for instance, the thinness of the drawer sides), but consistent with Boston-area practice. The secondary wood is red cedar in the larger drawers, and mahogany in the desk interior. Perhaps the most striking aspect of this monumental desk is its carved details.[54] Elegantly conceived and executed, they tie the composition together and emphasize its plastic architectural quality.

Colonel Quincy was a man of richly refined taste and a patron of the arts. His portrait by John Singleton Copley, painted in 1769, portrays a man of elegant solidarity, his dress highlighted by light rococo details (fig. 92). In similar fashion the solid, formal Queen Anne structure of the desk and bookcase is punctuated by airy, even whimsical touches in the carving. The American interpretation of the rococo mode in all the arts followed this pattern of fashionable, delicately rococo touches on an unmistakably solid structure. In this

53. "List of Pictures and Furniture etc. in the House built 1770 in 1879, by Eliza Susan Quincy," pp. 32–33 (current location unknown [photostat copy, Winterthur Libraries, Joseph Downs Manuscript Collection]).

54. Similar carving is found on the feet and drop of several other Boston-area blocked casepieces, including a small chest owned by Ginsburg and Levy, Inc., and the desk and bookcase illustrated in figure 83.

89. DESK AND BOOKCASE. Salem area, c. 1770–1800. Mahogany and white pine. H. 100 inches, W. 42 inches, D. 23 inches. (Ginsburg and Levy, Inc., New York City.) *Combined with other elements familiar to this group of desks (see fig. 84) are feet reminiscent of the classic Newport type.*

90. HIGH CHEST. Attributed to Joseph Hosmer, Concord, Massachusetts, c. 1769. Cherry, maple, and white pine; H. 88 inches, W. 40½ inches, D. 21 inches. (The Henry Francis du Pont Winterthur Museum.) *An unusual and inventive design, this rural adaptation of high-style blocking contributed to the worldly show of the Reverend William Emerson (1743–1776) in his Concord home now known as "The Old Manse."*

sense the Quincy desk and bookcase is as much a monument of its country and period as the great Philadelphia high chests. It is an artistic fabrication composed of diverse elements which are transformed and integrated into a successful whole. It represents the summit of Boston blockfront design and equals the celebrated blockfronts of Newport.

This survey of blockfronts attests to the vitality, diversity, and longevity of this form in the Boston area. From the 1738 Job Coit desk and bookcase through the developments of Joseph Davis, Abraham Watson, Nathaniel Treadwell, Benjamin Frothingham, Henry Rust, and Joseph Hosmer to the 1778 Quincy desk and bookcase, the fertility of design imagination seldom fails. The style of no single man, the blockfront was made by the polished urban professional and the rural cabinetmaker-farmer. Contemporary patrons from the Wasgatt sisters of Mount Desert, Maine, to the elegant Colonel Quincy of Braintree enjoyed its aesthetic and social attributes. Few other purely decorative design motifs knew such uniformity of principle yet such diversity of application.

Because the blockfronts of Boston antedate those of other regions, it might be assumed that it is from this center that the idea of blockfront case furniture spread to Newport, Connecticut, New York, Delaware, and Virginia. Nowhere except in Newport, however, did the enthusiasm for the form equal that of Boston. Curiously, these handsome, solid, baroque forms appealed to the New England temperament where, it has been thought, pragmatism, "plainness," and prim modesty prevailed.

The mistaken attribution of Boston blockfronts as Newport products will perhaps cease, yet the curious mystery of the source of the blockfronts continues. Nothing precisely like the style of blocking as it is known in this country has been found abroad. Undulating façades are often found on French furniture of the late seventeenth and eighteenth centuries, but the focal point is generally an advanced pavilion rather than a recessed niche. German and Spanish eighteenth-century cabinetwork exhibits a wide variety of vertically undulating façades, but these examples are usually undated and are not direct

prototypes. England produced some flatly blocked casepieces which exhibit a restraint and understatement of baroque movement similar to American blocking practice. The English desk and bookcase illustrated in figure 73 is not an isolated phenomenon. A small desk with a recessed central panel is similar, and a group of seven or eight British desks and bookcases is known which is related to one (in the Victoria and Albert Museum, London) said to have been bought by Dean Swift in 1710 (fig. 93). The recessed pedestal blocks of this last desk are reminiscent of American work. Unfortunately, even less is known about these European and English examples than about our own products. It is not likely that the mystery will be dispelled here before substantial research has been done abroad.

Boston, however, was distinctly the generative center for the creation and practice of the blockfront formula in this country. The groups of examples discussed in this study do not begin to exhaust the list of types and variations of blockfronts produced in the Boston area. By anchoring the discussion in the particular—and where possible the labelled, documented example—I have attempted to suggest (perhaps at the expense of the unique example or completely anonymous group) the general range of production and quality. Underlying the rich variety, however, are certain common design principles, construction techniques, and cultural preferences. The Boston cabinetmakers of the eighteenth century constituted a rich, inventive "school," and to them should go the credit for formulating and popularizing that significant American experiment in furniture design—the blockfront.

91. DESK AND BOOKCASE. Boston area, 1778. Mahogany, red cedar, and white pine; H. 96⅜ inches, W. 43 inches, D. 23 inches. (The Henry Francis du Pont Winterthur Museum.) *Perhaps the most ambitious and finest of Boston blockfronts, this desk was bought by Josiah Quincy (1710–1784) of Braintree, Massachusetts, in 1778, as the inscription on the desk indicates.*

92. JOSIAH QUINCY. Painted by John Singleton Copley, Boston, 1769. Oil on canvas; H. 35¾ inches, W. 28⅜ inches (excluding frame). (Dietrich Brothers Americana Corporation.) *A man of taste, Quincy is pictured here seated solidly in a Chippendale chair. The light rococo touches in the lace are reminiscent of the airy carving ornamenting the solid grace of the bookcase.*

93. DESK AND BOOKCASE. England or Ireland, c. 1700–1720. H. 87 inches, W. 49¼
inches, D. 21¾ inches. (Victoria and Albert Museum, London.) *One of a group of
similar desks, this one, said to have been owned by Jonathan Swift (1667–1745), displays the
use of recessed blocking on the pedestals.*

❧ GILBERT T. VINCENT ☙

The Bombé Furniture of Boston

T HE American bombé casepiece is among the most outstanding furniture forms produced by American eighteenth-century craftsmen. Bombé furniture is rare, well designed, and skillfully constructed. More importantly for the historian, its production was almost exclusively confined to the city of Boston and its immediate environs.[1] A study of this type of furniture will add to our understanding of the period leading up to the American Revolution and the Federalist era in Boston and its cultural dependencies from Salem in the north to Plymouth in the south.

Appearing on chests of drawers, chest-on-chests, desks, desks and bookcases, dressing tables, dressing glasses, and tea caddies, the form as produced in Boston is defined by a single bulge located near the base of the front and sides of a piece of furniture. Bombé furniture partakes of essentially the same refined spirit that produced turret-top tea tables (fig. 94), blockfront furniture, reverse serpentine casepieces (fig. 95), and furniture with a hollowed pediment composed of double ogee curves (fig. 96). These individual forms as well as American bombé design are either unique to or achieve their greatest popularity in Boston and its cultural dependents. When all the designs are considered as a group, they illustrate an aesthetic directly inspired by Great Britain. There was apparently little cross-exchange of design with the other colonial furniture-making centers of New York, Philadelphia, and Charleston; Boston furniture of this type relates almost directly with specific British prototypes.

1. At this date, there is only one known example of American bombé furniture that probably originated from outside the Boston area, a bombé dressing table probably from New Hampshire. See Samuel Chamberlain, *Salem Interiors: Two Centuries of New England Taste and Decoration* (New York, 1950), p. 37.

Bostonians' taste combined a Puritan and provincial background with a definite aspiration toward the cosmopolitan nature of the baroque age as interpreted in England. The tight, crisp verticality, attenuated proportions, and surface decoration of most Boston furniture express the Puritan and provincial aspects of Boston design, whereas the curvilinear character of Boston bombé, blockfront, and serpentine furniture strives for a sense of baroque form and movement in space.

PERIOD OF POPULARITY

The appearance of the bombé form in Boston poses a number of complex, unanswered, and perhaps unanswerable questions. What is the origin of the form that became so popular in Boston? How did

94. TEA TABLE. Boston area, c. 1750–1770. Mahogany and white pine; H. 27¾ inches, W. 32⅜ inches, D. 23⅜ inches. (Museum of Fine Arts, Boston, M. and M. Karolik Collection, 41.592.)

95. CHEST-ON-CHEST. Made by Nathan Bowen and Ebenezer Martin, Marblehead, 1780. Mahogany and white pine; H. 86 inches, W. 42 inches, D. 24½ inches. (Museum of Fine Arts, Boston, Gift of Miss Josie E. Prescott and Miss Mary E. Prescott, 33.373.)

the design arrive in Boston? Why does the form appear only in Massachusetts, an area resistant to the Counter-Reformation and its development of the baroque aesthetic?

A thorough study of Boston bombé furniture is handicapped by an absence of firm identification. Few of the more than fifty extant examples are signed, dated, or recorded in family histories. Only four bombé casepieces are known to be labelled by cabinetmakers. However, a number of generalizations can be drawn from the small amount of documentary information available. Major Benjamin Frothingham (1734–1809) signed a bombé desk and bookcase in four places in 1753 (fig. 97), the earliest dated American example. Although the signatures are probably that of Major Benjamin rather than that of his father (also named Benjamin), Frothingham would have been nineteen years old in 1753. There is a second signature, an unidentified "D Sprage." Whether both Major Benjamin and Sprage were working in the elder Frothingham's shop and this desk was a *chef d'oeuvre* made to demonstrate their competence, or whether this is one of the first products of a short-lived and previously unrecorded partnership is not known at this time. We only know that Frothingham was connected with the construction of this important and handsome desk in 1753. The latest dated example is a chest-on-chest made by John Cogswell for the Derby family in 1782 (fig. 125). That the Derbys, Salem's most fashion-conscious newly rich, chose to order a bombé chest from Boston shows the dominance of Boston cabinetwork in Massachusetts, and also the continuing appeal of the bombé form after the Revolution and perhaps as late as the turn of the century.

TERMINOLOGY

The word "bombé" is a recent term taken from the French verb *bomber*, meaning to bulge or jut out. The word had been used to describe both French and English furniture in the nineteenth century. The first publication to use the word to describe American furniture is Esther Singleton's *Furniture of Our Forefathers* (New York, 1901), where it is italicized and an obvious French importation. Luke Vin-

96. CHEST-ON-CHEST. Boston area, c. 1740–1760. Mahogany, chestnut, and white pine; H. 87⅞ inches, W. 43½ inches, D. 22⅛ inches. (Yale University Art Gallery, Mabel Brady Garvan Collection.)

97. DESK AND BOOKCASE. Made by Benjamin Frothingham and D. Sprage (signatures in pencil), Boston or Charlestown, 1753. Mahogany, red cedar, and white pine; H. 97⅜ inches, W. 44½ inches, D. 24⅝ inches. (The Department of State, Washington, D.C.: photo, Israel Sack, Inc., New York City.) See also fig. 162.

cent Lockwood uses "*bombé*-shaped" to describe a desk in *Colonial American Furniture* (New York, 1913). "Kettle shape," the other term used to describe the form, first appears in Frances Clary Morse's *Furniture of the Olden Time* (New York, 1902) and is often used by later authors such as Charles Over Cornelius (*Early American Furniture* [New York, 1926]) in conjunction with the word "bombé." Although it may seem stilted, "bombé" better connotes the original spirit which gave rise to the form than the word "kettle," and is thus used throughout this paper.

Eighteenth-century manuscripts demonstrate the lack of a specific designation for the bombé form. Inventories of individuals known to have owned bombé furniture offer an unilluminating file of "desks and bookcases" or "chests of drawers" occasionally prefaced by "large," "carved," or "mahogany." A bill for joiner's work on the pulpit of Christ Church, Spitalfields, London, in 1725–1726, offers one contemporary possibility. It states that the pulpit, which had a distinct bombé shape, is "of right Waint [wainscot] formed Oggee fashon the Pannells fineerd & inlaid."[2] In this case, the bombé design is called "Oggee fashon," ogee being an architectural term for the cyma reversa. The word "ogee" occasionally appears as a descriptive term in American documents, such as the 1776 shop inventory of the Charlestown cabinetmaker Thomas Wood,[3] but it is difficult to determine how inclusive the usage was or what furniture was being described.

The English seem to prefer the French word *commode* to describe the bombé shape, although this cannot be interpreted as a standard term. In the eighteenth century, the most popular use of the bombé form was on the casepiece of two or three drawers. First appearing in France, the new furniture form was given the name *commode en tombeau*—literally, "commode in the style of a sarcophagus." The design was derived from classical sarcophagi. The form was *plus commode*

2. Quoted in *Survey of London: Spitalfields and Mile End New Town*, XXVII (London, 1957), 293. Courtesy of Mr. Benno M. Forman.

3. Mabel M. Swan, "Furnituremakers of Charlestown," *Antiques*, XLVI (October, 1944), 203–204.

(more convenient) for storing clothes than the simple chest.[4] The fashionable French chest of drawers with bulging sides, simply called a commode, spread throughout Europe. Great Britain soon began producing the bombé form on chests of drawers, some of which copied French furniture while others took a profoundly British cast. The word "commode" entered the English vocabulary as a description of the new style of casepieces, a usage which became available in print to the American colonists in Thomas Chippendale's *The Gentleman and Cabinet-Maker's Director*. The 1754 edition illustrates both "French Commodes" (fig. 118) modelled on mid-eighteenth-century French furniture,[5] and a tall clock (fig. 98) described as having a commode pedestal which is identical in form to the bombé furniture of Boston.

The most logical explanation for the inexact terminology is that an individual word was unnecessary to describe a new furniture form that appealed to a small elite clientele isolated in colonial Boston. In eighteenth-century Boston inventories the word "commode" appears most frequently in reference to the commode chair. Occasional inventories list commode chests or other casepieces, but the exact form is impossible to determine. The adjective "swell'd" is known to have been used to describe both the blockfront and serpentine front on casepieces. Either of these terms may have been utilized for the bombé shape as well; the prospective purchaser would then describe the chosen "swell'd" or "commode" form to the cabinet-maker.

ORIGINS AND INFLUENCES

The sources of American bombé furniture present a complex problem. The first native manifestation of Bostonians' taste for the curvilinear baroque style is found in silver. With its easy transportability, inherent value, and strong dependence on Continental design, silver

4. Desmond Fitz-Gerald, *Georgian Furniture* (London, 1969), fig. 11.

5. Chippendale also imported French furniture; Edward Joy in an article in *Country Life*, cx (August, 1951), 569, draws attention to Chippendale's attempt to avoid the English customs.

was probably the vehicle for much of the importation of current English taste in the seventeenth and eighteenth centuries. In the 1650s John Hull and Robert Sanderson produced a caudle cup that has virtually the identical shape as the later bombé furniture (fig. 99). The same bombé form—often called "tulip-shape"—continued to be used in such silver objects as teapots, coffee pots, milk pots, and casters throughout the eighteenth century. Perhaps the greatest popularity of the form was achieved in canns and tankards. Indeed, the tulip-shaped cann may be considered one of the distinct marks of Boston silver just as the bombé casepiece is of Boston furniture. The parallel appeal of the form in two mediums is substantiated by Elias

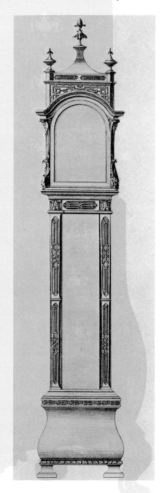

98. DESIGN FOR A TALL CLOCK. From Thomas Chippendale, *The Gentleman and Cabinet-Maker's Director*, plate CXXXV. London, 1754. (The Henry Francis du Pont Winterthur Museum Libraries.)

99. CAUDLE CUP. Made by John Hull and Robert Sanderson, Boston, c. 1660–1670. Silver; H. 3 3/16 inches, Diameter of base 2 5/8 inches, Diameter of lip 3 7/8 inches. (Museum of Fine Arts, Boston, Philip Leffingwell Spalding Collection, given in his memory by Katherine Ames Spalding and Philip Spalding, Oakes Ames Spalding, Hobart Ames Spalding, 42.226.)

Hasket Derby's purchase of two tulip-shaped canns from Paul Revere in 1783, one year after Cogswell completed the Derby chest-on-chest (fig. 100).

The popularity of the silver form seems to show the partiality of Bostonians to the shape but cannot be viewed as the direct source of inspiration for its use in furniture. The close similarity between American and English bombé furniture indicates a more probable source. Through the ties of immigration, trade, and government, England dominated colonial culture. Despite the various types of furniture upon which the bombé form was used, there remains a pervasive adherence in Boston to a single interpretation of bombé design that has a direct counterpart in English furniture dating as early as the

100. CANN. Made by Paul Revere, Boston, 1783. Silver; H. 6½ inches. (The Metropolitan Museum of Art, Purchase, 1958, Sandsbury-Mills Fund.) *This cann was originally owned by Elias Hasket Derby (1739–1799) of Salem.*

mid-1720s.[6] England produced a myriad of bombé forms, yet Boston steadfastly produced only one type. The lack of invention may indicate a single source or a number of very similar sources for the

6. The London cabinetmaker Samuel Bennett labelled a bombé desk and bookcase (c. 1720) that is illustrated in Percy Macquoid and Ralph Edwards, *The Dictionary of English Furniture*, 2nd ed., rev., 3 vols. (London, 1954), I, 136.

101. DESK AND BOOKCASE. Made by James McMillian, Boston, c. 1749–1769. Mahogany and white pine; H. 96 inches, W. 51 inches (before restoration). (Present location unknown. Sold at the American Art Association auction of the estate of Francis Shaw, December 12–14, 1935, lot 472. Restored and sold again at the American Art Association auction of the estate of Albert S. Hill, March 12, 1938, lot 100: photo [before restoration], Decorative Arts Photographic Collection, The Henry Francis du Pont Winterthur Museum.)

Boston patron and cabinetmaker to follow. More likely, it shows the essentially provincial nature of the Boston cultural milieu: Bostonians did not feel sufficiently secure to venture into new, inventive designs but, in the nature of a colonial society, selected, simplified, repeated, and perfected design motifs from the mother country.

Why Boston should have chosen only this design for the bombé shape is difficult to determine. There is the possibility that an English bombé casepiece of this design was imported to Boston by an influential person. By such means the form could have quickly acquired the symbolic aura of established social and economic stature that it seems to have enjoyed.

Possibly an English design book provided the source for the bombé furniture of Boston. Chippendale's *Director* offers a direct prototype. The publication is known to have been available in Boston and all editions contain a number of designs that would offer a simple solution to the question of a source (for example, fig. 98). However, since Frothingham constructed a bombé desk and bookcase a year preceding the publication of the first edition, the stimulus for the bombé form had appeared before the first possible pictorial source. Chippendale is thought to have published designs that were currently in vogue in London; the pieces of furniture that he illustrates were probably made by himself and other cabinetmakers before and after publication.

Thus, Frothingham probably imitated a bombé casepiece already in Boston. Either a London-trained cabinetmaker could have immigrated to Boston and produced an "American" bombé or an English casepiece could have been imported. At this date, a cabinetmaker fitting the necessary qualifications has yet to be identified; the only documented American bombé casepiece known that could predate the Frothingham desk is a desk and bookcase made by James McMillian (fig. 101). McMillian was probably born in Salem and worked in Boston between 1749 and 1769. However, it is unlikely that his desk and bookcase, an unusual example with enormous paw feet, served as the source for Frothingham. More likely, a piece of imported English furniture introduced the bombé form to Frothingham and the rest of Boston.

One English example, a bombé chest-on-chest made about 1740, has a tradition of ownership by Charles Apthorp (1698–1758) of Boston (fig. 102). His inventory lists "a Mohogony Beauro with Glass doors" in the great parlor and "a Mohogony Cabinet with glass doors" in the upstairs dining room;[7] either description could refer to the chest. Characterized as the "greatest and most noble merchant on the continent" at his death,[8] Apthorp would have given social stature to the new form.

The Apthorp chest may well have been the direct means by which the bombé form reached and became accepted in Boston. The external appearance has the identical bombé shape and use of straight drawer sides found in the Frothingham desk. In respect to overall design, Frothingham displayed a more powerful sense of baroque movement through the use of the swan's neck pediment. The English chest, distinctly architectural in design, relates to Palladian architecture and the furniture designs of William Kent with elaborate, almost oversized detailing and a heavy pedimented top. The similarity of the bombé base with that of Frothingham's desk, if it cannot prove the seminal importance of the Apthorp chest, certainly reinforces the theory of the English background of the bombé form as found in Boston. The construction of the lower sections of the pieces of furniture is identical. The differences in overall design and standard of finish are more striking, but are not unusual in any comparison of eighteenth-century Boston and London cabinetmaking. The chest has very fine dovetails, not found in Boston furniture until the nineteenth century; the secondary woods are finely cut oak and deal rather than white pine; dustboards are solid and the back is panelled rather than boarded.

Another example of European bombé furniture with a history of Boston ownership is a desk and bookcase made in the Netherlands about 1740 and said to have been owned by Governor Thomas

---

7. Suffolk County Registry of Probate, Boston, Massachusetts, docket 11871 (hereafter Suffolk Probate Records).

8. Quoted in James H. Stark, *The Loyalists of Massachusetts* (Boston, 1910), p. 352.

102. CHEST-ON-CHEST. England, c. 1740–1758. Mahogany, oak, and deal; H. 97 inches, W. 46¾ inches, D. 25½ inches. (Museum of Fine Arts, Boston, Gift of Albert Sack, 1971.737.) *According to family tradition, this chest was owned by Charles Apthorp (1698–1758), a wealthy merchant of Boston, and may have been the "Mohogony Beauro with Glass doors" listed in the 1758 inventory of the contents of his King Street house.*

Hutchinson (1711–1780) (fig. 103).[9] The furniture of a royal governor was necessarily impressive and as the governor's household would probably have been on view to most of the influential colonists, a new form of furniture introduced by the governor might be expected to have an impact on local taste and design. In addition, Governor Hutchinson, who belonged to one of the oldest Massachusetts families, lived in one of the handsomest houses in Boston.[10] Nonetheless, this desk and bookcase had virtually no direct impact on Boston bombé furniture. The presence of the bombé form has something of the same spirit found in Boston, but there the similarity ends. The construction of the Dutch desk has no counterpart in Boston cabinetmaking: the bombé form is contained within two bulges on the front of the piece of furniture; the sides are flat; the entire surface is veneered; and corner posts join the sides and the front rails—a feature never found in Boston cabinetwork. The interior construction of Dutch furniture is also quite different from that of Boston, with secondary woods often pieced together and roughly finished and drawers nailed together rather than dovetailed. The squat, heavy proportions and exuberant multiple curves characterizing Dutch furniture are also unrelated to the linear proportion of Boston furniture. The Netherlands is often considered a possible source for American bombé furniture, but the comparison of construction and proportion shows that there is actually very little direct connection between the cabinetmaking traditions.

English bombé design of the eighteenth century may have served as the inspiration for many craftsmen in Europe as well as in Boston. In a tea table (fig. 104) that has been considered one of the finest examples of eighteenth-century Dutch furniture,[11] the bombé design is related to the same tradition found in America, despite the typical Dutch emphasis on the corners. If indeed the table were made in the Netherlands, the simplified line and subdued curve are still

9. Joseph W. P. Frost, "Living with Antiques, Pepperrell Mansion, Kittery Point, Maine," *Antiques*, LXXXIX (March, 1966), 370.

10. Abbott Lowell Cummings, "The Foster-Hutchinson House," *Old-Time New England*, LIV (Winter, 1964), 59–76.

11. *World Furniture*, ed. Helena Hayward (London, 1965), p. 167.

103. DESK AND BOOKCASE. The Netherlands, c. 1740–1750. Walnut. (Collection of Mr. James W. P. Frost: photo, *Antiques*.) *According to family tradition, this desk was owned by Thomas Hutchinson (1711–1780), one of the last royal governors of Massachusetts.*

104. TEA TABLE. The Netherlands, c. 1745–1755. Walnut; H. 31¾ inches, w. 38¼ inches, D. 25⅜ inches. (Rijksmuseum, Amsterdam.)

profoundly English. The cross-exchange of furniture, designs, and craftsmen between England and the Netherlands became very complex in the seventeenth and eighteenth centuries. Dutch construction and bombé design seem to have had little influence on English cabinetmakers. But, so little is known about Anglo-Dutch furniture design that further research is necessary before any conclusive analysis can be reached.

The career of the German Abraham Roentgen (1711–1793), founder of the famous cabinetmaking firm located in Neuweid near Cologne, bears out the theory of English importance in the development of the bombé form in northern Europe. In his bombé furniture

105. DESK AND BOOKCASE. England or Ireland, c. 1750–1770. Mahogany. (Present location unknown. Illustrated in F. Lewis Hinckley, *A Directory of Queen Anne, Early Georgian and Chippendale Furniture* [New York, 1971], p. 244: photo, © 1971 by F. Lewis Hinckley. Used by permission of Crown Publishers, Inc.)

106. DESK AND BOOKCASE. Boston, c. 1760–1790. Mahogany and white pine; H.
102⅝ inches, W. 48½ inches, D. 23⅜ inches. (The Department of State, Washington,
D.C.) *According to family tradition, this desk and bookcase descended in the Hancock family
of Boston.*

Roentgen used the same contour that the Boston cabinetmakers borrowed from London. Roentgen worked in London between 1731 and 1738,[12] started the cabinetmaking business in Neuweid in 1750, and sent one of his assistants to be trained in London and to return with an English apprentice. The eminence attached to English cabinetmaking was demonstrated by his son, David Roentgen, who called himself an English cabinetmaker although he had never been in England.

English dominance of Boston design can be seen by comparing an English desk and bookcase (fig. 105) with a Boston example (fig. 106). The strong similarity of design between the two desks is immediately evident. In external appearance the English desk could have been made in Boston (except for the door and entablature fretwork and the rococo cartouche, which is more reminiscent of Philadelphia work). Another close resemblance is found in an English desk (fig. 107) and an American desk (fig. 108), which is stamped by G. Cade and which descended in the nineteenth century in the Sylvanus Plympton family of Woburn, Massachusetts.[13] The proportions of the two desks are different because of the addition of a fifth drawer in the English example, but the bombé form is much the same in both cases.

The bombé form was popular during the same period in England, Germany, and Boston. Frothingham was constructing his bombé desk and bookcase when Roentgen began to produce similar ex-

12. Hans Huth, "Roentgens—Cabinet-Makers," *The Connoisseur*, xcii (August, 1933), 85–91.

13. For an illustration of the Cade brand, see *American Antiques from Israel Sack Collection*, 3 vols. (Washington, D.C., 1969), ii, 340. "G. CADE" may refer to George Cade (1739–1789), a Boston ropemaker, or to his son, George Cade, Jr. (before 1769–1805), also a local ropemaker. The younger Cade's inventory included "1 Old Desk" valued at $2.00. If, in fact, Cade did own the bombé desk, then it probably passed to the Plympton family soon after his death in 1805. An inscription on the desk reads, "Augusta P. Plympton, Decr[?] 27 1830 / Formerly property of Dr. Plympton, Waban." For further information on the Cade and Plympton families, see Suffolk Probate Records, dockets 19402, 22390; *A Report of the Record Commissioners of the City of Boston, Containing the Statistics of the United States' Direct Tax of 1798, As Assessed in Boston*, xxii (Boston, 1892), 72, 306, 482; John Adams Vinton, *The Richardson Memorial* (Portland, Maine, 1876), p. 272.

amples. In 1761 Queen Charlotte of England ordered a bombé secretary from William Vile, the recently appointed cabinetmaker to George III (fig. 109). The invoice in the accounts of St. James's Palace describes the newly delivered piece of furniture as "an exceedingly ffine mahogy secretary with drawers and a writing drawer, a sett of shelves at Top, and the sides and back all handsome cuttwork."[14] It cost £71. When the Society of Upholsterers and Cabinetmakers of London published the second edition of *Genteel Household Furniture in the Present Taste* about 1762, they included designs for a bombé clothes press, clothes chest, and pedestal, all employing the form popular in Boston.[15]

Frothingham's creation of a bombé casepiece in 1753 demonstrates that Boston taste was concurrent with the London vogue. Boston's colonial status is reflected in the relative simplicity of decoration, in the repetition of the same form without change, and in the acceptance of this form with all its social import over nearly half a century. The persistent popularity of one furniture design indicates a certain cohesiveness of outlook in the Boston area. Boston was still a relatively small town in the eighteenth century; the confrontation of new, non-English cultural influences in the nineteenth century was still far off. Nor had the new political freedom obtained by the Revolution found expression in cultural life except in the most tentative manner.

Although England was the direct source for Boston bombé furniture, the form was not indigenous to the English sense of design. The interest in the classical past engendered by the Renaissance led to the imitation of Roman sources in Italian furniture. The medieval chest or *cassone* was brought up to date by incorporating the forms of Roman sarcophagi that often included curvilinear designs closely associated with eighteenth-century bombé furniture. The development of the baroque aesthetic reinforced and aggrandized the bombé character of Renaissance *cassoni*. Bombé chests spread throughout

14. Quoted in Anthony Coleridge, *Chippendale Furniture* (New York, 1968), p. 23.
15. *The IId. Edition of Genteel Household Furniture in the Present Taste with an Addition of Several Articles Never Before Executed* (London, n.d.), plates XLIV, XLV, LXXXVIII.

107. DESK. England, c. 1740–1760. Mahogany. (Present location unknown. Illustrated in H. Avray Tipping, *English Furniture of the Cabriole Period* [London, 1922], plate III: photo, The Henry Francis du Pont Winterthur Museum Libraries.)

108. D ESK. Stamped "G. CADE" (probably the name of an owner), Boston, c. 1755–1775. Mahogany and white pine; H. 42½ inches, W. 45½ inches, D. 25¼ inches. (The Hennage Collection: photo, Israel Sack, Inc., New York City.) See also figs. 119 and 120. *This desk was probably owned in the early nineteenth century by George Cade, Jr. (before 1769–1805), a Boston ropemaker, and later passed into the Plympton family of Woburn, Massachusetts.*

Europe.[16] By the mid-seventeenth century, picturesque ensembles in the baroque style incorporating the bombé form in chimney pieces, door surrounds, altars, tabernacles, memorials, and pedestals were published in France (fig. 110). In the 1680s the painter-designer-architect Charles Lebrun (1619–1690) designed a direct prototype of

16. Mario Praz, *An Illustrated History of Furnishing* (New York, 1964), p. 105, fig. 64.

109. SECRETARY. Made by William Vile, London, 1761. Mahogany and thujawood; H. 84 inches, W. 37 inches, D. 18 inches. (Buckingham Palace: photo by gracious permission of Her Majesty the Queen.) *This secretary was constructed for Queen Charlotte of England.*

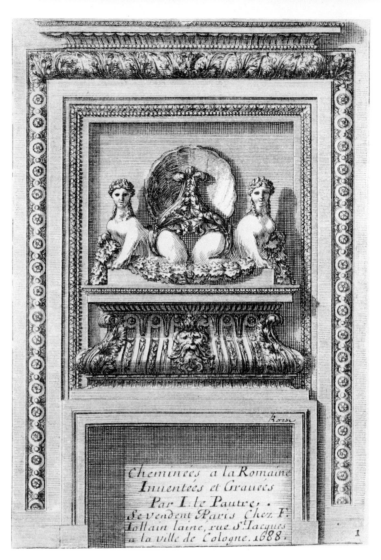

110. Design for a Chimney Piece. From Jean Le Pautre, *Cheminées à la Romaine*, plate I. Paris, 1688. (The Henry Francis du Pont Winterthur Museum Libraries.)

the first bombé casepieces in the bas-relief over the doors of the Salon de la Guerre at Versailles (fig. 111).[17]

The progenitors of the eighteenth-century bombé casepiece were built by the French cabinetmaker André-Charles Boulle (1642–1732).

17. For photographs of the bas-relief in the Salon de la Guerre, see André Pératé, *Versailles: Le Château, Les Jardins, Les Trianons, Le Musée, La Ville* (Paris, 1905), pp. 39, 41; *Key Monuments of the History of Architecture*, ed. Henry A. Millon (Englewood Cliffs, New Jersey, and New York, 1964), p. 402.

111. OVERDOOR DETAIL. By Charles Le Brun and Antoine Coysevox, Salon de la Guerre, Versailles, c. 1680–1685. (Drawing by Corinne Pascoe.)

In 1708 and 1709 he constructed a pair of bombé commodes for the King's bedroom at the Trianon in the Park of Versailles (fig. 112),[18] the earliest examples of casepieces with drawers in the bombé form. The novelty of the commodes lay in the use of drawers extending across the entire width of the chest and sliding into the frame. Although awkwardly suspending a sarcophagus pendant from a flat-topped table (both forms retain four legs), the design is an attempt to make the Italian *cassone* into a more functional and permanent piece of furniture. It was probably the designer Jean Berain (1638–1711)

18. Pierre Verlet, *French Royal Furniture* (London, 1963), p. 8.

who supplied the resolution to the new design in his *Ornemens Inventez par J. Berain*, published in Paris about 1710. Berain's successful unification of the tier of drawers and the supporting legs established the primary model for all eighteenth-century bombé casepieces (fig. 113).

The anglicization of the commode can be seen by comparing a later French commode in the tradition of Boulle (fig. 114) with a bombé chest of drawers made in England (fig. 115). Although the English example shows the indigenous propensity for a natural wood finish rather than the ornate *première-partie* inlay and ormolu decoration traditional in French cabinetwork, the underlying design of both casepieces is the same. The full English attainment which developed from this somewhat awkward attempt at the assimilation

112. COMMODE. Made by André-Charles Boulle, France, 1708–1709. Oak, tortoiseshell, ormolu, and brass; H. 34¼ inches, W. 51 inches, D. 25⅛ inches. (Versailles: photo, Musées Nationaux Français.) *Louis XIV ordered this commode for his bedroom at the Trianon in the Park of Versailles.*

of the bombé form is seen in the secretary by William Vile (fig. 109) and the clothes press designed by Thomas Chippendale (fig. 116). The best casepieces produced in Boston were only one step behind these English counterparts.

England continually responded to French developments in furniture design. By the mid-eighteenth century French cabinetmakers had refined the massive, rectilinear Boulle style into the delicate curvilinear furniture called Louis XV, a development soon adopted in England. A commode designed by William Vile's partner, John Cobb, in 1772, is a virtual copy of contemporary French furniture (fig. 117). Called French commodes in England, furniture of this type copied the French style with long, slender legs, flaring corners, and a serpentine and bombé front bulging in three dimensions. Although Cobb overlaid the Louis XV style carcass with a veneer in the neoclassical style, the design source is profoundly French.

113. DESIGN FOR A COMMODE. From Jean Berain, *Ornemens Inventez par J. Berain*, p. 41. Paris, c. 1710. (The Henry Francis du Pont Winterthur Museum Libraries.)

Designs for similar commodes were available to Bostonians. The *Director* includes a number of plates in all three editions illustrating French commodes that vary from direct copies of French furniture to heavily anglicized chests of drawers (fig. 118). No variation of style was ever adopted in Boston. Whether the methods of construction were beyond the capabilities of the Boston cabinetmakers or whether the design itself failed to awaken a response in Bostonians is difficult, if not impossible, to determine. All that can be said is that a number of choices for bombé casepieces were available to Bostonians, yet they continually chose one variety.

114. COMMODE. France, c. 1715–1730. Oak, tortoiseshell, ormolu, and brass; H. 34½ inches, w. 51 inches, D. 23 inches. (The Wallace Collection, London: photo by permission of the Trustees of the Wallace Collection.)

CONSTRUCTION

Any study of Boston bombé furniture is dependent upon correct identification. Since few examples bear labels or other inscriptions identifying makers, a close inspection of the inner construction and identification of the different woods is as necessary for the full understanding of a piece of furniture as is the analysis of the exterior proportions and design.

The construction of American bombé furniture bears out the

115. COMMODE. England, c. 1730–1740. Mahogany and oak; H. 36 inches, W. 56 inches, D. 31½ inches. (Victoria and Albert Museum, London.)

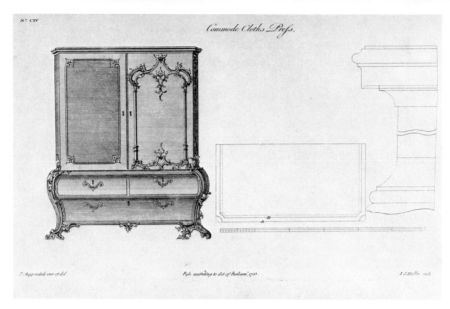

116. DESIGN FOR A COMMODE PRESS. From Thomas Chippendale, *The Gentleman and Cabinet-Maker's Director*, plate CIV. London, 1754. (The Henry Francis du Pont Winterthur Museum Libraries.)

117. COMMODE. Made by John Cobb, London, 1772. Satinwood, harewood, mahogany, and ormolu; H. 35 inches, W. 39 inches, D. 24½ inches. (Victoria and Albert Museum, London.)

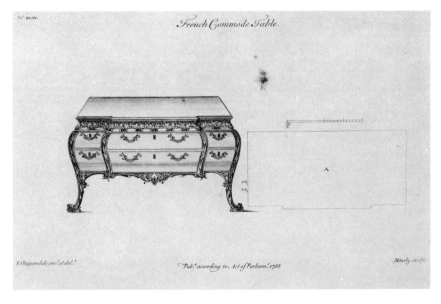

French Commode Table.

118. DESIGN FOR A FRENCH COMMODE TABLE. From Thomas Chippendale, *The Gentleman and Cabinet-Maker's Director*, plate XLIV. London, 1754. (The Henry Francis du Pont Winterthur Museum Libraries.)

tradition that it was made in Boston or certainly in nearby areas that used the same woods and traditions of craftsmanship. While the primary wood is mahogany, the secondary wood is ordinarily *Pinus strobus*, or white pine, the wood so favored by Boston cabinetmakers. The small differences in construction—size and number of dovetails, type of moldings, direction of the grain in the bottom of drawers, etc.—can serve as a guide to the identity of the cabinetmaker. The wide variance found in such details in bombé furniture belies the theory that the form was the specialty of only one or two shops. In fact, the names of six cabinetmakers have been linked to American bombé furniture and the list must include at least twice as many as yet unidentified men.

Boston bombé furniture is understandably unified in its general

119. INTERIOR OF DESK. Stamped "G. CADE." (The Hennage Collection.) See also figs. 108 and 120. *This desk is an example with straight-sided drawers.*

construction (fig. 119). The sides are cut from solid pieces of mahogany. The front rails, also mahogany, are dovetailed into the sides; in most cases, a strip of white pine is glued to the back of the rail for added strength and economy. A complete set of solid dust boards is rarely found, but in the traditional Boston manner the rail and attached secondary wood average about six inches in depth. Occasionally a single solid dust board is placed between the second and third drawers to strengthen the sides. The back is composed of vertically or horizontally lapped white pine boards nailed to the top,

120. DETAIL OF DESK INTERIOR. Stamped "G. CADE." (The Hennage Collection.) See also figs. 108 and 119.

sides, and bottom. The bottom, also composed of white pine boards, is either flush with or set down from the base rail. Additional strength was provided by glue blocks of various sizes and shapes between the sides and the back, and sometimes between the sides and bottom.

The major differences of Boston-area bombé work are found in the construction of the bombé itself, which can be divided into two major categories and assigned a chronological order. The earliest and least sophisticated method can be seen in the 1753 Frothingham desk (fig. 97). In casepieces of this type, the bulge is contained wholly within the solid mahogany sides. The interior of the bulge is either roughly hacked out to allow for wider and stronger drawer supports or simply smoothed to the vertical surface found in traditional casework construction (fig. 120). Drawer sides are straight in the standard manner; the bombé shape is encompassed only in the forward bulge of the lower two or three drawers. Bombé furniture with straight-sided drawers is the rarer of the two major methods of construction, appearing on about fifteen percent of known American bombé furniture. Since six bombé casepieces with firm dates before the Revolution are constructed in this manner, it is undoubtedly the earlier type of construction. Many desks and bookcases of this type relate stylistically to early eighteenth-century design in the retention of the vestigial molding separating the desk portion of the case from the drawers in the manner of the earlier desk-on-frames. The interior arrangement is usually in the Queen Anne rather than the Chippendale style. The doors of the upper sections have rounded arched panels in the manner of the Queen Anne style, and there is often little or no carving.

In the second major category, the curve of the case side is echoed in the curved construction of the drawer side (fig. 121). This method of construction is basically the same as the earlier method with the exception that the solid pieces of mahogany making up the sides are cut out on the inside to follow the exterior curve. The drawer construction therefore differs by the inclusion of curved sides built to fit the curve of the interior shape of the casepiece.

Although the curved sides of the drawer require greater sophistication of craftsmanship, that fact alone would not necessarily imply a later date. While the majority of bombé casepieces have curved-sided drawers, few can be dated prior to the Revolution. In addition, the aesthetic sense of the second type of bombé is more highly de-

121. INTERIOR OF CHEST OF DRAWERS. Salem. (The Henry Francis du Pont Winterthur Museum.) See also fig. 136. *This chest is an example with curved-sided drawers.*

veloped. When viewed from the front, the curving line of the drawer sides gives a unified and organic movement to the bombé bulge that is disrupted by the straight line of the straight-sided drawers of the earlier type. Most of the bombé furniture with curved-sided drawers is more developed in the Chippendale idiom, with details such as dentil molding, Chinese fretwork, rococo carving, and, in a few cases, serpentine fronts.

Both types of construction, the curved- and straight-sided drawer techniques, are found in a rare bombé form, the dressing glass (figs. 122 and 123).[19] In both glasses the concept of design is unified

19. Other examples are owned by John Walton, Inc., New York, and the Sargent-Murray-Gilman-Hough House, Gloucester, Massachusetts. See also Wallace Nutting, *Furniture Treasury* (1928; rpt. New York, 1954) figs. 3206, 3210.

122. DRESSING GLASS. Boston area, c. 1755–1780. Mahogany and white pine; H. 23⅜ inches, W. 18¾ inches, D. 9½ inches. (The Henry Francis du Pont Winterthur Museum.)

through the echoing curves of the spiral supports and bombé base. This particular unity of curvilinear form and detail is a hallmark of Boston bombé cabinetwork. In desks and bookcases the curve of the bombé sides is often repeated in the ogee bracket feet or small cabriole legs, in the door panels of the upper section composed of continuous ogee curves, and in the swan's neck pediment. In a few of

123. DRESSING GLASS. Salem area, c. 1765–1780. Mahogany and white pine; H. 28¾ inches, W. 18¾ inches, D. 9½ inches. (The Henry Francis du Pont Winterthur Museum.)

the more ambitious examples, a serpentine curve is added to the front of the base, incorporating the bombé and serpentine curves into a powerful three-dimensional form (fig. 135).

MAKERS

The makers of only four pieces of Boston bombé furniture have been identified. A desk and bookcase, signed by Benjamin Frothingham and dated 1753, is the earliest documented example of the bombé form in Boston (fig. 97). An unusual bombé desk and bookcase with paw feet and a squatty upper section is labelled by James Mc-Millian of Boston and was made sometime before 1769 (fig. 101). Another desk and bookcase is signed by George Bright, a cabinet-maker of Boston, and was constructed sometime between 1770 and 1792 (fig. 124). A chest-on-chest, signed by John Cogswell and dated 1782, is the latest documented example in Boston (fig. 125).

An outstanding example of the bombé casepiece with curved drawer sides is the desk and bookcase made by George Bright for the Boston merchant Samuel Barrett (figs. 124 and 140). Born in Boston in 1726 and trained by his father, Bright was one of the most success-ful cabinetmakers in late eighteenth-century Boston.[20] His extensive patronage included such important merchants as Thomas Hancock and Caleb Davis. In 1797 he supplied thirty chairs to the new Mas-sachusetts State House.[21] The superb quality of craftsmanship evident in the desk and bookcase directly illustrates the reason behind Bright's immensely successful career. In effect, the desk is truly a Boston creation in all aspects of cabinetmaking, carving, and construction. The bombé shape, short cabriole legs, continuous ogee panels, and swan's neck pediment create a unity of curvilinear design. Although a massive piece of furniture, the desk is carefully proportioned in the relationship between the lower or desk section and the upper or

20. Ethel Hall Bjerkoe, *The Cabinetmakers of America* (Garden City, New York, 1957), p. 49.

21. Mabel M. Swan, "Boston's Carvers and Joiners, Part II, Post-Revolutionary," *Antiques*, LIII (April, 1948), 281–285; Richard H. Randall, Jr., "George Bright, Cabinetmaker," *The Art Quarterly*, XXVII (1964), 134–149.

124. DESK AND BOOKCASE. Made by George Bright, Boston, c. 1770–1792.
Mahogany and white pine; H. 99½ inches, W. 43 inches, D. 24 inches. (Museum of
Fine Arts, Boston, Bequest of Miss Charlotte Hazen, 56.1194.) See also fig. 140.
*According to family tradition, Samuel Barrett, a Boston merchant, presented this desk to
his daughter Ann on her marriage to Isaac Green in 1792.*

bookcase section. Much of the detail is composed with respect to the desk or to the bookcase, but the heavy carved feet and double entablature unite the object into a carefully balanced whole. The finely carved garlands in the pediment and the egg and dart molding on the base are examples of elaboration found only on the very finest Boston furniture.

Samuel Barrett, the original owner of the Bright desk and bookcase, was born in 1738, the son of the Boston merchant John Barrett. His first wife was Mary Clarke, daughter of one of Boston's richest citizens and the sister of Sukey Clarke, wife of John Singleton Copley. Barrett married his second wife, Elizabeth Salisbury, in 1771; the desk and bookcase is said to have been a wedding present to their daughter Ann when she married Isaac Green in 1792. The desk is signed by George Bright but is not dated. Whether it was made in 1792 as a wedding present or whether it was an inheritance, the desk is an example of the fully developed Chippendale style.

John Cogswell was another Boston cabinetmaker who produced bombé furniture of the highest quality. Born in Ipswich in 1738, he married Abigail Goodwin of Boston in 1762 and established his residence in or near the city at that time. He was working as a cabinetmaker in Boston in 1769, when he rendered a bill to Caleb Davis, merchant of Boston.[22] Cogswell rose to a certain amount of prominence and held town offices from 1778 to 1809. The identification of his cabinetwork is based upon a chest-on-chest signed "Made By John / Cogswell in middle Street / Boston 1782" (figs. 125, 139, and 143). Ordered by Elias Hasket Derby of Salem, the chest-on-chest, the first of five made for the Derby family, was probably intended for the new house "by the Wharf" which was then under construction but was later abandoned just before completion.[23] A desk and bookcase (fig. 126) neither signed nor supporting a provenance has been attributed to Cogswell because of the close similarity

22. M. Ada Young, "Five Secretaries and the Cogswells," *Antiques*, LXXXVIII (October, 1965), 484–485.

23. Joseph Downs, "John Cogswell, Cabinetmaker," *Antiques*, LXI (April, 1952), 324.

125. CHEST-ON-CHEST. Made by John Cogswell, Boston, 1782. Mahogany and white pine; H. 97 inches, W. 44¼ inches, D. 23½ inches. (Museum of Fine Arts, Boston, William Francis Warden Fund, 1973.289.) See also figs. 139 and 143. *According to family tradition Cogswell constructed this chest for Elias Hasket Derby (1739–1799) of Salem.*

126. DESK AND BOOKCASE. Attributed to John Cogswell, Boston, c. 1770–1790. Mahogany and white pine; H. 95½ inches, W. 45½ inches, D. 22⅝ inches. (The Henry Francis du Pont Winterthur Museum.) See also fig. 127.

127. INTERIOR OF DESK AND BOOKCASE. Attributed to John Cogswell. (The Henry Francis du Pont Winterthur Museum.) See also fig. 126.

in construction and design with the chest-on-chest. The differences are many in the carving. The pattern of the fret on the upper section is quite different in design though not in scale, the knee brackets have dissimilar carved designs, the finials are totally different, and portions of the carving on the pediment are varied in pattern.

The bombé construction of the two casepieces presents a compromise between the two major techniques of American bombé construction.[24] Cogswell has maintained the traditional straight-sided drawer construction but has employed the outward design of curved-sided drawers by allowing only the fronts of the drawers to follow the bombé bulge of the sides (fig. 127). The construction of these

24. Two heavily restored secretaries with structural features similar to the Cogswell casepieces are now in the Winterthur Museum. Both secretaries have unusual upper sections, much different in appearance from the documented Cogswell chest. However, the structural similarities in the desk sections suggest attributions to Cogswell. See figure 135 and Joseph Downs, *American Furniture, Queen Anne and Chippendale Periods in the Henry Francis du Pont Winterthur Museum* (New York, 1952), no. 227.

128. CHEST OF DRAWERS. Attributed to John Cogswell, Boston, c. 1770–1790. Mahogany and white pine; H. 34¾ inches, W. 38½ inches, D. 24 inches. (Museum of Fine Arts, Boston, Bequest of Maria Theresa Burnham Hopkins, 37.34.) See also fig. 142.

two casepieces may be viewed as Cogswell's own, yet it must not be construed that Cogswell exclusively employed this individual method of construction.

Another variation in drawer construction is seen in a bombé chest of drawers attributed to Cogswell (figs. 128 and 142). The interior of the bulge is cut away in the manner of most American bombé casepieces; but the sides of the drawers are slanted to fit the interior space of the bombé bulge. This variation of the curved-sided drawer technique appears on about one-third of the bombé casepieces that

129. DESK AND BOOKCASE. Attributed to Gibbs Atkins, Boston, c. 1770–
1790. Mahogany and white pine; H. 100 inches, W. 46 inches, D. 23 inches.
(Museum of Fine Arts, Boston, M. and M. Karolik Collection, 39.181.) See
also fig. 130. *According to family tradition, this desk and bookcase was owned originally by Gibbs Atkins (1739–1806) and may have been the "desk and bookcase"
(valued at £20) listed in the inventory of his estate.*

have the interior bulge hollowed out.[25] It makes no difference to the outward appearance as the drawer fronts extend very slightly to fill out the curve of the side, but is probably easier to construct. All the other evidence regarding this chest of drawers is so conclusive that it can be safely attributed to Cogswell, but such changes in the method of construction are difficult to interpret without more factual evidence. The elimination of the solid bulge in the chest of drawers may show a developing sophistication in Cogswell's craftsmanship or the use of the solid bulge in the desk and bookcase and chest-on-chest may have been deemed necessary because of the increased weight of the upper section.

Furniture by or attributed to Cogswell portrays a refinement of outline and diminution of detail that is especially evident in the attenuation of the ionic pilasters and the compression of the bombé bulge. The robust circular curves of the Bright desk are transformed by Cogswell into smaller cabriole legs and ovoid openings in the flattened swan's neck pediment. The inclusion of fretwork in the entablature and base of the bookcase adds to the sense of linear delicacy. The fully articulated carving expresses the spirit of rococo design; the carving of the finials, unusual in Massachusetts furniture of this period, is a carefully considered balance to the carving on the feet. As with Federal period cabinetmakers, Cogswell carefully chose different colored mahogany to emphasize the various sections of the design. These pieces of furniture create the standard by which Cogswell can be judged as the creator of some of the most outstanding furniture made in late eighteenth-century America.

Although only four cabinetmakers, Bright, Cogswell, Frothingham, and McMillian, are known to have signed bombé casepieces, another cabinetmaker, Gibbs Atkins, may be considered for the list. Born in 1739, Atkins was trained as a cabinetmaker in Boston. Because of his loyalist sympathies, he moved to Halifax with members of his family in 1776, returned to Boston by 1787, and died there in

25. The Gay family desk and bookcase (fig. 131), attributed to Gibbs Atkins, has slanted drawer sides; the overlapping drawer front is cut to follow the contour of the sides of the case.

130. INTERIOR OF DESK AND BOOKCASE. Attributed to Gibbs Atkins. (Museum of Fine Arts, Boston, M. and M. Karolik Collection, 39.181.) See also fig. 129.

1806. A desk and bookcase (figs. 129 and 130) that descended in his family has been attributed to him. This alone does not substantiate the attribution, but a similar desk and bookcase with the tradition of being made by Atkins descended in the family of his brother-in-law,

Martin Gay (fig. 131).[26] The Gay family desk and bookcase has a history that aids in dating the popularity of the bombé form in Boston. Family tradition states that when the loyalist Martin Gay fled Boston in 1776, he took the desk with him to Halifax, Nova Scotia.[27] That he would take such a cumbersome piece of furniture on board a British transport points to the relative value of such a desk, for many of the fleeing Tories took only silver and abandoned their furnishings. Gay could have left the desk with his wife, Ruth Atkins Gay, who remained in Boston.[28] When he returned in 1792, Gay brought the desk with him. In addition to the historical background, the statement that the desk was taken to Halifax establishes a construction date prior to 1776.

Another piece of furniture with a history dating its construction to before 1774 is a bombé desk and bookcase which was originally owned by William Greenleaf, a wealthy merchant of Boston and New Bedford (figs. 132 and 133).[29] During the preliminary hostilities of 1774, William Greenleaf moved his possessions to Charlestown for storage. With the arrival of the Continental Army, the desk was lent as one of the furnishings of the commander's lodging, thus escaping the burning of Charlestown. The desk was moved again for

26. Both secretaries also have a strong relationship with the desk and bookcase made by George Bright. Until the history of both Atkins' and Bright's apprenticeships and their respective cabinetshops is determined, I am attributing the Gay and Atkins family desks to Gibbs Atkins.

27. Mabel M. Swan, "Furniture of the Boston Tories," *Antiques*, XLI (March, 1942), 187.

28. Stark, *Loyalists*, p. 323.

29. Another bombé desk and bookcase at the Metropolitan Museum also has a tradition of being owned by William Greenleaf. However, Greenleaf's inventory (Bristol County Registry of Probate, Taunton, Massachusetts, XL, 173) lists only one desk and bookcase (valued at $53). The Metropolitan's desk has no proven family history, though an extraneous letter in their files mentions that a desk was owned by William Greenleaf and lent to George Washington when he resided at the Vassall-Longfellow House in Cambridge (Daniel Greenleaf to William Pope, Quincy, Massachusetts, July 1, 1838 [American Wing, Metropolitan Museum of Art]). Since the desk and bookcase at the Whaling Museum has a documented history through the Greenleaf family and since the Metropolitan's letter of documentation is not tied directly to its desk, I feel that the Whaling Museum's desk was probably the one owned by William Greenleaf.

131. DESK AND BOOKCASE. Attributed to Gibbs Atkins, Boston, c. 1770–1776.
Mahogany and white pine; H. 100 inches (without center finial), W. 47$\frac{1}{8}$ inches,
D. 23$\frac{3}{4}$ inches. (Collection of Ebenezer Gay: photo, Richard Cheek.) *According to*
family tradition, this desk was owned by Martin Gay (1726–1809) and his wife Ruth
(Atkins) Gay, the sister of Gibbs Atkins. A gilded eagle and the lower portions of the
finials, both still in the hands of the present owner, were removed to fit the desk into its
current location.

132. Desk and Bookcase. Boston, c. 1770–1774. Mahogany and white pine; h. 97¼ inches, w. 47¼ inches, d. 23½ inches. (Old Dartmouth Historical Society, Whaling Museum, New Bedford, Massachusetts: photo, Richard Cheek.) See also fig. 133. *According to family tradition, this desk was owned by William Greenleaf (1725–1803), a merchant of Boston and New Bedford.*

133. INTERIOR OF DESK AND BOOKCASE. Boston. (Old Dartmouth Historical Society, Whaling Museum, New Bedford, Massachusetts: photo, Richard Cheek.) See also fig. 132.

134. DESIGN FOR A TEA CADDY. From Thomas Chippendale, *The Gentleman and Cabinet-Maker's Director*, plate CXXIX. London, 1754. (The Henry Francis du Pont Winterthur Museum Libraries.)

George Washington's use at the Vassall-Longfellow House in Cambridge. The desk is one of the few examples of curved-sided drawer construction to date before the Revolution. A drawer in the bookcase section bears the inscription "June . . . 1771."

Other bombé casepieces dating before the Revolution are a desk and bookcase given to Abigail Phillips upon her marriage to Josiah Quincy, Jr., in 1769;[30] a desk and bookcase belonging to Sir William Pepperrell;[31] and a tea caddy copied directly from plate CXXIX in the first edition of Chippendale's *Director* (fig. 134). The tea caddy

30. A partial view of the desk and bookcase appears in an 1880s photograph of the left parlor of the Josiah Quincy House, Quincy, Massachusetts, on file in the library of the Society for the Preservation of New England Antiquities, Boston, Massachusetts.

31. Sack, *Fine Points*, p. 161, bottom.

135. DESK AND BOOKCASE. Boston, c. 1780–1795. Mahogany and white pine; H. 95½ inches, W. 37½ inches, D. 20½ inches. (The Henry Francis du Pont Winterthur Museum.) *According to family tradition, this desk was owned by Joseph Barrell (1739–1804), a wealthy merchant of Boston who constructed an elegant two-story house at Lechmere Point between 1792 and 1793.*

136. CHEST OF DRAWERS. Salem, c. 1765–1790. Mahogany and white pine; H. 35¼ inches, W. 40 inches, D. 22½ inches. (The Henry Francis du Pont Winterthur Museum.) See also fig. 121. *According to family tradition, this chest was owned by the Waters family of Salem during the late eighteenth century.*

has the date 1765 written in two places.[32] With the acceptance of the bombé form well established by the time of the Revolution, Cogswell's chest-on-chest demonstrates that the form was favored by the most fashionable clientele into the 1780s. Bombé casepieces with serpentine fronts have a reduction of detail and scale that suggest the delicacy and refinement of the neoclassical style and may well date as late as the 1790s (fig. 135).

A sixth cabinetmaker may be tentatively added to the list of men

32. *Antiques*, LXIII (May, 1953), 385. Another Massachusetts bombé tea caddy made of mahogany and white pine is illustrated in Israel Sack, Inc., *Opportunities in American Antiques*, XXII (November, 1972), 43.

137. CHEST OF DRAWERS. Salem area, c. 1765–1790. Mahogany and white pine; H. 37½ inches, w. 37¼ inches, D. 21½ inches. (The Bayou Bend Collection of the Museum of Fine Arts, Houston.)

known to have constructed bombé furniture. A blockfront desk signed by the cabinetmaker Henry Rust (figs. 84 and 85) has construction, detailing, and proportional organization similar to a group of bombé furniture (figs. 136–138). Born in Ipswich, Rust received his training from Jonathan Gavet of Salem[33] and could have been the

33. Benno M. Forman, "Salem Tradesmen and Craftsmen Circa 1762: A Contemporary Document," *Essex Institute Historical Collections*, CVII (January, 1971), 81.

138. DESK. Salem area, c. 1765–1790. Mahogany and white pine; H. 43½ inches, W. 43⅞ inches, D. 20⅞ inches. (Museum of Fine Arts, Boston, M. and M. Karolik Collection, 41.574.)

source of the bombé furniture generally attributed to Salem. This furniture is distinguished by a finely carved and strongly realistic quahog shell on the center drop. The greatly elongated knee brackets are shaped in a distinct pattern of two reverse curves balancing a semicircle with small breaks. A chest of drawers in the Winterthur Museum (fig. 136) has a history of descent in the Waters and Osgood families of Salem. A nearly identical chest in the Marblehead Historical Society also descended in the Osgood family. From the history of ownership, stylistic connection with a Salem cabinetmaker, and the peculiarities of form and design that separate this group from other American bombé furniture, it seems likely that case-pieces with the above characteristics are indeed a product of Salem and not Boston proper. Since Rust was working from 1762 to 1800,[34] it is impossible to determine if construction predates or postdates the Derby chest-on-chest.[35] The bombé form is obviously similar, but the Salem-attributed examples are not constructed with hidden straight-sided drawers (fig. 121). In addition, the so-called "quahog school" has a definite development of increasing sophistication in the design that implies a relatively uneducated first attempt. In the chest of drawers at Winterthur the bombé bulge begins abruptly after the second drawer, thus dividing the visual balance and losing the overall unity of the sides. A chest of drawers at Bayou Bend (fig. 137) in-corporates the curve at the second drawer, but the curve is still too pronounced. Other examples from the same group achieve the flowing curve characteristic of the best American design (fig. 138).[36]

CONCLUSION

To summarize, the antecedents of Boston bombé furniture arose on the Continent. Stemming from Italian design sources, the bombé casepiece was transformed into contemporary usage by French cabi-netmakers, then adopted and reinterpreted by English taste, tradi-tion, and craftsmanship before it was accepted in colonial America. In the manner peculiar to the arts, the bombé form cut across ideo-logical and political barriers to appear in both colonial and post-Revolutionary Boston with virtually the same status. The same

34. Rust was working in Salem from 1762, removed to Boston by 1773, and was located in Beverly in 1782. He later returned to Salem where he died about 1800. Henry Wyckoff Belknap, *Artists and Craftsmen of Essex County, Massachusetts* (Salem, 1927), p. 68; Forman, "Salem Tradesmen and Craftsmen," p. 65.

35. Rust's only dated piece of furniture is a desk which bears the inscription: "This desk Made By Henry Rust of Salem / Salem, New England / One Thousand seven Hundred and Seventy." Sack, *Opportunities*, XXII (November, 1972), 28–29.

36. See also a desk illustrated by Ginsburg and Levy, Inc., *Antiques*, XLVI (Novem-ber, 1944), 255.

source in England was open to all the colonies, yet a unique combination of emigrating craftsmen, imported furniture, perhaps Chippendale's *Director*, and a response in Bostonian taste resulted in the conscious choice of one furniture form that never appeared in the other colonies.

Although Boston furniture is not comparable to the finest European examples, it is certainly equal to objects owned by the merchant class of London. The overall quality of Boston bombé furniture is representative of the best cabinetwork produced in eighteenth-century Boston. Woods were carefully chosen either for color or for complexity of graining. Carving, when included, usually ranks among the most ornate found on Boston furniture. Construction is light yet accomplished, in the best tradition of Boston cabinetwork. The individuality of many of the examples reflects the number of craftsmen involved in its production, and their number probably increased during the fifty years the form was in demand.

An analysis of ownership shows that the original owners of bombé furniture were among the wealthiest people in Massachusetts. The list includes loyalists such as Governor Hutchinson, Sir William Pepperrell, Charles Apthorp, Edward Brinley, Martin Gay, Gibbs Atkins, and the Vassall family; and patriot and post-Revolutionary merchants such as Joseph Barrell, William Greenleaf, Samuel Barrett, Josiah Quincy, and Elias Hasket Derby. The confines of the Puritan aesthetic seem to have been no barrier to the ownership of relatively ostentatious material possessions; Greenleaf, for example, was the son of a Congregational minister. However, from the few definite family histories, it seems that Anglicans were more disposed to the bombé form than were Congregationalists.

The bombé form was as popular after the Revolution as it was under colonial rule. This continuity demonstrates that the aspirations of the American Revolution were political; a revolution in cultural values was apparently not considered, as many of the revolutionaries took up the outward trappings of the departed loyalists. Thus the bombé furniture of Boston stands as a profound and vivid representation of the taste of eighteenth-century Bostonians.

◆❀ MARY ELLEN HAYWARD YEHIA ❀◆

Ornamental Carving on Boston Furniture
of the Chippendale Style

A T least three major furniture carvers, each with his own particular style of carving, worked in Boston between the years
1755 and 1785. One style of carving, seen on a chest-on-
chest signed by John Cogswell, is notable for its three-dimensionality
and the wide shallow grooves articulating the surface of the leaves
(fig. 139). Another style, distinguished by two-dimensionality and
the thin, narrow grooves used to indicate leaf forms, is evident on a
desk and bookcase by George Bright (fig. 140). A third style, seen on
a distinctive group of chairs and settees, is notable for its amorphous
quality and lack of sharp articulating lines (fig. 141).

Personal and business papers relating to the activities of furniture
craftsmen in eighteenth-century Boston are scarce. No record of a
transaction between a cabinetmaker and carver in the Chippendale
period in Boston has yet come to light. Whether cabinetmakers
carved some or all of the products of their shops, hired specialized
carvers for individual, specific jobs, or arranged for carving on a con-
tract basis has yet to be discovered. Certainly in the Boston of the
1770s and 1780s *cabinetmakers* were the prestige segment of the furniture-making population. It was the cabinetmaker's name that appeared on a bill for furniture and if any name appeared on a piece of
furniture it was more likely the cabinetmaker's than the carver's. If
the cabinetmaker himself did not do the skillfully carved decorations,
he certainly took credit for the finished product.

The pre-eminence of the cabinetmaker is well illustrated by the
correspondence between David Spear and his fiancée, Marcy Hig-

139. DETAIL OF CARVED FOOT OF CHEST-ON-CHEST. Made by John Cogswell. (Museum of Fine Arts, Boston, William Francis Warden Fund, 1973.289.) See also figs. 125 and 143.

gins.[1] David Spear wrote to Marcy excitedly telling her that his father was going to get "Mr. Bright" to make the mahogany furniture for their new home. David was pleased because he knew that George Bright was "esteemed the neatest workman in town." The "very

1. Quoted in Richard H. Randall, Jr., "George Bright, Cabinetmaker," *The Art Quarterly*, XXVII (1964), 136, 138.

good Furniture" from Bright's shop that the Spears were antici-
pating was probably being, at that very moment, decorated by
someone far less exalted than Mr. Bright—someone who would
have received a very small sum for his very skillful services. In the
1780 tax lists for Suffolk County, George Bright and the equally
successful cabinetmaker Alexander Edwards were assessed £120
apiece whereas the carver Joshua Bowles paid £10 and carvers Simeon and John Skillin paid only £20 and £15 respectively.

It is comparatively easy to sort, sift, and separate visual data, but no
carved work can yet be associated with the name of a known carver.
Therefore, this discussion of ornamental carving on Boston furniture
emphasizes the carving styles. The names of some craftsmen likely
to have executed the carved work will be suggested.

John Cogswell apparently employed more than one carver since
carved work of very different styles is found on casepieces made by
this cabinetmaker. The carver of the bracket feet on the signed
Cogswell chest-on-chest (fig. 139) favored a general three-dimensional style of carving, with C-scrolls carved in high relief, dense
leaves lapping one over the other, and shallow grooves used to
articulate the surface of the leaves. Similarly carved feet are found on
a chest of drawers at the Museum of Fine Arts, Boston (figs. 128 and
142), which, on the basis of the carving style and construction details, is attributed to Cogswell. A different carver undoubtedly executed the sophisticated decoration applied to the pediment (fig. 143)
of the signed Cogswell chest-on-chest as the rich, highly three-
dimensional style of the carving is quite different from that of the
carving on the bracket feet.

Another type of three-dimensional carving is seen on a side chair
in the Museum of Fine Arts, Boston (fig. 144), from the James Prince
Mansion in Newburyport and probably made for Nathaniel Tracy
(1751–1796), a prosperous merchant and previous owner of the
house. The chair is part of a set including four other chairs and a sofa
which was exhibited as American at the Girl Scout Loan Exhibition
of 1929. (The sofa is in the collection of Colonial Williamsburg.)
There is now doubt as to the origin of the group of furniture. The

140. DETAIL OF CARVED FOOT OF DESK AND BOOKCASE. Made by George Bright. (Museum of Fine Arts, Boston, Bequest of Miss Charlotte Hazen, 56.1194.) See also fig. 124.

seat frames are beech and thin, open seat braces are used. If the beech can be identified by micro-analysis as American beech, this elaborately carved group of furniture from the Boston area will present a new area of study in Boston carving of the three-dimensional type.

The craftsman who carved the George Bright desk and bookcase had a distinctive style of his own characterized by an overall two-dimensionality (fig. 140). On the carved feet and brackets he used long narrow grooves to articulate the surface of sparse, hatchet-shaped leaves. A star-punched background partially fills the uncarved surface. The carving on the bracket is contained by a smooth band along the lower edge.

Two-dimensionality characterizes much of the carving on Massachusetts Chippendale furniture, but some ornamentation relates directly to the work on the Bright desk and bookcase. A bombé chest of drawers with serpentine front in the Museum of Fine Arts, Boston, has claw and ball feet and brackets with similarly fashioned leaves, a star-punched background, and a smooth band forming a border along the bracket's lower edge.[2] It is unlikely, however, that the two pieces of furniture were carved by the same hand for different punches were used on the two backgrounds and the smooth bordered edge extends much further along the bracket on the chest than on the desk and bookcase. The similarities suggest that the craftsman who executed the carving on the chest was familiar with, if not trained by, the craftsman responsible for the carving on the Bright desk and bookcase.

The third major style of furniture carving seen in Boston in the Chippendale period appears on a very interesting and sophisticated group of furniture notable for its unusual, asymmetrically designed carved decorations. The group consists of: matching settees in the Winterthur Museum (fig. 145) and the Metropolitan Museum of Art; a card table in a private collection; two armchairs and ten side chairs at the Yale University Art Gallery (fig. 141); a side chair at the Winterthur Museum (fig. 146); and an armchair in the collection of Israel Sack, Inc. (fig. 147). For the sake of convenience, Chart I lists various pieces of seating furniture belonging to this group, giving secondary woods, construction methods, and pertinent measurements.

The most distinctive feature of the pieces of furniture in this group, a feature that they all have in common, is the unusual carved ornamentation on the knees. The decorative motif is markedly asymmetrical. (Most carved designs on American Chippendale furniture are totally symmetrical in spite of the rococo penchant for asymmetry.) It consists of a large C-scroll with leafy appendages placed

---

2. For an illustration of the serpentine-front bombé chest, see Edwin J. Hipkiss, *Eighteenth-Century American Arts, The M. and M. Karolik Collection* (Cambridge, 1941), fig. 35.

CHART I

Location	Type	Construction; woods	Measurements
1. Winterthur 51.80	Armchair knee with asymmetrical carving; hairy paw feet	*beech* seat frame; thin *beech* open seat braces	H. 37¼″, W. 25½″, D. 20½″
2. Israel Sack, Inc.	Armchair knee with asymmetrical carving; claw and ball feet	*maple* rear seat rail veneered with mahogany; triangular corner blocks (3½″×1½″) with thin chamfered edge, held in place by 2 round-headed nails ⅜″d.	H. 37½″, W. 29″, D. 19″ *W. top rail:* 20⅜″ *Splat:* H. 19¾″ w. at rosettes 8½″, w. at base 4⁹⁄₁₀″ *Seat:* w. rear 17⅞″, w. front 22¾″, D. 17″ *H. of leg:* 14⅝″
3. Yale University 1967.28.1	Side chair knee with asymmetrical carving; claw and ball feet	*maple* seat frame; *white pine* triangular corner blocks (3¼″×1½″) with thin chamfered edge, held in place by 4 round-headed nails ¼″d.; *American black ash* and *maple* open seat braces held in place with round-headed nails ⅜″d.	H. 37⅝″, W. 22⅞″, D. 18¾″ *W. top rail:* 20½″ *Splat:* H. 19¾″ w. at rosettes 8½″, w. at base 4⁹⁄₁₀″ *Seat:* w. rear 17⅞″, w. front 22⅞″, D. 17¼″ *H. of leg:* 14⅝″
4. Yale University 1967.26	Armchair knee with asymmetrical carving; claw and ball feet	*maple* seat frame; *birch* rear triangular corner blocks (3¼″×1½″) with thin chamfered edge, held in place by 2 round-headed nails ⅜″d.; *maple* open seat braces	H. 37⅜″, W. 26½″, D. 19⁹⁄₁₆″ *W. top rail:* 21½″ *Splat:* H. 19¾″, w. at rosettes 9¼″, w. at base 5⁸⁄₁₀″ *Seat:* w. rear 18⅞″, w. front 25½″, D. 18¼″ *H. of leg:* 14⅝″
5. Winterthur 52.242	Side chair knee with asymmetrical carving; hairy paw feet	*oak* rear seat rail veneered with mahogany; triangular corner blocks *cherry* (3½″×1½″) with thin chamfered edge, held in place by screws that have replaced original nails	H. 37″, W. 21½″, D. 17¾″ *W. top rail:* 20⅜″ *Splat:* H. 19¼″, *H. of leg:* 14⅝″
6. Winterthur 59.1877	Settee knee with asymmetrical carving; claw and ball feet	*maple* seat rail and rear legs, also top of scroll arms; *cedar* top rail, side rail, front and sides of arms; *birch* brace of top rail; triangular corner blocks (4⁵⁄₁₆″×2⅛″) with thin chamfered edge, held in place by 4 round-headed nails ⅜″d.	H. 36″, L. 57″, D. 24″ *H. of leg:* 14⅝″

141. ARMCHAIR. Boston area, c. 1760–1780. Mahogany, maple, and birch; H. 37⅜ inches, W. 26½ inches, D. 19 9/16 inches. (Yale University Art Gallery, Mabel Brady Garvan Collection.)

diagonally across the surface of the knee. Beneath the C-scroll hangs a wilted and drooping leaf.

An armchair at Winterthur (fig. 148 and no. 1, chart 1) seemingly identical to the group of chairs at Yale University (fig. 141 and nos. 3 and 4, chart 1)—with the same asymmetrical knee decoration and the same splat design—proves on closer inspection, however, to have been carved by a different hand than all of the other pieces of furniture in the group. A close look reveals many subtle differences.

The Winterthur armchair has stiles fluted in an a,b,a pattern with the center flute rising higher than those to the sides. Its carved leafage across the top rail descends to various levels on the rail. The flutes on the splat's central figure-eight motif are closely spaced and subtly varied in direction to follow the curve of the figure-eight.

In contrast, the carving on the set of chairs at Yale (fig. 141 and nos. 3, 4, chart 1) and that on an armchair owned by Israel Sack (fig. 147 and no. 2, chart 1) show a less artistic hand at work. The flutes in the stiles all reach the same height. The carved leafage across the top rail is equidistant from the lower edge of the rail. There are far fewer flutes on the figure-eight motif on the splat and these are rather carelessly arranged.

One may conclude that the chairs at Yale and the chair owned by Israel Sack, Inc., were copied from the chair owned by Winterthur, but copied by a craftsman who was not so particular in carrying out the details of execution. There has long been speculation about whether the Winterthur chair is American. Acting on the authority of an antiques dealer in Massachusetts who told him that the chair was found in a Massachusetts house, Joseph Downs considered the chair as American despite its beech seat frame and traditionally English seat braces.[3]

It seems quite likely that the armchair at Winterthur is English[4] and that it or a member of its set (the Museum of Fine Arts, Boston,

3. Joseph Downs, *American Furniture, Queen Anne and Chippendale Periods in the Henry Francis du Pont Winterthur Museum* (New York, 1952), no. 55.

4. See also F. Lewis Hinckley, *Directory of the Historic Cabinet Woods* (New York, 1960), pp. 120, 133.

142. DETAIL OF CARVED FOOT OF CHEST OF DRAWERS. Attributed to John Cogswell. (Museum of Fine Arts, Boston, Bequest of Maria Theresa Burnham Hopkins, 37.34.) See also fig. 128.

owns a seemingly identical side chair) was used as the model for the rest of the furniture in this group. Particularly intriguing in this context are the thick, wide, open seat braces found on the twelve chairs at Yale. It seems as though the Boston chairmaker attempted to copy not only the design and carving of the English chair, but also its method of construction. The open seat braces on the Boston-made versions are much heavier and cruder than on the imported model, and the Boston chairmaker refused to abandon his own traditional method of supporting the chair seats with triangular corner blocks, so that the seats are supported by both open braces and corner blocks.

Consistent construction methods indicate that chairmaker and

143. DETAIL OF PEDIMENT OF CHEST-ON-CHEST. Made by John Cogswell. (Museum of Fine Arts, Boston, William Francis Warden Fund, 1973.289.) See also figs. 125 and 139.

carver (and they may have been the same person) worked on all of the members of this particular group of furniture. In each chair and in the settees the maker used triangular corner blocks with thinly chamfered edges, approximately $3\frac{1}{2}$ inches wide, held in place with either four or two large, round-headed nails. The Yale chairs (fig. 141 and nos. 3, 4, chart 1) are upholstered over the frame; the Sack chair (fig. 147 and no. 2, chart 1) and a side chair at Winterthur (fig. 146 and no. 5, chart 1) have slip seats with rear seat rails veneered with mahogany. Although the splat of the Winterthur side chair is not the same design as that of the other chairs in this group, its cresting rail was made with the same template used for the top rails of the other chairs (they all measure $20\frac{1}{2}$ inches in width). All of the legs belonging to the group of chairs and settees measure $14\frac{5}{8}$ inches in height, indicating that the craftsman worked on a piece basis, turning out carved leg after carved leg (thirty-two legs in all). Only the center legs of the settees differ in style.

More modest types of chairs produced in Boston in the 1770s and 1780s also show interesting carved work by three or more different

144. SIDE CHAIR. England or Boston area, c. 1760–1780. Mahogany and beech; H. 37¼ inches, W. 22½ inches, D. 19 inches. (Museum of Fine Arts, Boston, Gift of Mrs. Guy Currier, 35.1977.) *According to family tradition, this chair was owned by Nathaniel Tracy (1751–1796) of Newburyport, Massachusetts.*

CHART II

Location	Type	Construction; woods	Measurements
1. Winterthur 59.2639.40	Side chair, *splat A* (intertwined scrolls) carved knees, stretchers, claw and ball feet	*pine* triangular corner blocks held in place with 2 round-headed nails	H. 36¾″, W. 21½″, D. 17¼″ *W. top rail:* 20″ *H. splat:* 20⅝″ *Central leaf:* H. 4 3/16″, w. 2⅞″
2. Museum of Fine Arts 60.1176	Side chair, *splat A* (intertwined scrolls) carved knees, stretchers, claw and ball feet	*maple* seat frame; *pine* triangular corner blocks held in place with 2 round-headed nails ¼″d.	H. 37″, W. 21⅜″, D. 17⅝″ *W. top rail:* 19¾″ *H. splat:* 20¾″ *Central leaf:* H. 4 3/16″, w. 2⅞″
3. Winterthur 64.662	Side chair, *splat A* (intertwined scrolls) Marlborough legs	no corner blocks; no secondary woods	H. 36¾″, W. 21¼″, D. 18″ *W. top rail:* 19¼″ *H. splat:* 21″ *Central leaf:* H. 4⅜″, w. 3 1/16″
4. Metropolitan Museum of Art 10.125.289	Side chair, *splat A* (intertwined scrolls) Marlborough legs (set of six)	*cherry* seat rail; *pine* triangular corner blocks	H. 37″, W. 21″, D. 18″
5. Winterthur 61.140.1 and 6. Metropolitan Museum of Art 44.55	Side chair, *splat B* (Gothic arch and trefoil) carved knees, stretchers, claw and ball feet	no corner blocks; no secondary woods	H. 38″, W. 23½″, D. 19″ *W. top rail:* 22¼″ *H. splat:* 21½″ *Central leaf:* H. 2 13/16″, w. 4¾″
7. Winterthur 53.166.3	Side chair, *splat B* (Gothic arch and trefoil) Marlborough legs	*pine* rear triangular corner blocks	H. 38¾″, W. 22″, D. 19⅛″ *W. top rail:* 22⅜″ *H. splat:* 22″ *Central leaf:* H. 2 9/16″, w. 4″
8. Metropolitan Museum of Art 39.88.2	Side chair, *splat C* (from Manwaring) carved knees with punched ground, claw and ball feet	*maple* seat rails, *pine* triangular corner blocks	H. 38⅝″, W. 23½″, D. 17½″

Location	Type	Construction; woods	Measurements
9. Massachusetts Historical Society on loan to Museum of Fine Arts 132.60	Side chair, *splat C* (from Manwaring) carved knees with punched ground, claw and ball feet	*maple* seat rails, *pine* triangular corner blocks, rear ($5'' \times 2\frac{1}{8}''$), front ($4\frac{1}{2}'' \times 1\frac{7}{8}''$) held by 4 nails	H. $38\frac{1}{4}''$, W. $23\frac{5}{8}''$, D. $17\frac{3}{4}''$
10. Museum of Fine Arts Res. 28.78	Side chair, *splat D* (two-tiered Gothic) plain knees, claw and ball feet (set of six)	*maple* seat frame, *pine* triangular corner blocks, rear ($4\frac{1}{2}'' \times 1\frac{7}{8}''$), front ($5'' \times 2\frac{1}{2}''$) held by 4 nails	H. $38''$, W. $22\frac{15}{16}''$, D. $19''$
11. Winterthur 54.532	Side chair, *splat D*, (two-tiered Gothic) plain knees, claw and ball feet	*pine* triangular corner blocks in front	H. $38''$, W. $22\frac{1}{4}''$, D. $18\frac{1}{2}''$

145. SETTEE. Boston area, c. 1760–1780. Mahogany, maple, cedar, and birch; H. 36 inches, w. 57 inches, D. 24 inches. (The Henry Francis du Pont Winterthur Museum.)

hands. A variety of chairs arranged by splat type are listed in Chart II giving details of construction, secondary woods, and measurements.

A Boston-made chair popular among those who could afford mahogany furniture was one with a splat of intertwined scrolls, splat A. Examples are located in the Winterthur Museum (no. 1, chart II), the Museum of Fine Arts, Boston (fig. 149 and no. 2, chart II), and the Metropolitan Museum of Art (no. 4, chart II). Chairs of this type, found frequently in New England, appear not only with ornamental carving, but also in a plain, undecorated form.

Chairs numbers 1 and 2 (fig. 149) on Chart II with this splat design appear identical to chairs numbers 3 (fig. 150) and 4 with the same splat, but subtle differences in the size of the carved motifs indicate that the chairs were carved by different hands. Differences in construction further indicate that chairs numbers 3 and 4 were not produced in the same shop as numbers 1 and 2, emphasizing the popularity of the chair design.

Numbers 5 (fig. 151) and 6 are two chairs from a large set with unusual splat designs of attenuated C-scrolls, a central Gothic arch, and a small solid trefoil near the base, splat B. They were probably made by the same chairmaker who fashioned chairs numbers 3 (fig. 150) and 4, or, at least, carved by the same hand.

Chairs numbers 8 and 9 with splat C (fig. 152) are copied from plate 9 in Robert Manwaring's *The Cabinet and Chair-Maker's Real Friend and Companion* (London, 1765). A very differently designed chair with a two-tiered Gothic splat (fig. 153 and no. 10, chart II), splat D, shows a similar two-dimensional style of carving and similar construction, making tenable an attribution to the same shop and carver. The carving on the chair with the two-tiered splat relates in its two-dimensional character to that on the Bright desk and bookcase (fig. 140).

Although as yet no carver can be identified with a specific piece of furniture, there is an accumulating body of documentary material relating to a number of craftsmen known to have been working in Boston between 1755 and 1785.

146. SIDE CHAIR. Boston area, c. 1760–1780. Mahogany, oak, and cherry; H. 37 inches, W. 21½ inches, D. 17¾ inches. (The Henry Francis du Pont Winterthur Museum.)

147. ARMCHAIR. Boston area, c. 1760–1780. Mahogany and maple; H. 37½ inches, w. 29 inches, D. 19 inches. (Israel Sack, Inc., New York City.) *According to family tradition, this chair was owned by Elias Hasket Derby (1739–1799) of Salem.*

One of the most important identifiable carvers of pre-Revolutionary Boston was John Welch. Born in 1711, Welch is famed for carving the "Sacred Codfish" for the Hall of Representatives in the Boston State House in 1736.[5] In 1733 he purchased a lot of land forty by eighty feet in Green Lane, or in Green Street,[6] presumably in anticipation of his marriage to the granddaughter of the prosperous carver George Robinson. The association with the Robinson family was an important one for Welch. He may have served an apprenticeship under Robinson. The unfortunate death of Welch's young wife in 1736 left Welch with a substantial portion of the Robinson estate.[7] In 1738 and 1743 Welch increased his holdings in the Green Street area.[8] He made his home on Green Lane, but from 1733 until 1758 he kept a shop on the town dock, a good location for a man who was probably primarily a ship carver.

In 1758 Isaac Dupee, a ship carver, petitioned to have the use of the "Town's shop that John Welch occupied."[9] In the same year Welch advertised the sale of many household possessions because he proposed "to go to England in a short time." He did travel to England, presumably on business, but returned to Boston about 1760.[10]

The 1789 inventory of Welch's estate indicates that he was involved in the sale of imported looking glasses. A list of shop goods includes a gilt framed glass, a mahogany framed glass, and four looking glass frames as well as carving tools and "5 ps Carved Work."[11] The inventory of his personal property lists "A Marble slab and frame" and "2 Busts,"[12] an intriguing reference when one

5. Mabel M. Swan, "Boston's Carvers and Joiners, Part I, Pre-Revolutionary," *Antiques*, LIII (March, 1948), 198.

6. Suffolk County Registry of Deeds, Boston, Massachusetts, XLVII, 196 (hereafter Suffolk Deeds).

7. Swan, "Boston's Carvers and Joiners, Part I," p. 198.

8. Suffolk Deeds, LVIII, 4–6; LXVI, 194–195.

9. Quoted in Swan, "Boston's Carvers and Joiners, Part I," p. 199.

10. Ibid.; *The Boston News-Letter*, April 20, 1758; *The Boston Gazette*, April 24, 1758.

11. Suffolk County Registry of Probate, Boston, Massachusetts, docket 19253 (hereafter Suffolk Probate Records).

12. Ibid.

148. ARMCHAIR. England, c. 1760–1780. Mahogany and beech; H. $37\frac{1}{4}$ inches, W. $25\frac{1}{2}$ inches, D. $20\frac{1}{2}$ inches. (The Henry Francis du Pont Winterthur Museum.)

recalls the popularity of carved busts as ornaments for casepieces in Boston in the 1770s and 1780s.

Welch was a very prosperous carver in pre-Revolutionary Boston. The list of his household furniture before the 1758 trip to England included: "Large and Small Sconces, Looking Glasses, Chimney and Dressing Glasses, a very handsome japanned Chest of Drawers and Bureau, a Marble topped table supported by Carved Eagles."[13] Numerous real estate transactions established Welch as a shrewd businessman. In May, 1774, for example, John Welch bought a lot adjoining his own in Green Lane from John Singleton Copley for £153 and resold it a few weeks later for £253.[14] He also had property in the Bowdoin Square–Sudbury Street area and in 1780 he paid the large tax of £50, more than double the sum paid by any other Boston carver.[15]

Most of the other men designated as carvers in public records seem, like Welch, to have been primarily ship carvers. Joshua Bowles and Thomas Luckis had been keeping shop together along the wharf when their inventory was destroyed by the great fire of 1760. They were also engaged in other aspects of the shipping trade for in addition to the "3 Carved heads and carving tools," they lost two boat masts, fifteen cod and mackerel lines, and three barrels of flour.[16] A bill from Bowles and Luckis to John Hancock further identifies these carvers as ship carvers. Mr. Hancock was charged £28 for a woman's head "7 foot long" and £13 more for brackets, a trail board, and two scrolls.[17] By 1780, Joshua Bowles and Thomas Luckis were working separately. At that time Bowles appears to have been slightly more successful, but by Luckis' death in 1808 he had im-

13. *The Boston News-Letter*, April 20, 1758; *The Boston Gazette*, April 24, 1758.

14. Suffolk Deeds, CXXVI, 121.

15. "Assessors' 'Taking Books' of the Town of Boston, 1780," The Bostonian Society, *Publications*, IX (1912), 33.

16. *A Volume of Records Relating to the Early History of Boston Containing Miscellaneous Papers*, XXIX (Boston, 1900), 16–17.

17. Swan, "Boston's Carvers and Joiners, Part I," p. 199.

149. SIDE CHAIR. Boston, c. 1760–1780. Mahogany, maple, and white pine; H. 37 inches, W. 21 3/8 inches, D. 17 5/8 inches. (Museum of Fine Arts, Boston, Gift of Mrs. F. Carrington Weems, 60.1176.) *This chair descended in the Lane family of Boston. The splat of this chair is an example of splat A.*

150. SIDE CHAIR. Boston area, c. 1760–1780. Mahogany; H. 36¾ inches, W. 21¼ inches, D. 18 inches. (The Henry Francis du Pont Winterthur Museum.) *Splat A.*

151. SIDE CHAIR. Boston, c. 1760–1780. Mahogany; H. 38 inches, W. 23 ½ inches, D. 19 inches. (The Henry Francis du Pont Winterthur Museum.) *This chair descended in the De Wolf family of Boston. The splat of this chair is an example of splat B.*

152. SIDE CHAIR. Boston or Salem, c. 1760–1780. Mahogany, maple, and white pine; H. 38¼ inches, W. 23⅝ inches, D. 17¾ inches. (Massachusetts Historical Society: photo, Richard Cheek.) *Splat C.*

153. SIDE CHAIR. Boston, c. 1760–1780. Mahogany, maple, and white pine; H. 38 inches, W. 22 15/16 inches, D. 19 inches. (Museum of Fine Arts, Boston, Gift of Mary W. Bartol, John W. Bartol, and Abigail W. Clark, Res. 28.78.) *According to family tradition, this chair was owned by James Swan (1754–1830) of Boston and Dorchester. The splat of this chair is an example of splat D.*

proved his financial situation and had a house and land on Scotts Court worth $3000.[18]

Another known carver is Simeon Skillin, Sr., who was in business by 1741 in Salutation Alley.[19] Simeon Skillin's activities as a ship carver are well documented but no evidence has been found to show that he carved for cabinetmakers.

Joshua Bowles, Thomas Luckis, and Simeon Skillin may have sometimes carved furniture for the great Boston cabinetmakers, but probably they did not permanently associate themselves with one particular cabinetmaker.

One prominent Boston cabinetmaker who may have employed carvers is Alexander Edwards. Although little is known about his life, his economic success in the cabinetmaking trade associates him with a high-style, highly decorated type of furniture.

Alexander Edwards' father, Benjamin Edwards, a mariner, arrived in Boston in 1716 and three years later bought a large piece of property in Back Street.[20] During his thirty-five years in Boston Benjamin Edwards became a successful merchant, owning at the time of his death in 1751 a "Mansion House" with warehouse and wharf worth £800, four other houses in Back Street, Ship Street, and White Bread Alley, and two Negro slaves.[21]

When his father died, Alexander was eighteen years old and still considered a minor. The cabinetmaker Thomas Sherburne, a neighbor, was made his guardian and probably Edwards was apprenticed to Sherburne in the cabinetmaking trade.[22] Upon his maturity Alexander Edwards inherited his father's Back Street property and set up shop there as a "Gentleman-Cabinetmaker." He was a patriot and in March, 1777, was appointed to a committee of public safety repre-

18. Suffolk Probate Records, docket 23075.

19. Leroy L. Thwing, "The Four Carving Skillins," *Antiques*, XXXIII (June, 1938), 327.

20. Suffolk Deeds, XXXIV, 112–113.

21. Suffolk Probate Records, docket 9826.

22. Suffolk Probate Records, docket 9902.

senting Ward 4.[23] In 1780 he was taxed the considerable sum of £120, the same amount as George Bright.[24]

As with the other Boston cabinetmakers, no carver's name can be linked to Alexander Edwards. The difficulty of associating known carvers with existing carved furniture is compounded by the inability to readily discriminate in documentary sources among furniture, ship, or sign carvers.

This analytical study has attempted to isolate the different styles of the craftsmen who carved Boston furniture during the Chippendale period. Eventually, further study may link these styles with identifiable craftsmen and clarify the relationship between carvers and cabinetmakers.

23. *A Report of the Record Commissioners of the City of Boston, Containing the Boston Town Records, 1770 through 1777*, xviii (Boston, 1887), 276–277.
24. "Assessors' 'Taking Books'," p. 25.

◄❦ RICHARD H. RANDALL, JR. ❦►

Benjamin Frothingham

SO few American cabinetmakers have left behind a broad variety of signed work that the picture of normal daily production cannot be easily examined by the student. William Savery of Philadelphia, John Townsend of Newport, and Benjamin Frothingham of Charlestown are three major exceptions in the eighteenth century, each having liberally labelled his furniture, while others as competent did not seem to do so. Among the many famous cabinetmakers of Boston, like John Cogswell, George Bright, and Ebenezer Hartshorne, sometimes only one or two pieces have retained signatures or maker's marks, while in the case of Alexander Edwards, who paid as high a tax as Bright, not a single example is known. The signed furniture of Benjamin Frothingham is, therefore, worth considering as giving the broadest view of a typical workshop of the Boston region in the eighteenth century.

Benjamin Frothingham (April 6, 1734 – August 19, 1809) was the son of the joiner Benjamin Frothingham (1708–1765) of Boston. The father had a shop in Milk Street, recorded to have burned in the great fire of March 20, 1760, and presumably the younger Benjamin was trained in that shop. In 1756, our Benjamin Frothingham bought a parcel of land in Charlestown where he seems to have been established from at least 1754 until his death in 1809.[1] At the time of the Revolution, his shop in Walker Street was one of twenty-nine cabinetmakers' establishments which were destroyed when the town of Charlestown was burned by the British on June 17, 1775. He was a member of Captain Gridley's militia from 1754 and served in the

1. Mabel M. Swan, "Major Benjamin Frothingham, Cabinetmaker," *Antiques*, LXII (November, 1952), 392–395.

154. HIGH CHEST. Made by Benjamin Frothingham (signature in chalk), Charlestown, c. 1755–1790. Mahogany and white pine; H. 87⅜ inches, W. 42 inches, D. 22⅛ inches. (The Henry Francis du Pont Winterthur Museum.) *This chest and matching dressing table (fig. 155) may have been owned by Nathaniel Richards (1712–1788), an innholder and saddler of Roxbury. His name appears in chalk on the bottom of the long drawer in the lower section.*

Revolution becoming a major by war's end. He retained the title of "Major" all his life, and it has often been noted that George Washington visited Frothingham, "whom he had known in the army," in 1789 in Charlestown. The cabinetmaker was also a member of the Society of the Cincinnati.[2] His wife was Mary Deland by whom he had seven children, one of whom, Benjamin (born 1774), followed the family trade.

The example of John Townsend's labelled furniture gives fair warning to all who would date furniture purely on the basis of style, since his work includes pieces in the styles of the mid-century dated in the 1790s. His three-shell chest in the Metropolitan Museum (fig. 49) is dated 1765, for instance, and a second labelled three-shell chest, now in the State Department, is dated 1792.[3] There are minor concessions to the new neoclassicism, in the choice of plain bail handles and a slight change of proportion and lightening of the moldings of the top, but the answer to dating furniture probably lies in the taste of the man who commissioned it, not in the taste of the cabinetmaker.

Hence, the furniture of Frothingham to be examined is placed in the order of stylistic sequence for simplicity, with no intention of implying dates, early or late. The first examples to consider are in the pad-foot cabriole style of the mid-century.[4] There is a dressing table and matching high chest of drawers, now in the Winterthur Museum and formerly in the Charles K. Davis Collection, with simple cabriole legs and "plain feet," as they were called (figs. 154 and 155). Each piece has a nicely executed fan in one drawer, the proportions

2. A summary of Frothingham's military exploits and the earliest notes on his life are found in Dexter Edwin Spalding, "Benjamin Frothingham of Charlestown, Cabinetmaker and Soldier," *Antiques*, XIV (December, 1928), 536–537. Frothingham's certificate of membership in the Society of the Cincinnati, signed by George Washington and Henry Knox and dated May 5, 1784, has survived and is presently owned by Ginsburg and Levy, Inc., New York.

3. Clement E. Conger and Jane W. Pool, "Americana in the Diplomatic Reception Rooms at the Department of State, Washington, D.C.," *The Connoisseur*, CLXXIV (July, 1970), 220, figs. 7, 8.

4. I would like to acknowledge the great help of Albert Sack in acquiring photographs and information for this paper. His many years of observing details in furniture related to Frothingham have been of signal help, as has the firm's photograph collection.

are good, and the high chest terminates in a well-shaped bonnet with three corkscrew finials. The pieces are made of an unusual burl wood, formerly called curly walnut, but now identified as a type of plum pudding mahogany. The wood is very beautiful and gives considerable interest to the surface, as do the pierced fret brasses on the drawers. Two of the brasses are unusual in that they are stamped clearly on the lower edge of the face "I. Gold," presumably the name of the maker or supplier. Interior construction is of white pine throughout. One drawer in the high chest is signed in chalk: "Benjamin Frothingham" and "Nathanael Richards" (probably the name of the owner).[5]

In the cabriole style are two examples at Winterthur having claw feet with raked talons, typical of the Boston region. One is a card table with reverse blocked sides, nicely emphasizing the corners of the table and accommodating the candle pockets (fig. 156). The legs are long and lean with a sophisticated curve and unusually delicate ankles. The piece is labelled in the drawer with one of the labels engraved for Frothingham by Nathaniel Hurd, the silversmith of Boston (fig. 157). Its secondary woods are white pine and maple.[6]

The second claw table at Winterthur is unusual in itself, since so few of the type survive (fig. 158). It is a six-legged claw foot dining table with two swinging gates to support each large leaf. It is built of light-hued mahogany with white pine and maple as its secondary woods, and is labelled beneath with Hurd's paper label. The legs are well shaped, but not as delicate as those of the card table, nor are the carved talons as acutely raked.[7]

Two secretaries with plain bracket feet number among Frothingham's labelled works. One is made of cherry, an unusual wood in Boston-area practice, and was formerly in the collection of Ernest

5. Helen Comstock, "Frothingham and the Question of Attributions," *Antiques*, LXIII (June, 1953), 502, fig. 3 showing signature; see also Charles F. Hummel, "Queen Anne and Chippendale Furniture in the Henry Francis du Pont Winterthur Museum, Part III," *Antiques*, XCIX (January, 1971), 98–101.

6. Joseph Downs, *American Furniture, Queen Anne and Chippendale Periods in the Henry Francis du Pont Winterthur Museum* (New York, 1952), no. 349.

7. Swan, "Major Benjamin Frothingham," p. 393.

155. DRESSING TABLE. Attributed to Benjamin Frothingham, Charlestown, c. 1755–1790. Mahogany and white pine; H. 31½ inches, W. 33⅞ inches, D. 20¾ inches. (The Henry Francis du Pont Winterthur Museum.) *This table is a mate to the chest illustrated in fig. 154.*

Lo Nano (fig. 159). The base has a straight front, and the bookcase top has doors with fielded panels terminating in flattened arches. The bonnet top resembles the Winterthur high chest with three corkscrew finials. The interior of the bookcase is divided into eight compartments with two rows of eight ogee-headed pigeonholes above. The desk interior has three reverse blocked sections, containing drawers at each end and a central door, each carved with a fan at the

156. CARD TABLE. Made by Benjamin Frothingham (paper label), Charlestown, c. 1755–1790. Mahogany, white pine, and maple; H. 28 inches, W. 34⅛ inches, D. 16¾ inches (closed), 33½ inches (open). (The Henry Francis du Pont Winterthur Museum.) See also fig. 157.

top (fig. 160). These, like the fans of the Davis-Winterthur examples, have a notched or as it is sometimes called a "thumbprint" profile. There are two round-headed pigeonholes between, with a blocked drawer below. The bracket feet have a simple single spur for decoration.[8]

The second secretary, belonging to William T. Earls in 1952, is rather similar (fig. 161). It is broader in proportion and made of mahogany, but the details of the bookcase interior, the desk, and the

8. Ibid.

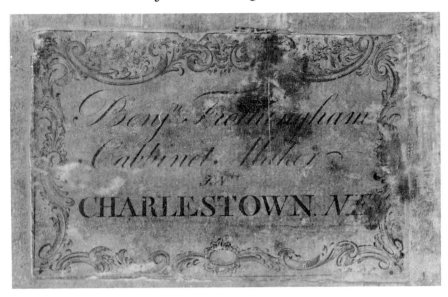

157. DETAIL OF PAPER LABEL ON CARD TABLE: "Benjn. Frothingham / Cabinet Maker / IN / CHARLESTOWN. NE." (The Henry Francis du Pont Winterthur Museum.) See also fig. 156.

feet are nearly identical. It is furnished with only a single middle finial, while the central opening of the bonnet is somewhat wider and rounder in proportion to the breadth of the secretary. There is also a shaped drop in the center of the skirt to accommodate the width of the piece. The mahogany is rather black, and the secondary wood is pine. It is marked with the Hurd paper label in an inside drawer.[9]

The third secretary is, like the Davis–Winterthur high chest, signed on the drawers, this time in four places (figs. 97 and 162). It is an unusual mahogany bombé secretary with molded bracket feet. The bookcase upper section again has fielded panels in the doors, with round, rather than flattened arches at the top, and the bonnet is shaped like those already illustrated with three corkscrew finials. The

9. Ibid., p. 392.

158. DINING TABLE. Made by Benjamin Frothingham (paper label), Charlestown, c. 1755–1790. Mahogany, maple, and white pine; H. 28⅛ inches, W. 59 inches (open), D. 60⅛ inches. (The Henry Francis du Pont Winterthur Museum.)

upper case is divided by three fluted pilasters with capitals of the Corinthian order. They are richly carved with acanthus leaves against a punched ground. In the interior of the case are two intaglio fans at the top, three drawers at the bottom and a series of pigeonholes running up each side. In the center are three movable book shelves. The desk is contrived in an amphitheatre arrangement with two tiers of drawers below four pigeonholes at each side. The central door is reverse blocked with a round-headed panel. There are two narrow document drawers with plain pilasters and acorn finials. The long lower drawers have normal straight sides, and the bombé form is carried out by the shaping of the exterior of the case. Red cedar is the major secondary wood.[10]

The signatures on the bombé secretary are interesting from several points of view. On the back of the top large drawer is the following

10. The information and photographs were kindly supplied by Clement Conger, Chairman of the Fine Arts Committee, the Department of State, Washington, D.C.

159. DESK AND BOOKCASE. Made by Benjamin Frothingham (paper label), Charlestown, c. 1755–1790. Cherry. (Present location unknown. Formerly in the collection of Ernest Lo Nano: photo, Israel Sack, Inc., New York City.) See also fig. 160.

160. INTERIOR OF DESK AND BOOKCASE. Made by Benjamin Frothingham. (Present location unknown. Formerly in the collection of Ernest Lo Nano: photo, Israel Sack, Inc., New York City.) See also fig. 159.

161. DESK AND BOOKCASE. Made by Benjamin Frothingham (paper label), Charles-town, c. 1755–1790. Mahogany and white pine. (Present location unknown. Formerly in the collection of William T. Earls: photo, *Antiques*.)

162. INTERIOR OF DESK AND BOOKCASE. Made by Benjamin Frothingham and D. Sprage. (The Department of State, Washington, D.C.) See also fig. 97.

inscription: "Do D Sprage Benj. Frothingham." On two small interior desk drawers on the bottom is "Benj. Frothingham," and on the side of one document drawer is "Do Sprage 1753." The placement of the inscription on the big drawer is certainly appropriate only to those involved in the construction of the piece, and implies, since Sprage's initials appear, that he was either a partner or workman in its construction. If the date is correct, it is the only dated example of Frothingham's work, and is very early in his career. One might surmise that young Benjamin had gone into partnership before his father's shop burned in 1760, and that he may have already moved from Boston to Charlestown since he is recorded there in 1754. Another possibility might be that Frothingham and Sprage were apprentices nearing the end of their training with the elder Benjamin Frothingham. The construction of the secretary could then have represented the culmination of their apprenticeships and have shown to others their mastery of the craft of cabinetmaking. A final possibility is that the signature is not that of the younger Frothingham, but that of his father. At the moment, however, since no other work attributable to the father is known, it is difficult to subtract this dated and fascinating piece from the work of the man who signed other pieces in a similar fashion. The discovery of facts relating to D. Sprage might settle the matter.[11]

Frothingham employed the ogee bracket foot on occasion, as seen on three reverse serpentine mahogany desks. On the first, formerly in the collection of Mrs. Sidney Harwood (fig. 163),[12] the foot has a bracket with a simple spur profile. The projecting sections of the reverse serpentine terminate with round blocking in the upper drawer and with a depressed arch in the central area. Such a treatment occurs on a desk by Joseph Hosmer of Concord[13] and on a number of pieces

11. Two Spragues are known to have worked in the cabinet business in Boston at later dates, one of whom, Holmes Sprague, is recorded as working after the Revolution. See Mabel M. Swan, "Boston's Carvers and Joiners, Part II, Post-Revolutionary," *Antiques*, LIII (April, 1948), 285.

12. This desk was sold in the Philip Flayderman sale of January 2–4, 1930. See *The Collection of the Late Philip Flayderman* (New York, 1930), lot 418.

13. Ethel Hall Bjerkoe, *The Cabinetmakers of America* (Garden City, New York, 1957), plate XVIII, no. 2.

from the Northampton area,[14] as well as on a chest-on-chest with Boston details in the Henry Ford Museum.[15] The interior of the desk has a projecting shelf with three drawers, above which is a pair of drawers below four ogee-headed pigeonholes on each side of the central section. The central door is treated with a reverse-blocked panel with a carved fan, and the two document drawers have plain pilasters with urn finials. The mahogany was chosen for its figure.[16]

Remarkably similar to the Harwood desk is a second example, now in a private collection (figs. 164 and 165). With the exception of a slight variation in the brasses and the addition of a shaped drop to the center of the skirt, this desk repeats virtually line for line the exterior shape and interior details of the Harwood desk. In addition, the blond mahogany of both desks compares quite closely in wood color and surface grain, suggesting that perhaps a single piece of mahogany was used for the drawer fronts of both pieces. According to the present owner, the second desk was purchased by her father in the Boston area about 1901. Like the Harwood desk, it bears a Hurd label in the small reverse blocked central drawer of the interior.

A third labelled desk with ogee bracket feet is in the collection of the Currier Gallery of Art (figs. 166 and 167). The shape of the brackets and brasses is reminiscent of those on the two previous desks. However, the desk front has a less pronounced bow with only a hint of blocking on the upper drawer. The desk interior also differs, containing a double tier of drawers above a row of pigeonholes. A column of three central drawers is decorated with string inlay and, on the upper drawer, with an inlaid fan. The use of inlay, a characteristic of Federal period work, suggests a date of manufacture of 1790 to 1800. A Hurd paper label appears in the middle drawer of the central section. According to David Brooke, Director of the Currier Gallery, the desk descended in the Nichols family of Wiscasset, Maine, before coming to the Gallery in 1967.

14. Wallace Nutting, *Furniture Treasury* (1928; rpt. New York, 1954), figs. 718, 719.

15. Helen Comstock, *American Furniture* (New York, 1962), fig. 304.

16. The interior is shown by Spalding, "Frothingham," p. 537, fig. 3.

A more elaborate desk is at Historic Deerfield (figs. 78, 79, 168, and 169). It is of rich mahogany with square blocking and short cabriole legs carved with hairy claws. The desk interior duplicates that of the Lo Nano secretary. The feet are the most extraordinary features. All four feet are carved with four great talons grasping a

163. DESK. Made by Benjamin Frothingham (paper label), Charlestown, c. 1755–1790. Mahogany and white pine; H. 43¾ inches, W. 44½ inches, D. 23⅜ inches. (Private collection: photo, Richard Cheek.)

round ball, and the fleshy parts of the foot are rendered so as to represent the effect of pin feathers. The brackets are blocked on the front and have the spur profile. The foot is smaller and more compact than the examples of hairy claw feet by George Bright and other cabinetmakers of the Boston area.[17]

Two blockfront chests of drawers with plain bracket feet bear the

17. Richard H. Randall, Jr., *American Furniture in the Museum of Fine Arts, Boston* (Boston, 1965), fig. 64d.

164. DESK. Made by Benjamin Frothingham (paper label), Charlestown, c. 1755–1790. Mahogany and white pine; H. 43½ inches, W. 41¾ inches, D. 21⅞ inches. (Private collection.) See also fig. 165.

165. INTERIOR OF DESK. Made by Benjamin Frothingham. (Private collection.) See also fig. 164.

166. DESK. Made by Benjamin Frothingham (paper label), Charlestown, c. 1780–1800. Mahogany and white pine; H. 43 ¼ inches, W. 44 inches, D. 24 inches. (The Currier Gallery of Art.) See also fig. 167.

167. INTERIOR OF DESK. Made by Benjamin Frothingham. (The Currier Gallery of Art.) See also fig. 166.

label of Frothingham. The first example (fig. 170) has square block-ing similar to the Deerfield desk; the bracket has the same spur detail seen on other examples. The top of the piece, which I have never examined, has almost no overhang, a feature unusual in Boston practice, and suggests that this might have been the base of a chest-on-chest originally. The piece bears the Hurd paper label in the drawer and was in the collection of Mrs. Ernest L. Rueter in 1952.[18]

The second chest, documented by a fragmentary Hurd label in the upper drawer, has rounded blocking and a molded top which follows the contours of the front. It closely resembles a chest signed in chalk by Walter Frothingham, an unidentified member of the Frothingham family. Mr. and Mrs. Stephens Croom of Mobile, Alabama, owned the chest in 1964.[19]

A chest-on-chest, now in a private collection, is one of the most masterful of Frothingham's works (fig. 1). It again carries the Hurd paper label. The lower case is square blocked, and its lines carry down into a blocked ogee bracket foot of a type rarely met outside of Rhode Island. The upper case is flanked by fluted pilasters with pulvinated caps. The carved fan in the central upper drawer is of the most elaborate type found in the Boston area. It is based on stylized acanthus leaves; the main area of the fan is a leaf with undulating edges. Its surface is decorated with punched ovals and at the lower center is a smaller leaf in high relief and a row of scrolling leaves across the base. The richness of carving is continued into the open bonnet with its two floral rosettes, and the three corkscrew finials have pierced bases, giving them a weightlessness and a richness of light and shade. The lower case is supplied with side brasses, matching the large pine-tree type of the drawers.[20]

Having worked in the styles of the middle and third quarter of the century, Frothingham turned his attention to those of the last years

18. Swan, "Major Benjamin Frothingham," p. 395.

19. For illustrations of the chest and label, see Margaret Rose Ingate, "History in Towns: Mobile, Alabama," *Antiques*, LXXXV (March, 1964), 309. For illustrations of the Walter Frothingham chest, see Comstock, "Frothingham and the Question of Attributions," p. 505, figs. 13, 14.

20. *Antiques*, LXII (November, 1952), frontispiece. This type of richly carved fan exists in a number of Boston examples including the Hancock dressing table, now in the John Hancock Insurance Company Collection (Albert Sack, *Fine Points of Furniture: Early American* [New York, 1950], p. 198, bottom); a pad-foot high chest now at the Metropolitan Museum of Art (Luke Vincent Lockwood, *Colonial Furniture in America*, 3rd ed., 2 vols. [New York, 1926], I, 97, fig. 94); and a blockfront chest-on-chest (Lockwood, *Colonial Furniture*, I, 360, fig. XXVII); all perhaps by the same carver.

of the century. He is known to have made three pieces of labelled furniture in the new neoclassical manner of Hepplewhite. One is a characteristic New England chair with an urn-decorated back, of a type made in Newport, Providence, Salem, and Boston (fig. 171).

168. DESK. Made by Benjamin Frothingham. (Historic Deerfield, Inc., Deerfield, Massachusetts.) See also figs. 78, 79, and 169.

The Boston-area chairs are usually uncarved on the lower semicircle of the back splat, as is the case with this chair. The legs are molded, and across the underside of the rear seat rail is lettered "Mr Benjan. Frothingham / Charlestown" in ink. If it is not a mark of ownership, it is likely that this was the inscription of an upholsterer who wished to know to whom the chair should be returned. While it is one of only two surviving chairs associated with Frothingham, his shop inventory listed "6 chears" indicating that he had always made a certain number. The chair is owned by the Toms Foundation of Knoxville, Tennessee.[21]

Another chair, which descended in the Frothingham family, is in the Museum of Fine Arts, Boston, and carries the legend that it was made in the shop of Benjamin Frothingham. As it is a Windsor

21. Swan, "Major Benjamin Frothingham," p. 394 showing inscription.

169. DETAIL OF FOOT OF DESK. Made by Benjamin Frothingham. (Historic Deerfield, Inc., Deerfield, Massachusetts.) See also figs. 78, 79, and 168.

170. CHEST OF DRAWERS. Made by Benjamin Frothingham (paper label), Charlestown, c. 1755–1790. Mahogany. (Present location unknown. Formerly in the collection of Mrs. Ernest L. Rueter: photo, *Antiques.*)

chair, with bow back and continuous arms, it seems hardly likely to have been the product of Frothingham's shop. Windsor chair making was a specialty in the cabinet trade; it is far more likely that Frothingham purchased the chair for his daughter. It is interesting in being a documented example of furniture which did belong to a cabinetmaker's family.[22]

The second neoclassical example, which has been in unknown hands since the Philip Flayderman sale of 1930 where it was lot 417, is a serpentine-front sideboard (fig. 172). The unfortunate brasses of

22. Randall, *American Furniture,* p. 239.

the photograph distract one from the quality of this unusual New England board with three central drawers. The doors and drawers are well veneered and banded, with the door keyholes carried out as diamond inlays. The stiles and tapering legs have long round-headed panels of stringing, those of the legs having a single bellflower at the top of each panel. The cuffs are banded, and the top is finished with a double-beaded edge. It was described in the Flayderman catalogue as being of "fine figured mahogany, banded with cross-cut wood of beautiful color."[23]

The third example is a typical D-shaped card table in a characteristic Massachusetts manner. It has good stringing in the legs with a small panel of lighter wood at the top of the leg, and a checkered band across the bottom of the skirt. It is built of good, well-figured mahogany, but has few characteristics that indicate its origins in Frothingham's shop, other than a finely preserved label on the underside. It is in the collection of Joseph Kindig III.

While I do not wish to discuss the attributions to Frothingham, of which many have been made, I would like to point out that certain pieces such as the secretary in the William Rockhill Nelson Gallery with its bracket feet, similar bonnet, and identical desk interior show such affinity to Frothingham that it is hard to interpret them as merely regional similarities.[24] The fall-front square blocked desk at Colonial Williamsburg again shares the general features, with minor variations in the pen drawers of the desk interior, and is one of only a few Boston-area casepieces having blocked ogee bracket feet with scroll returns. This is related to the treatment of the Frothingham chest-on-chest and bears an obvious indirect relation to Newport sources.[25]

Three surviving bills from Frothingham indicate the variety of work performed in his shop. On June 12, 1788, he billed Colonel

23. *Flayderman*, lot 417.

24. Bjerkoe, *Cabinetmakers*, plate XVII, no. 2.

25. The information was kindly supplied by Barry Greenlaw, Curator of Furniture at Colonial Williamsburg. For further information and illustrations, see Barry Greenlaw, *New England Furniture at Colonial Williamsburg* (Williamsburg, 1974), no. 98.

171. SIDE CHAIR. Made or owned by Benjamin Frothingham (inscription in ink), Charlestown, c. 1790–1809. Mahogany, beech, and maple; H. 33 inches, W. 22 inches, D. 18 inches. (The Toms Foundation, Craighead–Jackson House, Knoxville, Tennessee.)

Ervin for two field bedsteads, and, on April 17, 1789, William Stearns for a coffin and furniture.[26] On January 16, 1797, he charged General Henry Knox of Thomaston, Maine, £57:8:0 for the following:

To 2 large mohogany Card Tables	£ 6:12:0
To 2 D[itt]o Do Pembrook Do	6:12:0
To 1 large mohogany Bedsted foot &	
Side Boards	12:10:0
To 1 Do without foot Board	11: 0:0
To large mohogany ward Robe	16:10:0
To 2 Cornish & Painting	4: 4:0[27]

The contents of his shop, destroyed by fire in 1775, shed further light on the general size of Frothingham's production where the following items were listed:

1 Mahogany Case draws	[£] 7: 0:0
1 Burow tabel	4: 0:0
3 Walnut Case draws	17:10:0
12 tabels of sortes	20: 0:0
. . .	
6 chears	0:14:0

The wood inventory of the same year includes cherry and "yallowsander wood," probably American gumwood which Frothingham's inventory clerk put down as sandalwood because of its similar yellow color. This seems more likely than the interpretation that it was "palisander" or rosewood, which is purplish in hue. The list is as follows:

a Quantity of Mahogany boards & planks	[£]34: 0:0
Walnut boards	14: 0:0
Cherrytree boards	1: 0:0
Mapole planks. pineboards. planks	8: 0:0
. . .	
a Quantity of Yallowsander wood	3:10:0[28]

26. Swan, "Major Benjamin Frothingham," p. 395.

27. General Henry Knox to Benjamin Frothingham, Charlestown, January 16, 1797, Henry Knox Papers (Maine Historical Society). Courtesy of Earle Shettleworth.

28. Quoted in Swan, "Major Benjamin Frothingham," p. 394.

While we certainly have today only a fragment of the production of Benjamin Frothingham from his career of more than fifty years, the pieces that survive with his label show a man working in the best traditions through three phases of style. He was therefore both skilled and aware of his customers' needs. His use of unusually beautiful or colored woods—plum pudding mahogany, cherry, and "yallow-sander"—indicate either that there may have been some differences in taste between Boston and Charlestown or that the cabinetmaker himself enjoyed unusual woods. His choice of brasses, also, judging from the evidence of two sets of pierced ones, is something more than ordinary.

However, it is very difficult to attribute the richness of taste in details to the cabinetmaker of the eighteenth century. The taste was more often that of the customer. While we know a certain amount about Frothingham, we have, except for three bills, very little knowledge of his clientele. For them it appears that he produced mostly casepieces—desks, secretaries, and chests of drawers—though tables formed a good portion of his 1775 inventory and account for two of his surviving pieces. That he also made chairs is implied by the inventory and affirmed by the Hepplewhite shield-back example.

A number of details remain to be discovered. Who was the I. Gold whose name appears on the brasses of the Davis-Winterthur examples, and who was the D. Sprage who signed the bombé secretary? To judge from the majority of his cabinetwork, it would be interesting to know if he was a carver himself or if, more likely, he employed a carver to produce the elaborate fan of the privately owned chest-on-chest and the hairy paw feet of the Deerfield desk.

Certainly, Major Benjamin Frothingham was a man well known and honored in his own day. He was also financially successful. His claims of 1775 show that he owned a shop valued at £26, a barn at £40, and a house of £220 value. In 1809 he died possessed of twenty-seven square rods of land and a building valued at $2500. He has left behind what many other Boston-area makers have denied us, a series of labelled examples ranging from the mid-eighteenth century to the early nineteenth century. While this tells much about Frothingham

172. SIDEBOARD. Made by Benjamin Frothingham (paper label), Charlestown, c. 1790–1809. Mahogany and white pine; H. 38 inches, W. 59 inches, D. 25 inches. (Present location unknown. Sold at the American Art Association auction of the estate of Philip Flayderman, January 2–4, 1930, lot 417: photo, *Antiques*.)

as an individual, it tells an equal amount about his contemporaries in Boston and vicinity, and what one may expect to have emerged from their shops. There has yet to be discovered a daybook of a Boston maker, where one can learn the day-to-day business of the cabinetmaker as that of the silversmith is outlined by Paul Revere's accounts. However, the labelled furniture of Frothingham comes closest to showing the range and variety of the Boston cabinet-maker's work.

New England Timbers

BOSTON CABINET WOODS
OF THE EIGHTEENTH CENTURY

I N 1634 William Wood in his promotional tract *New England Prospects* described Boston as "bare of wood," the residents "being constrayned to fetch their building-timber, and fire-wood from the Ilands in Boates."[1] Furniture craftsmen relied on local merchants, ship captains, inland farmers, and traders for their lumber. During the eighteenth century craftsmen principally used black walnut, mahogany, cedar, and maple as primary woods and white pine as a secondary wood. Less frequently they chose birch, cherry, white oak, red oak, and chestnut. The 1797 inventory of the estate of Samuel Fisk, one of Boston's wealthiest cabinetmakers, included not only a "Pile of Bay Mahogany" valued at $325.29 and "235 feet Jamaica Mahy" valued at $42.30, but also:

51 feet black Walnut at [$].–4 [per foot] [$]	2.–4
2 Logs of d[itt]o in the Shed	2.—
720½ feet of Mahy at the Mill in	
Watertown at .14½ pr foot	104.47
292 feet Chesnut at 1.50 pr hund	4.38
194 feet Cherry tree boards at 2.50 pr hund	4.85
573 feet clear pine boards at 12.0 pr M [thousand]	6.87
1023 feet Maple joysts at 1.50 pr hundd	15.34
844 do boards at 1. pr hundred	8.44
2 birch planks	3.—
. . .	
Ebony & wood for Inlays	3.—[2]

1. Quoted in Nathaniel B. Shurtleff, *A Topographical and Historical Description of Boston*, 3rd ed. (Boston, 1891), pp. 40–41.
2. Suffolk County Registry of Probate, Boston, Massachusetts, docket 20668.

Black walnut, popular throughout most of the century, was imported largely from the southern and middle colonies. In 1774 while travelling through New Jersey, John Adams spotted a row of four large black walnut trees and commented, "It seems that these Trees are plenty in these Southern Provinces—all the black Walnut Timber which is used by our Cabinet Makers in Boston is brought from the Southern Provinces."[3]

By the 1730s mahogany had become a fashionable wood in Boston. Shipped from the West Indies and Central America, the wood was sold by the piece at local vendues or marketed by merchants.[4] According to the Boston physician William Douglass (c. 1691–1752), "Mahogany wood of the West-Indies" was excellent for cabinet and joiners' work, "much surpassing the red cedar of Carolina and Bermudas, which has a disagreeable perfume."[5]

Despite Douglass' comments, Boston cabinetmakers occasionally used red cedar in their furniture. Merchants imported some cedar from the South; however, much more came from the lowlands and swamps of eastern Massachusetts. Based on surviving evidence, the wood seems to have gained popularity between about 1720 and 1760. In the November 28 – December 5, 1728, issue of *The Boston News-Letter*, the printer advertised "A *Fine Red New Cedar Desk*" for sale. After the disastrous fire of 1760, Thomas Foot, a local cabinetmaker, listed among his losses, "36 foot Cedar Logs" valued at £2:17:6.[6]

Boston craftsmen easily obtained native hardwoods such as cherry

3. *Diary and Autobiography of John Adams*, ed. L. H. Butterfield, 4 vols. (Cambridge, 1961), II, 114.

4. A vendue announcement appears in *The Boston Gazette*, November 21–28, 1737; an advertisement by the merchant Nathaniel Cunningham appears in *The Boston Evening-Post*, September 6, 1742.

5. William Douglass, *A Summary, Historical and Political, of the First Planting, Progressive Improvements, and Present State of the British Settlements in North-America*, 2nd ed., 2 vols. (London, 1755), II, 61.

6. Documents and Correspondence in the Boston Public Library Concerning the Boston Fire of 1760, part II, document 29 (microfilm copy, Henry Francis du Pont Winterthur Museum Libraries, Joseph Downs Manuscript Collection).

or maple. Yeomen in surrounding towns often traded lumber with merchants or craftsmen for imported foodstuffs and cloth. While documented Boston furniture of cherry is scarce, John Adams noted during a visit to the Braintree home of John Borland that "The Wood [cherry] is very good for the Cabinet-Maker. . . . It is a tree of much Beauty."[7] Maple, on the other hand, is seen in many pieces of Boston furniture. Japanned high chests, for example, are almost always constructed of maple. The close-grained wood provided an excellent base for the many layers of white lead, vermilion, lamp-black, and gold leaf used by the japanner.

White pine, "the tallest and most stately tree of our forests,"[8] was common throughout New England. Beginning early in the seventeenth century, merchants and millwrights established sawmills in coastal settlements and shipped cargoes of sawn pine boards and planks to Boston.[9] White pine was, according to William Douglass, "much used in framing of houses and in joiners work, scarce any of it to be found south of New-England. In joiners work, it is of a good grain, soft, and easily wrought."[10]

Gordon Saltar has prepared the following list of New England woods available to furniture craftsmen in the eighteenth century. He has included those properties which might have been of concern to cabinetmakers. The log diameters represent the average. The geographical ranges represent coastal regions only. An annotated bibliography on the identification of woods is presented at the end of the article.

BROCK JOBE

7. *Adams Diary*, ed. Butterfield, I, 228. See also Douglass, *A Summary*, II, 66.

8. George B. Emerson, *A Report on the Trees and Shrubs Growing Naturally in the Forests of Massachusetts* (Boston, 1846), p. 60.

9. Benno M. Forman, "Mill Sawing in Seventeenth-Century Massachusetts," *Old-Time New England*, LX (Spring, 1970), 118–120.

10. Douglass, *A Summary*, II, 54.

New England Timbers

CONIFER TIMBERS

ARBORVITAE, *Thuja occidentalis*, also called Northern White Cedar

Diameter 2′–3′. Light; soft; brittle; very coarse to fine-grained; somewhat harsh under tools, but can be worked to a smooth finish and holds paint well; faint bitter taste; pale brown. It ranged from New Brunswick to southern New Hampshire and central Massachusetts.

FIR, *Abies balsamea*, also called Balsam Fir

Diameter 12″–18″. Light; soft; not strong; coarse-grained; pale brown streaked with yellow; is used for sugar and butter tubs because of absence of objectionable taste. It ranged through northern New England and western Massachusetts.

HEMLOCK, *Tsuga canadensis*

Diameter 2′–4′. Light; soft; not strong; brittle; coarse-grained; harsh and splintery under tools; glues easily; uneven and frequently spiral-grained; light brown tinged with red. It ranged from Nova Scotia to northern Delaware.

JACK PINE, *Pinus banksiana*, also called Grey Pine

Diameter under 2′. Light; soft; not strong; close-grained; refractory under tools; clear pale brown. It ranged from Nova Scotia to coast of Maine, northern New Hampshire and Vermont.

PITCH PINE, *Pinus rigida*

Diameter under 3′. Light; soft; not strong; brittle; coarse-grained; light brown or red. It ranged from Mount Desert, Maine, to southern Delaware.

RED PINE, *Pinus resinosa*, also called Norway Pine

Diameter 2′–3′. Light; moderately soft to hard; high in shock resistance; works easily with tools; very close-grained; glues well; pale red to orange-brown. It ranged from Nova Scotia to eastern Massachusetts.

WHITE PINE, *Pinus strobus*

Diameter 3′–4′. Light; not strong; straight-grained; medium-textured; moderately soft; moderately low in shock resistance; works easily with tools; glues well; takes paint extremely well; light brown often tinged with red which darkens a great deal on exposure. It ranged from Newfoundland to northern Delaware.

RED CEDAR, *Juniperus virginiana*

Diameter 3'–4'. Light; close-grained; brittle; not strong; works easily under tools; high in shock resistance; fine-textured; very fragrant; very resistant to decay; purplish or rose-red when first exposed, aging rapidly to a dull red or reddish brown. It ranged from New Brunswick to the coast of Georgia.

BLACK SPRUCE, *Picea mariana**

Diameter 6"–12". Light; soft; not strong; glues well; easy to work; pale yellow-white.

WHITE SPRUCE, *Picea glauca**

Diameter under 2'. Same general properties as the Black Spruce.

RED SPRUCE, *Picea rubra**

Diameter 2'–3'. Same general properties as the Black and White Spruces, except somewhat closer-grained and slightly tinged with red.

TAMARACK, *Larix laricina*, also called Eastern Larch

Diameter 18"–20". Very heavy; moderately to exceedingly hard; strong; coarse-grained; moderately high in shock resistance; a slightly oily feel to the touch; often spiral-grained; yellowish to light reddish brown. It ranged from Labrador to eastern Pennsylvania.

WHITE CEDAR, *Chamaecyparis thyoides*, also called Atlantic White
Cedar and Southern White Cedar

Diameter 3'–4' (probably much smaller in New England). Light; soft; straight-grained; fine-textured; low in shock resistance; works well under tools; takes a smooth finish; holds paint well; slight bitter taste; pale brown with red or pink in the late wood of each annual ring. It ranged from near Concord, New Hampshire, and southern Maine to the coast of northern Florida.

POROUS WOOD TIMBERS

WHITE ASH, *Fraxinus americana*

Diameter 5'–6'. Heavy; hard; strong; works well under tools; close-grained; tough; brown heartwood; very thick light straw-colored sapwood. It ranged from Nova Scotia to Florida.

---

* Spruce wood, though little used in the construction of furniture, has long been a favorite in the making of musical instruments, especially sounding boards, for it has exceptional resonance. All of these trees ranged through all of the New England states.

RED ASH, *Fraxinus pennsylvanica*

Diameter 18″–20″. Heavy; hard; fairly strong; works well under tools; brittle; coarse-grained; light brown heartwood; very thick lighter brown sapwood with yellowish streaks. It ranged from Nova Scotia to central Georgia.

BLACK ASH, *Fraxinus nigra*, also called Brown Ash

Diameter up to 20″. Heavy; fairly soft; not strong; tough; coarse-grained; straight-grained; separates easily along its annual rings, especially in its thick sapwood, into thin flexible layers—basket, splint-seat material. Heartwood is grey-brown to dark brown, lusterless compared to other Ashes. Sapwood is very light brown, sometimes nearly white. It ranged from Newfoundland to northern Delaware.

BASSWOOD, *Tilia americana*, also called Linden

Diameter 3′–4′. Soft; weak; low in shock resistance; works well under tools; valued for hand carving; finishes smooth; holds paint well; glues well. Heartwood pale brown with very slight touches of red, merging gradually with the paler sapwood. It ranged from New Brunswick to Pennsylvania.

BEECH, *Fagus grandifolia*

Diameter 3′–4′. Hard; strong; tough; high in shock resistance; difficult to work with hand tools, but excellent for turning; stays smooth when subjected to friction; pale rose to reddish brown. It ranged from New Brunswick to northern Delaware.

BLACK BIRCH, *Betula lenta*, also called Sweet Birch and Cherry Birch

Diameter 2′–5′. Heavy; very strong; hard; close-grained; very high in shock resistance; turns well; takes a smooth finish; dark brown tinged with red. It ranged from southern Maine and northwestern Vermont to northern Delaware.

YELLOW BIRCH, *Betula lutea*, also called Grey Birch

Diameter 3′–4′. Heavy; very strong; hard; close-grained; high in shock resistance; turns well; takes a smooth finish; light brown tinged with red. It ranged at its best in northern New England; small and rare in southern New England.

PAPER BIRCH, *Betula papyrifera*, also called Canoe Birch

Diameter 2′–3′. Light; strong; hard; tough (but less so than the Black Birch and the Yellow Birch); very close-grained; turns extremely well; takes a smooth finish; light brown tinged with red. It ranged over northern New England; small and rare in the coastal region of southern New England.

BLACK GUM, *Nyssa sylvatica*, also called Sour Gum, Tupelo, and
         Pepperidge

Diameter up to 5′. Usually heavy; soft; strong; very tough; usually with interlocking grain; moderately high in shock resistance; difficult to split; refractory under hand tools; finishes very well; takes paint well; stains well; glues satisfactorily; light yellow to almost white. It ranged from the valley of the Kennebec River, Maine, to northern Florida.

BLUE BEECH, *Carpinus caroliniana*, also called American Hornbeam, Water Beech, and Ironwood

Diameter up to 2'. Hard; moderately strong in bending; exceedingly high in shock resistance; splits with great difficulty; stiff; good for handles, vehicle parts, levers; William Noyes wrote in *Wood and Forest* (Peoria, Illinois, 1912), p. 125, "No other wood so good for levers, because of stiffness"; pale yellowish to light brown. It ranged from Nova Scotia to Florida.

BUTTERNUT, *Juglans cinerea*, also called White Walnut

Diameter 2'–3'. Light; soft; not strong; coarse-grained; straight-grained; moderately high in shock resistance; works well; takes stain well; light brown turning darker with exposure. It ranged from New Brunswick to eastern Virginia.

BLACK CHERRY, *Prunus serotina*, also called Wild Cherry and Rum Cherry

Diameter 4'–5'. Light to moderately heavy; moderately strong; rather hard; close-grained; straight-grained; strong in bending and endwise compression; high in shock resistance; works well with tools; finishes smoothly; glues satisfactorily; satiny surface; light to dark reddish brown. It ranged from Nova Scotia to central Florida.

CHESTNUT, *Castanea dentata*, also called American Chestnut

Diameter 3'–4'. Light; soft to moderately hard; not strong; easily split; moderately low in shock resistance; works well under tools; glues very well; very resistant to decay; greyish brown to reddish brown. It ranged from Southern Maine to Delaware.

DOGWOOD, *Cornus florida*, also called Flowering Dogwood

Diameter 12"–18". Heavy; hard to very hard; strong; close-grained; strong in bending and in endwise compression; very high in shock resistance; difficult to work with tools; wears smooth with use; turns well; glues poorly. Uses of this wood have always been contingent upon its extreme hardness and fine texture which let it work and stay smooth under continuous wear—mallet heads, pulleys, vehicle parts, hubs of wheels, and machine bearings. Sapwood is very wide pinkish brown; heartwood, when present, dark brown variegated with shades of green and red. It ranged from southern Maine to central Florida.

PIGNUT HICKORY, *Carya cordiformis*, also called Bitternut

Diameter 2'–3'. Heavy to very heavy; very hard; strong; tough; close-grained; straight-grained; strong to very strong in bending and endwise compression; high to exceedingly high in shock resistance; works satisfactorily under tools; finishes well; below average for gluing; dark brown heartwood with thick lighter sapwood. It ranged from southern Maine to northwestern Florida.

SHELLBARK HICKORY, *Carya ovata*, also called Shagbark Hickory

Diameter 3'–4'. Same general properties as Pignut Hickory, but a definitely lighter brown. It ranged from southern Maine to western Florida.

HICKORY, *Carya alba*

Diameter up to 3'. Very heavy; hard; tough; strong; flexible; close-grained; rich dark brown like the Pignut. It ranged from eastern Massachusetts to Florida.

HOLLY, *Ilex opaca*

Diameter 2'–3'. Light; tough; not strong; close-grained; moderately strong in bending; high in shock resistance; stains well; carves well; works well under tools; turns well; nearly white when first cut, turning brownish with time; thick lighter-colored sapwood. It ranged from the coast of Massachusetts to Florida.

HOP HORNBEAM, *Ostrya virginiana*, also called Ironwood

Diameter up to 2'. Very heavy; very hard; very strong in bending and in endwise compression; stiff; very high in shock resistance; durable; light brown tinged with red to nearly white; a thick pale sapwood of forty years or more. It ranged from western New England to northern Florida.

GREAT LAUREL, *Rhododendron maximum*, also called Rose Bay

Diameter 10"–12". Heavy; hard; strong; somewhat brittle; fine-grained; light brown. It ranged from Nova Scotia through New Hampshire and southern New England and eastern New York.

SUGAR MAPLE, *Acer saccharum* Marsh., also called Rock Maple
(of "Hard" group)

Diameter 3'–4'. Heavy; hard; strong; close-grained; tough; usually straight-grained (occasionally curly- or wavy-grained or bird's-eye); very strong in bending and endwise compression; stiff; high in shock resistance; works well under tools; turns well; stays smooth under abrasion; takes a high polish; takes stain satisfactorily; splits radially; glues medium well; light reddish brown. It ranged from Nova Scotia to northern Georgia.

BLACK MAPLE, *Acer nigrum* Michx. (of "Hard" group)

Diameter up to 3 '. Similar to the *Acer saccharum*. It ranged from Montreal to the valley of Cold River, New Hampshire, through western Vermont and Massachusetts and northwestern Connecticut.

RED MAPLE, *Acer rubrum* L., also called Scarlet Maple (of "Soft" group)

Diameter 3 '–4½'. Very heavy; close-grained; not strong; usually straight-grained (sometimes curly-grained); moderately hard to hard; moderately weak to strong in bending and in endwise compression; limber to stiff; moderately high in shock resistance; works well under tools; glues satisfactorily; takes a smooth finish; light brown often slightly tinged with red. It ranged from Newfoundland to Florida.

SILVER MAPLE, *Acer saccharinum* L. (of "Soft" group)

Diameter 3 '–4'. Hard; strong; close-grained; easily worked; rather brittle; pale brown; thick sapwood of forty to fifty years' growth. It ranged from New Brunswick through western Vermont and central Massachusetts.

SOME TYPICAL OAKS OF THE "RED" GROUP, CALLED "ERYTHROBALANUS"

RED OAK, *Quercus borealis* Michx. (*Quercus rubra* L.)

Diameter 2 '–3 '. Heavy; hard; strong; close-grained; usually straight-grained; strong in bending and endwise compression; high in shock resistance; stiff; tendency to have casehardening; machines well; finishes well; average in gluing; some tendency to split along the rays; light reddish brown. It ranged from New Brunswick through northern New England.

SCARLET OAK, *Quercus coccinea*, also called Spanish Oak

Diameter 2 '–3 '. Much like the *O. borealis* except that its grain is coarser, its sapwood much thicker and darker. It ranged from the valley of the Androscoggin River, Maine, through southern New Hampshire and Vermont.

PIN OAK, *Quercus palustris*, also called Swamp Spanish Oak

Diameter 2 '–3 '. Like *Q. coccinea* except that it has less sapwood. It ranged over the valley of the Connecticut River in western Massachusetts and Connecticut.

BLACK OAK, *Quercus velutina*, also called Yellow-Bark Oak

Diameter 3 '–4 '. Like *Q. palustris* except that the color is usually brighter and redder. It ranged over the coast of southern Maine through northern Vermont.

SOME TYPICAL OAKS OF THE "WHITE" GROUP, CALLED "LEUCOBALANUS"

BURR OAK, *Quercus macrocarpa*, also called Mossy Cup Oak

Diameter 6′–7′. Heavy; strong; tough; close-grained; strong in bending and end-wise compression; high in shock resistance; stiff; tendency to have casehardening; machines well; finishes smooth; glues well; tendency to split along the rays; very durable; dark or rich light brown. It ranged from New Brunswick to the valley of the Penobscot River, Maine, Vermont, western Massachusetts.

WHITE OAK, *Quercus alba*

Diameter 3′–4′. Same properties as Q. *macrocarpa*. It ranged from southern Maine to Florida.

POST OAK, *Quercus stellata*

Diameter 2′–3′. Same properties as above species, but also somewhat like the Black Ash (*Fraxinus nigra*); splits well tangentially; used for making baskets and splint seats. It ranged from Cape Cod and islands of southern Massachusetts to Florida.

BALSAM POPLAR, *Populus tacamahacca*, also called Poplar and Tacamahac

Diameter 6′–7′. Light; moderately soft; weak; low in shock resistance; usually straight-grained; easy to moderately hard to work with tools; glues well; takes paint fairly well; light brown with thick nearly white sapwood. It ranged from Labrador through northern New England.

SWAMP POPLAR, *Populus heterophylla*, also called Swamp Cottonwood and Black Cottonwood

Diameter 2′–3′. Same properties as the above except that it is a much darker brown. It ranged from Connecticut and Rhode Island to Florida.

QUAKING ASPEN, *Populus tremuloides*, also called Trembling Aspen

Diameter 18″–20″. Same properties as the above except that the color is creamy to very light greyish brown; has a silken luster and a finer texture. It ranged from Labrador to Pennsylvania.

RED GUM, *Liquidamber styraciflua*, also called Sweet Gum and Bilsted

Diameter 4′–5′. Heavy; fairly hard; straight and sometimes interlocked grain; moderately strong in bending and endwise compression; moderately high in shock resistance; works fairly well with hand tools; turns exceedingly well; takes paint and stains well; has an unusually thick sapwood (sixty to seventy layers of annual growth) of light yellow to almost white; heartwood of carneous grey to varying shades of reddish brown. It ranged from Fairfield County, Connecticut, to southeastern Pennsylvania.

RED MULBERRY, *Morus rubra*

Diameter 3 '–4 '. Heavy to light; hard to soft; strong; rather tough; coarse-grained; very durable; machines well; works well under tools; glues well; orange-yellow to golden brown, turning a reddish brown upon exposure. It ranged from western Massachusetts, Connecticut, and Long Island to Florida.

SASSAFRAS, *Sassafras albidum*

Diameter up to 6 '. Moderately heavy; moderately hard; very high in shock resistance; coarse-grained; machines well; finishes well; very durable; dull orange-brown to greyish brown or dark brown. It ranged from southern Maine and eastern Massachusetts and southern Vermont to central Florida.

SERVICE BERRY, *Amelanchier canadensis* Med., also called Shad Bush

Diameter 12″–18″. Heavy; exceedingly hard; close-grained; dark brown sometimes tinged with red. It ranged from the valley of the Penobscot River, Maine, the valley of the Connecticut River (central Vermont, southern New Hampshire, Massachusetts, and Connecticut) through western Massachusetts to Florida.

SERVICE BERRY, *Amelanchier laevis* Wieg.

Diameter 12″–18″. Same as *A. canadensis* except that it ranges from Newfoundland through New England to northern Georgia.

STAGHORN SUMACH, *Rhus typhina* L.

Diameter 12″–14″. Light; brittle; soft; coarse-grained; orange-colored; streaked with green. From its young shoots, pipes are made for drawing sap of the Sugar Maple. It ranged from New Brunswick to northern Georgia.

SUMACH, *Rhus copallina*

Diameter 8″–10″. Light; soft; coarse-grained; light brown streaked with green and often tinged with red. It ranged from northern New England to southern Florida. In *North American Sylva* by F. Andrew Michaux (Philadelphia: J. Dobson, 1842), III, 205: "Among the native trees, in the Northern States, the Black Birch, the Yellow Birch, the Canoe Birch, the Red-flowering Curled Maple, the Bird's-eye Maple, the Wild Cherry Tree and the Sumac, are chiefly employed in cabinet-making."

SYCAMORE, *Platanus occidentalis* L., also called Buttonwood and
American Plane-Tree

Diameter up to 10'. Moderately heavy; hard; moderately strong in bending and
endwise compression; moderately stiff; moderately low in shock resistance; difficult to split because of interlocked grain; turns well; glues satisfactorily; light to
dark brown or reddish brown. It ranged from southeastern Maine and northern
Vermont to Florida.

TULIP TREE, *Liriodendron tulipifera*, also called Yellow Poplar, Tulip
Poplar, Whitewood

Diameter up to 9'. Light; fairly soft; brittle; straight-grained; moderately weak in
bending and endwise compression; fairly stiff; moderately low in shock resistance;
easy to work under tools; glues well; takes and holds paint exceptionally well;
clear yellow to tan or greenish grey or brown, occasionally with shades of purple,
dark green, or black. It ranged from Worcester County, Massachusetts, south-
western Vermont to Florida.

BLACK WALNUT, *Juglans nigra*

Diameter 4'–6'. Heavy; hard; strong in bending; very strong in endwise compression; stiff; high in shock resistance; works easily with tools; finishes very smoothly;
takes and holds stains well; glues well; very durable; light brown to rich chocolate
or purplish brown; dull; straight- or irregular-grained. It ranged from western
Massachusetts to Florida. A natural hybrid of *J. nigra* and *J. regia* (English Walnut)
has appeared in the United States and Europe, and on the banks of the James River
in Virginia has grown to a larger size than any other recorded Walnut tree.

BLACK WILLOW, *Salix nigra* Marsh.

Diameter up to 4'. Light; soft; weak in bending; exceedingly weak in endwise
compression; moderately high in shock resistance; usually with straight grain;
works well with tools; glues well; does not split readily; stains and finishes well;
light brown to pale reddish or greyish brown, frequently with darker streaks along
the grain. It ranged from southern New Brunswick through South Carolina.

WHITE ELM, *Ulmus americana* L.

Diameter 6'–11'. Moderately heavy; moderately hard; straight or sometimes interlocked grain; moderately weak in endwise compression, with excellent bending
qualities; high in shock resistance; tough; difficult to split; difficult to work with
tools; used as the hubs of wheels and vehicle parts; brown to dark brown, frequently with shades of red. It ranged from Newfoundland to Florida.

ANNOTATED BIBLIOGRAPHY
FOR THE IDENTIFICATION OF WOODS

Brown, Harry Philip, Panshin, A. J., and Forsaith, C. C. *Textbook of Wood Technology*. 2 vols. New York: McGraw-Hill, 1949 and 1964. (Carl de Zeeuw collaborated with Brown and Panshin in the preparation of the second edition of vol. 1, 1964, and is listed as one of the authors.)

Vol. 1 contains straight technology, excellent glossary of identification factors, good illustrations, and is the more useful of the two volumes. Deals exclusively with timber woods of the United States.

Carpenter, Charles H., and Leney, Lawrence. *382 Photomicrographs of 91 Papermaking Fibers*. Rev. ed. Syracuse, New York: State University of New York, College of Forestry, 1952.

Good illustrations of longitudinal vessels of major pulp woods, most of which are easily identified under the microscope.

Edlin, Herbert L. *Trees, Woods and Man*. London: Collins, 1956.

A history of British woodlands from the viewpoints of men using these woods throughout changing times and environments.

Emerson, George B. *A Report on the Trees and Shrubs Growing Naturally in the Forests of Massachusetts*. Boston: Dutton and Wentworth, 1846. 2nd ed., rev., 2 vols. Boston: Little, Brown, and Company, 1875.

An excellent account of the native woods of Massachusetts. Emerson stresses the appearance and uses (particularly by cabinetmakers) of various woods and in the second edition inserts numerous illustrations.

Greguss, Pál. *Holzanatomie der Europäischen Laubhölzer und Sträucher* [Wood Anatomy of European Leaf Woods and Shrubs]. Budapest: Akademiai Kiadó, 1959.

An important contribution, especially for the identification of European hardwoods.

Identification of Hardwoods. London: Her Majesty's Stationery Office, 1952.

A worldwide study of so-called hardwoods, that is, nonconiferous trees. Factors for identification and keys are difficult and less precise than those in Phillips' *Softwoods*. An auxiliary *Atlas of End-Grain Photomicro-*

graphs, sold separately, can be useful in conjunction. Together they are somewhat useful.

Jane, Frank W. *The Structure of Wood*. London: Adam & Charles Black, 1956. (A second edition, revised by Karl Wilson and Donald J. B. White, appeared in 1970.)
Deals with gross and microscopic structures of many woods of different continents. Beautifully illustrated and useful for a beginner in wood analysis by microscope.

Phillips, E. W. J. *Identification of Softwoods*. London: Her Majesty's Stationery Office, 1948.
A most thorough work published on the identification of coniferous woods throughout the world.

Sargent, Charles S. *Manual of the Trees of North America*, 1905. New ed., 2 vols. New York: Dover Publications, 1961.
Very useful for determining those areas in which most species of American trees grow. The inclusion of average dimensions (diameter and height) enables one to estimate whether a particular species is (was) used for lumber.

United States Department of Agriculture. *Wood: Colors and Kinds*. Agricultural Handbook No. 101. Prepared by Forest Products Laboratory, Forest Service. October, 1956.
Excellent for colored illustrations of common woods.

van Ravenswaay, Charles. "A Historical Checklist of the Pines of Eastern North America." *Winterthur Portfolio 7*. Charlottesville, Virginia: University Press of Virginia, 1972. Pp. 175–215.
An excellent historical guide to the uses and commercial importance of Eastern pines. Van Ravenswaay identifies 13 species of pine and 167 common names applied to these species.

APPENDICES

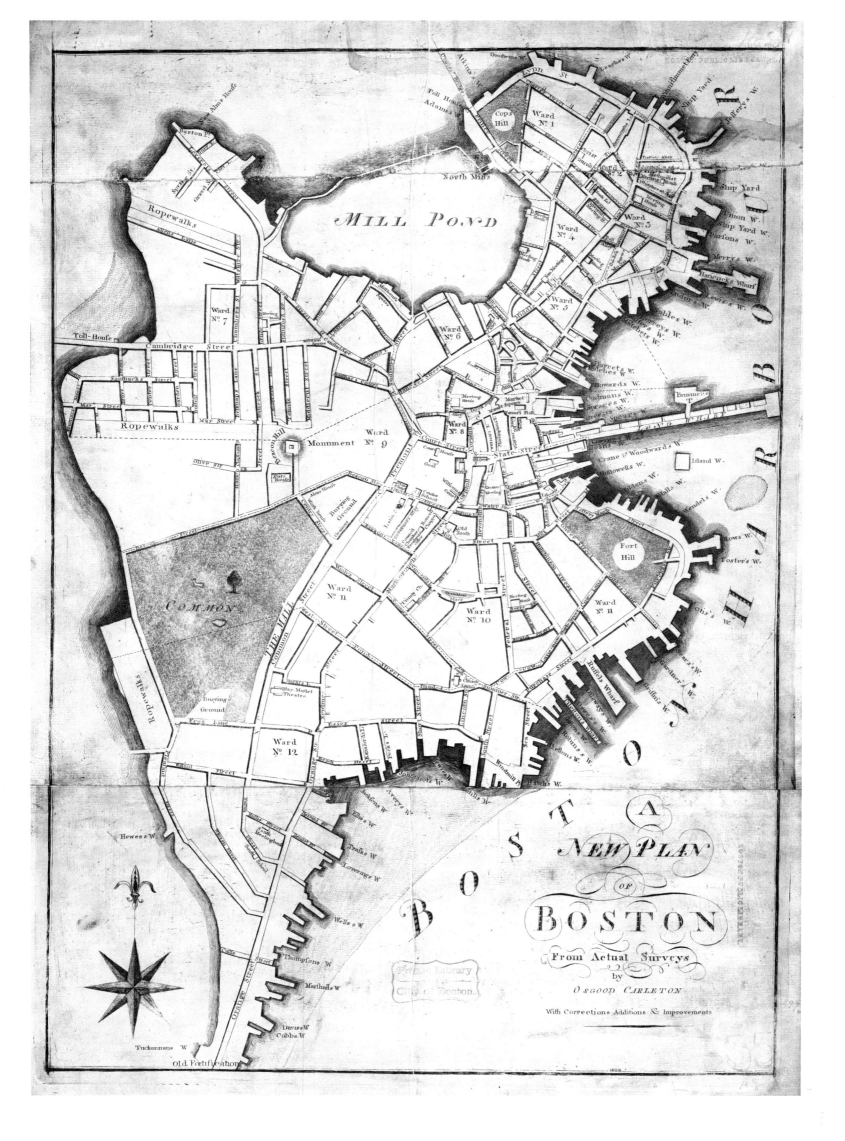

173. A New Plan of Boston from Actual Surveys by Osgood Carleton, with Corrections, Additions and Improvements. 1800. Copperplate engraving; H. 28⅛ inches, w. 19⅝ inches (engraved surface only). (Boston Public Library.)

Appendix A

EIGHTEENTH-CENTURY BOSTON FURNITURE CRAFTSMEN

THIS list comprises Boston craftsmen engaged in furniture making during the eighteenth century (1701–1800). It includes men still working in the Jacobean style of the seventeenth century as well as those working in the William and Mary style fashionable in the first quarter of the century, in the Queen Anne and Chippendale styles popular for about seventy years, and in the fashion of the American Federal period of the last fifteen years of the century when Boston finally recovered from the depression and depopulation of the war and postwar years.

Joiners, turners, japanners, cabinetmakers, chairmakers, Windsor chair makers, upholsterers, and even a few specialists who made picture frames are included. Occasionally several occupations are listed for one man; secondary occupations are in parentheses.

Craftsmen endowed with ability and financing often engaged in several trades; more often men were forced by lack of ability and financing to try various trades. Some trades were closely related. The men who joined furniture, joiners and shop joiners, were often also housewrights, house joiners, house carpenters, or ship joiners. Japanners were often painters. Upholsterers sold fabric and so were usually shopkeepers, often attaining the rank of merchant. And everyone who became wealthy became a gentleman, an appellation usually omitted on this list. Some crafts were almost indistinguishable: turner and chairmaker, joiner and cabinetmaker, and, in the late eighteenth-century, chairmaker and Windsor chair maker.

Furniture craftsmen of surrounding towns (e.g., Charlestown, Roxbury, Dorchester) are not included unless they worked at some time within Boston. The men who made and sold pulls and other hardware for furniture are omitted. Also omitted are the house-

wrights, carpenters, and ship joiners, who, masters of the art of joinery, no doubt occasionally made a piece of furniture.

Information considered uncertain is bracketed. To simplify use of
the list, parenthesized "Sr." and "Jr." were added to names of men
not necessarily so designated in their lifetimes.

Addresses are most often of house and shop. Addresses known to
have been of homes alone are omitted. Known addresses of shops are
so designated. Documented pieces of furniture are noted. For more
information on individual craftsmen, additional reading references
are indicated. Author's complete name and title are given in a bibliography at the end of the list.

Abbreviations are as follows: b. (born), bapt. (baptized), i.m.
(published intention to marry), and d. (died). The reader may assume that most craftsmen were working at their trade by the year of
their marriage and usually were still working at the time of death.

Working dates given are documented dates during which craftsmen worked in Boston at the furniture trade. Working dates before
1701 and after 1800 have been omitted.

Data was gleaned from records of the Suffolk County Inferior
Court of Common Pleas; Registry of Probate; Registry of Deeds;
Superior Court of General Sessions; Boston Directories for 1789,
1796, 1798, 1800; Boston Assessor's List of 1780. Additional information came from "Boston Inhabitants," compiled by Annie Thwing,
at the Massachusetts Historical Society; "Craftsmen List" (unpublished), compiled by Kathryn C. Buhler, at the Museum of Fine Arts,
Boston; "List of Furniture Craftsmen" (unpublished) by Brock Jobe;
and genealogies. Published lists (i.e., Paul Burroughs, *American Collector*, September, 1937; Mabel M. Swan, *Antiques*, March and April,
1948; and Ethel Hall Bjerkoe, *The Cabinetmakers of America* [Garden
City, New York, 1957]) were used, and names were omitted of men
now believed to have had other occupations.

MYRNA KAYE

174. TRADE CARD OF ZIPHION THAYER. Drawn and engraved by Nathaniel Hurd, Boston, c. 1765–1777. Copperplate engraving; H. 7⅜ inches, w. 5⅜ inches (engraved surface only). (Worcester Art Museum, Worcester, Massachusetts.)

LIST OF BOSTON FURNITURE CRAFTSMEN

working dates

Acres, George; *Cabinetmaker*; Back Street. 1789

Adams & Todd; *Cabinetmakers*; partners Samuel Adams & William 1798
Todd; Cambridge Street; labelled card table (*Antiques*, LXXXI
[April, 1962], 412); ref. Randall "Works II."

Adams, Elisha; *Cabinetmaker*; partner Abner Guild (Guild & 1796–1800
Adams) (1796–1798); partners' shop 48 Orange Street (1796–
1798), jointly owned land on Federal Street (1798), Adams
property on Hollis Street (1800).

Adams, Jacob; *Cabinetmaker*, (*Auctioneer*); shop Dock Square. 1788–1789

Adams, John; *Joiner*; [possibly b. 1704 (Newbury); in Littleton, 1758
Acton, Chelmsford (1737), in Newbury (1753)].

Adams, Joseph; *Windsor Chair Maker, Cabinetmaker*, (*Hackney* 1789–1800
Coachman), (*Hostler*); m. Mary ———— by 1782; Center Street.

Adams, Samuel; *Cabinetmaker*; partner William Todd (Adams & 1794–1800
Todd) Southack's Street (1796), Cambridge Street (1794–1800);
for labelled table see Adams & Todd; ref. Randall "Works II."

Aimer (Amer), Thomas; *Cabinetmaker*; d. 1798; worked for Samuel 1791–1798
Stratford (1791–1795), in 1796 Aimer sued saying he "reasonably
deserved" payment of $682 for four years' labor.

Alcock, John; *Chairmaker*; [probably son of Mylam Alcock] m. 1740–1746
Hannah Walker 1733, m. Mary Souther 1749; Orange Street.

Alcock, Mylam; *Chairmaker*; b. 1680, m. Elizabeth Gent 1704, m. 1738
Mary Hodgen 1712, m. Ester Androse 1716.

Alexander, Giles; *Cabinetmaker*; partner Samuel Stone (Stone & 1792–1800
Alexander) (1796); shop Back Street (1798–1800); for labelled
furniture see Stone & Alexander.

Alexander, William (Jr.); *Cabinetmaker*; Back Street. 1780–1796

Allen, Henry; *Joiner, Turner*. 1719

Allen, Jonathan; *Joiner*. 1717

Allen, Samuel; *Upholsterer*; [possibly trained by Samuel Ridgway, 1800
chairmaker 1758–1764] Federal Street.

Andrews, ————; *Cabinetmaker*; arrived from London 1716. 1716

Apthorp, Charles; *Upholsterer, (Merchant)*; b. 1698, m. Grizzelle   1721
Eastwicke 1727, d. 1758.

Armstrong, John; *Cabinetmaker*; m. Christian Bass 1747, d. 1785;   1747–1785
estate £24:16:1.

Armstrong, Richard; *Chairmaker*; m. Mary Fairfield 1714; rented   1717–1719
shop and cellar near Town Dock (1717–1719).

Arnit, William; *Joiner*; arrived from Scotland 1766.   1766–1780

Arnold, John; *Cabinetmaker*; i.m. Abigail Foster 1763, d. 1784;   1783
estate £54:7:4.

Atkins, Gibbs; *Cabinetmaker*; b. 1739, left Boston for Halifax 1776,   1775–1800
state sued to take Atkins' property because he was Tory (1781),
in Boston 1787, d. 1806; owned property Middle Street, Prince
Street; documented desk and bookcase (figs. 129, 130), documented desk and bookcase (fig. 131); ref. Hipkiss.

Audebert, Isaiah; *Chairmaker*; b. 1724, m. Sarah Pattin 1751,   1752–1769
d. 1769; shop Milk Street and Battery March Street (1760),
house and shop Summer Street (1769); estate £407:8:5.

Austin, John; *Carver*; m. Susanna Screech 1750; worked in   1770–1786
Charlestown (1750–1770).

Badger, Benjamin; *Joiner*; b. 1712 (Charlestown), m. Rebecca   1734–1740
Jones 1733, d. 1757.

Baker, Joseph; *Joiner*; [probably m. Hannah Barnes 1727] rented   1733–1735
shop Fish Street.

Ballard, Daniel; *Shipjoiner, (Joiner)*; d. 1741; estate £1472:0:3   1720–1740
excluding house and pew; ref. Singleton.

Barnard (Burnard), Thomas; *Housewright, House Carpenter, Joiner*;   1713
father and son of same name; father b. 1657, m. Elizabeth ———
about 1680, d. 1716; son b. 1684, [probably m. Sarah Parker
1713;] [possibly father was housewright and carpenter; son was
housewright and joiner].

Bass, Benjamin Jr.; *Cabinetmaker*; d. 1803; Orange Street.   1798

Bass, Joseph; *Upholsterer*; shop 3 Newbury Street.   1800

Bass, Moses Belcher; *Upholsterer*; bapt. 1735, m. Elizabeth Wimble   1757–1800
1769, m. Margaret Sprague 1773, d. 1817; shop Ann Street
(1757–1762), 66 Orange Street; ref. Smith.

Baston, Gershom; *Joiner.*   1733

Batson, John; *Joiner.*   1719

Baxter, Thomas; *Upholsterer*; ref. Singleton.   1751

Beath, Joseph; *Carver*; carved bed headboards and cornices for   1760–1761
Samuel Grant, upholsterer.

Belknap, Samuel; *Joiner, Housewright*; owned house Sudbury Lane   1714
until 1715; in Hartford, Connecticut, 1718.

Bennett, Thomas; *Joiner*; worked with Thomas Tippin (1723).   1723–1729

Bent, William & Adam; *Instrument Makers & Carvers*; 26 Orange   1800
Street.

Bickner, Benjamin; *Joiner.*   1718

Bisby, Jonathan; *Cabinetmaker*; Washington Street.   1798

Blackford, Thomas; *Chairmaker.*   1784

Blair, Bethel; *Joiner*; m. Elizabeth Snelling 1745; Purchase Street;   1750
declared incompetent 1757.

Blake, Samuel; *Chairmaker*; Newbury Street.   1789

Blake, William; *Cabinetmaker, Windsor Chair Maker*; m. Sarah   1789–1800
Gandell 1792; shop Fore Street next to Draw-Bridge (1789),
Lynn Street (1800); ref. Fraser "Painted."

Bleigh (Bligh), Samuel; *Joiner*; m. Ann East 1709, d. 1766.   1720–1727

Bobb, John; *Turner.*   1741–1742

Bowler, James; *Upholsterer*; worked with a Mr. Paine.   1736

Bowles, Joshua; *Carver*; Ward 1.   1760–1780

Bramley, Benjamin; *Joiner*; m. Dorcas ——— about 1710.   1717

Breck, Nathaniel; *Joiner, Shopkeeper*; m. Martha Ireland 1707;   1715–1726
[possibly worked with Thomas Odell (1724)] shop west side of
Union Street until 1726, moved to east side of Union Street at
the sign of the Cornfields.

Brewer, John; *Joiner.*   1704

Brickhead, William; *Upholsterer*; arrived from London 1716.   1716

Bridge (Bridges), George; *Turner*; [possibly m. Anna Crump 1721,   1724–1734
m. Sarah Earle 1723].

Bright, George; *Cabinetmaker, (Chairmaker)*; b. 1727 son of John   1760–1800
Bright (Sr.), m. Eunice de Larue 1750, m. Amy Adams Vincent,
daughter of John Adams, 1789, d. 1805; John Johnston & Daniel
Rea, painters, decorated some furniture for Bright (1788); shop
Fish Street; called upon by courts as arbiter of cases involving
other cabinetmakers (1780, 1789); estate $8459.75; signed desk
and bookcase (figs. 124, 140), documented chair, one of thirty
made for Massachusetts State House (Montgomery, no. 134);
ref. Montgomery, Randall *American Furniture*, Randall "Bright,"
Swan "Johnstons."

Bright, John (Sr.); *Chairmaker*; b. 1681, m. ——— about 1726,   1734–1766
m. Elizabeth Pierce 1740, m. Sarah Batt 1747, d. 1766; billed
(1734) Samuel Samber £18:3:8 for frames of twelve
"ordnerey Chairs," four easy chairs, and eight other chairs; Fort
Hill vicinity; ref. Randall "Bright."

Bright, John; *Upholsterer*; [probably son of George Bright]   1788–1800
m. Mary Adams 1788; partner William Bright (1796–1799);
shop 17 Marlborough Street (1789), shop 44 Marlborough Street
(1796–1800); ref. Randall "Bright."

Bright, John & William; *Upholsterers & Lace Manufacturers*;   1796–1799
44 Marlborough Street.

Bright, Joseph; *Cabinetmaker, Upholsterer, (Chairmaker)*; bapt. 1767,   1797–1800
son of George Bright; Franklin Street; ref. Randall "Bright."

Bright, Richard; *Cabinetmaker, Joiner*; son of John Bright (Sr.),   1780–1789
m. Ann Ingersoll 1753; partner Thomas Bright; 44 Marlborough
Street; ref. Randall "Bright."

Bright, Thomas; *Cabinetmaker, Chairmaker*; son of George Bright;   1789–1800
partner Richard Bright (1789); 44 Marlborough Street (1789),
Spring Street (1796), Franklin Street (1798), Water Street
(1800); ref. Randall "Bright."

Bright, William; *Upholsterer*; bapt. 1752, son of George Bright,   1796–1799
m. Sally Malcolm-Butler 1797, d. 1799; partner John Bright;
44 Marlborough Street.

Brimmer, Andrew; [possibly *Cabinetmaker*] 62 Cornhill; only evi-   [1789]
dence of Brimmer as a cabinetmaker is a questionably labelled
desk (*Antiquarian*, xiv [May, 1930], 60). Label does not mention
cabinetmaking.

Brocas (Broccas), John Sr.; *Cabinetmaker*; d. 1740; Union Street   1701–1740
(1708); estate £259:19:5 old tenor.

Brocas, John Jr.; *Joiner*; i.m. Abigail Coker 1729, d. 1751.   1728

Brown & Thayer; *Upholsterers*; partners William Brown and   1798
William Thayer; shop Hanover Street.

Brown (Browne), Benjamin; *Joiner*.   1708–1720

Brown, Enoch; [possibly *Cabinetmaker*] only evidence of Brown as   [1783]
a cabinetmaker is a questionably labelled desk and bookcase
(*Antiquarian*, xiv [March, 1930], 88; xiv [May, 1930], 12).
Label does not mention cabinetmaking.

Brown, Joseph; *Joiner*.   1723

Brown, Joseph; *Cabinetmaker*; Marlborough Street (1798),   1798–1800
45 Orange Street (1800).

Brown (Browne), William; *Joiner*; b. 1671, i.m. Anne Frost 1696,   1711–1737
d. 1745; Prince Street; estate £1659:2:3.

Brown, William; *Upholsterer, Merchant*; partner William Thayer   1798
(Brown & Thayer); shop Hanover Street.

Buck, James; *Picture Frame Maker, Print Seller, Glazier*; Queen Street   1747–1751
(1748–1751); ref. Dow.

Budd (Bud), Edward; *Carver*; m. Dorothy ——— about 1664,   1701–1709
m. Elizabeth Samms 1705, d. 1710; shop and wharf Ann Street
between Cross Street and Mill Creek.

Bull, Charles; *Cabinetmaker*; arrived from North Carolina 1716.   1716

Bumstead, Jeremiah; *Joiner*; [probably b. 1678] m. Elizabeth   1701–1710
Bridges 1705, m. Bethia Sherrer 1726.

Bumstead, Josiah; *Upholsterer, (Paper Stainer)*; 53 Marlborough   1795–1800
Street.

Burbeck, Edward; *Carver*; carved capitals on Faneuil Hall (1768).   1715–1785

Burrill, George; *Chairmaker*.   1721

Burrows, William; *Frame Maker*.   1751

Bushell (Bushnell) (Bushel), John; *Joiner, Housewright*; m. 1711,   1713–1720
d. 1731.

Byles, Jonas; *Upholsterer*.   1782

Cabot, George; *Joiner, (Housewright)*.   1701–1714

Call, Isaac; *Chairmaker*; inventory 1790 £14:16:10 included no   1790
tools.

Campbell & Ward; *Cabinetmakers*; partners James Campbell and Moses Ward.   1791

Campbell, Henry; *Upholsterer*; Spring Lane.   1798–1800

Campbell, James; *Cabinetmaker, Chairmaker*; d. 1809; partner Moses Ward (Campbell & Ward) (1791); Spring Lane (1796–1800).   1791–1800

Cary, Edward; *Cabinetmaker*; North Street.   1796–1797

Chamberlain, William; *Chairmaker*; b. 1755, m. Sarah Cox 1779, [possibly m. Ruth New 1795].   1798

Cheever, Daniel; *Joiner*; tools in inventory £4:2:10.   1771

Cheever, Joseph; *Cabinetmaker*.   1775

Clarke, Daniel; *Cabinetmaker*; moved to Salem 1794.   1768–1794

Clasbey, Robert; *Chairmaker*.   –1778

Claxton, Salmon Grave (Salmagrave); *Joiner*; m. Margaret Woodmancy-Richardson 1715, d. by 1745.   1714–1715

Clement, Thomas; *Cabinetmaker*.   1768

Cleveland (Cleaveland), Samuel; *Joiner, Mariner*; b. 1704 (Charlestown), m. Hannah Belcher 1732.   1732

Clinton, Francis; *Joiner*; b. Ireland, given permission with William Freeland to practice joinery in Boston 1730.   1730

Clough, Ebenezer; *Joiner*; [probably b. 1716] m. Elizabeth Welch, daughter of Thomas Welch, Charlestown joiner, 1738, d. 1751; estate £200:9:7¾.   1739

Clough, Samuel; *Joiner*; b. 1665, m. Ruth ——— about 1688, d. 1707; estate £241:1:1.   1701–1702

Clow (Clough), Joseph; *Joiner*.   –1776

Codner, William; *Carver*.   1711

Coffin, William; *Cabinetmaker, Tavernkeeper*; Bunch of Grapes Tavern (1731); [probably moved to Marblehead 1759].   1731–1758

Cogswell, John; *Cabinetmaker, (Surveyor of Boards)*; b. 1738, m. Abigail Gooding 1762, i.m. Abiel Page 1782, d. 1818; shop 49 Middle Street (1782–1800); estate $39,235.57; signed chest-on-chest (figs. 125, 139, 143); ref. Downs "Cogswell," Downs *American Furniture*, Randall *American Furniture*, Young.   1767–1800

Coit, Job (Sr.); *Cabinetmaker, Joiner*; b. 1692, m. Lydia Amie   1718–1742
1713, d. 1742; apprentice Joseph Davis (1726); owned house,
shop, land Ann Street between Mill Creek and Cross Street;
estate £1747:9:8 old tenor; signed desk and bookcase (figs. 62, 63,
64); ref. Evans, Mooz, Winchester.

Coit, Job (Sr.), & Company; *Joiner*.   1720

Coit, Job Jr.; *Joiner*; b. 1717 son of Job Coit (Sr.), m. Rebecca   1738–1745
Parkman 1739, d. 1745; estate £82:8:0 old tenor; signed desk
and bookcase (figs. 62, 63, 64); ref. Evans, Mooz.

Coit, Joseph; *Cabinetmaker, Joiner*; b. 1721 son of Job Coit (Sr.),   1747–1758
m. Dorothy Vesey 1745; apprentice Joseph Booker (1748–1758).

Coit, Nathaniel; *Joiner*; b. 1714 son of Job Coit (Sr.), m. Elizabeth   1745
Ricks 1738, d. 1747.

Collins, Daniel; *Cabinetmaker*; b. 1717 younger brother of Samuel   1751
Collins, i.m. Hannah Cherritoe 1750, d. about 1757; estate
£318:2:1.

Collins, Samuel; *Cabinetmaker*; b. 1706 older brother of Daniel   1737
Collins, m. Hannah Palfry 1731, d. 1751, estate £22:4:1¼.

Collins, Thomas; *Joiner*; arrived in Boston 1718.   1718–1719

Collins, William; *Joiner*; i.m. Elizabeth Gaar 1728; Middle Street.   1722–1729

Colvill, John; *Cabinetmaker*.   1765–1767

Conerry, William; *Joiner*.   1736

Coney, Daniel; *Joiner, Cabinetmaker*; b. 1709, d. after 1774;   1733–1768
charged £20 for teaching joinery to David Stimpson for
fifty-one weeks (1733–1734).

Courser (Corsser) (Corser), John; *Joiner*; m. Sarah Wakefield 1703,   1713–1729
d. 1756; apprentice John Whitehorne (1714–1721); shop
Union Street.

Cosely, William; *Cabinetmaker*.   1797

Cox, Lambert; *Joiner*; m. Elizabeth Hinchcomb 1726.   1728

Crafts, Thomas; *Painter, Japanner, Justice, County Treasurer*; b. 1740,   1763
m. Frances Pinckney Gore 1763, d. 1799; Cornhill (1789–1796).

Crockford, William; *Turner*; d. about 1756; estate £166:11:3.   1738–1756

Crouch, Jacob; *Carver, Merchant*; warehouse and land Merchants   1719
Row at Shippens Dock.

Crouch, Jacob, & Company; *Carvers*; [Crouch and William 1719
Shute, jointly sued (1719), probably constitute company]
Merchants Row at Shippens Dock.

Cumber, John; *Carver, Picture Frame Carver*; rented shop Back 1735–1750
Street (1737).

Cummings (Cummins) (Cummens), William; *Cabinetmaker*; 1798–1800
worked with Alexander Edwards Jr. (1799); 10 Orange Street.

Cunnabell (Cunabel) (Cunable), John (Sr.); *Joiner*; d. 1724; 1701–1724
practiced joinery in London before coming to Boston;
ref. Singleton.

Cunnabell (Cunable), John Jr.; *Joiner*; son of John Cunnabell (Sr.), 1705
joiner, d. 1705.

Cunnabell, John; *Joiner*; [probably b. 1725 son of Samuel 1746–1752
Cunnabell, joiner, m. Sarah Crafts 1748] apprentice John Bell.

Cunnabell (Cunable), Samuel; *Joiner, Housewright*; b. 1689 son of 1710–1725
John Cunnabell (Sr.), m. Abigail Treadway 1710, m. Mary
Diamond 1713, i.m. Hannah Blanchard 1739, inherited father's
tools 1724, d. 1760; owned property Mill Pond; estate
£118:18:2½.

Dalton, William; *Windsor Chair Maker*. 1800

Darrell (Dorrell), John; *Joiner, Housewright*; [probably b. 1685, m. 1713–1722
Rachel Thwing 1706, d. 1746].

Davies, Samuel; *Cabinetmaker*; furniture warehouse Newbury 1792
Street.

Davis, Benjamin; *Chairmaker (Turner)*; m. Elizabeth ——— about 1714–1718
1700, d. 1718; estate £850 included a lot of thirty-four chairs
£3:1:0.

Davis, John; *Cabinetmaker*. 1719–1741

Davis, Joseph; *Cabinetmaker*; m. Sarah Parsons 1728; apprenticed 1729–1732
to Job Coit (Sr.) (1726); signed dressing table (fig. 68).

Davis, Robert; *Japanner*; m. Elizabeth Randle, daughter of 1735–1739
William Randle, japanner, 1735, d. 1739; signed high chest
(fig. 35); ref. Rhoades and Jobe.

Dearborn, ———; *Carver, Gilder, Picture Frame Maker*; shop 1799
Milk Street; labelled picture frame (Winterthur).

DeCosta, Anthony; *Carver*. 1729

Dell, John; *Upholsterer.*   1729

Deshon, Moses; *Carver, (Auctioneer)*; m. Percis Stevens 1731, m.   1743
Mehetabel Gerrish 1739; carved Peter Faneuil's coat of arms
for Faneuil Hall (1743).

Dewing, Francis; *Engraver, (Carver), (Calico Printer)*; arrived   1716–1727
from London 1716; King Street (1716); principally an engraver,
"He Likewise Cuts Neatly in wood."

Dillaway, John; *Cabinetmaker*; m. Mary Cook 1740, d. 1779;   1758
rented building from Mrs. Bethel Blair (see Blair) (1761–1762);
estate £838:0:0.

Dillaway, Thomas; *Chairmaker, Carpenter.*   1795

Doak (Doaks), William; *Windsor Chair Maker*; Back Street.   1787–1789

Dogget, William; *Housewright, Printers' Furniture Maker*; d.   1789
between 1795 and 1798; Milk Street.

Down, Thomas; *Upholsterer*; 44 Cornhill.   1796

Downe, Samuel; *Upholsterer*; brother of William Downe,   1759–1783
upholsterer.

Downe (Downes) (Donn) (Downs), William; *Upholsterer, (Shop-*   1720–1753
keeper); b. 1676 brother of Samuel Downe, upholsterer, d.
about 1753; inventory 1753 £1777:15:0.

Drew, John; *Joiner*; in Portsmouth, New Hampshire, 1723.   1714–1716

Drinker, Edward; *Joiner, Innholder*; [possibly b. 1680] m. Tabitha   1730–1734
Baker 1718, d. 1783; originally of Philadelphia; returned
Philadelphia 1745; inn Salutation Alley and Ship Street
(1736–1741).

Dupee, Isaac; *Carver, (Merchant), (Gentleman)*; d. 1766; *Boston*   1758–1766
Gazette February 9, 1761, "since the late Fire (on Dock Square)
he has opened a Shop the North side of the Swing-Bridge
. . . ," shop Oliver's Dock (1763–1765).

Edes, Edward; *Joiner, (Shipjoiner)*; father and son of same name   1709–1733
and trade; father m. Martha Frothingham 1704, m. Susannah
Welch 1714, d. by 1733; son b. 1705, m. Sarah Mills 1728.

Edwards, Alexander (Sr.); *Cabinetmaker*; b. 1733, i.m. Sarah   1760–1798
Greenough 1757, d. 1798; shop Back Street.

Edwards, Alexander Jr.; *Cabinetmaker*; worked with William   1799
Cummings 1799.

Ennesly, William; *Carver, Gilder*; shop Theatre Alley. 1800

Everard, Jonathan; *Upholsterer*. 1703

Evory (Ivory), James; *Turner*. 1727

Fearservis, Robert Jr.; *Chairmaker*. 1780

Fernside (Farnside), Jacob; *Joiner*; d. 1716. 1701–1716

Ferris, Samuel; *Joiner*. 1719

Finch, Caleb; *Joiner*; m. Mercy Alkin 1714. 1722

Fisk (Fiske), Samuel; *Cabinetmaker*; d. 1797; [probably worked 1792–1797
with Stephen Badlam, cabinetmaker, Dorchester] partner son
William Fisk; estate excepting real property $1589.28; signed
card table (Israel Sack Brochure Number Eighteen no. 1468),
[probably maker of chair (fig. 7) stamped "S.F," card table
stamped "S.F" and "WF" (DAPC), chair stamped "S. Badlam"
and "S.F" (Montgomery no. 30), lolling chair stamped "S.
Badlam" and "S.F" (Montgomery no. 110)].

Fisk (Fiske), William; *Cabinetmaker*; b. 1770, d. 1844; partner father 1797–1800
Samuel Fisk (1797) [probably maker of chair stamped "WF"
(Randall *American Furniture* no. 158), card table stamped "S.F"
and "WF" (DAPC)]; shop Washington Street, on the neck;
ref. Randall *American Furniture*.

Fitch, Thomas; *Upholsterer, Merchant*; b. 1669, m. Abiel Danforth 1701–1736
1697, d. 1736; estate excepting real property £3388:8:11.

Foot, Thomas; *Cabinetmaker*; m. Ruth Mecom 1760; shop Oliver's 1754–1796
Dock (until fire 1760), after fire shop in house Horn Lane,
Creek Square (1796).

Forrest (Forest), John; *Upholsterer;* Newbury Street. 1796

Forrester, Robert; *Joiner*. 1714–1729

Forsyth, John; *Upholsterer*; d. 1764; estate £4:0:6. 1761

Foster, Abraham (Sr.); *Joiner*; b. 1716, m. Elizabeth Davis 1742, 1742
d. by 1749.

Foster, Abraham (Jr.); *Cabinetmaker*; b. 1744 son of Abraham 1762–1796
(Sr.), joiner; Fish Street; estate $2519.70.

Foster, James Hiller; *Upholsterer*; shop 56 Marlborough Street. 1796–1800

Foster, Jesse; *Windsor Chair Maker, Chairmaker*; shop Water Street. 1796–1799

Francis, Abraham; *Cabinetmaker*; d. 1720; estate £2658:12:0; ref. Singleton.   1720

Francis (Frances), Joseph; *Chairmaker*; Water Street; stamped easy chair and stamp illustrated (*Antiquarian*, XIV [May, 1930], 56), privately owned stamped lolling chair.   1789

Francis (Frances), Simon; *Cabinetmaker*; shop Middle Street.   1798–1800

Freeland, James; *Cabinetmaker*; [possibly son of William Freeland] m. Ann Armstrong 1769, d. 1802; North End; estate $9374.50.   1764–1800

Freeland (Fryland), William; *Joiner, Retailer*; b. Ireland, [probably m. Jane Miller 1732] permit to practice joinery in Boston 1730; shop Milk Street and Battery March Street; tools and furniture destroyed in fire (1760); retailing near Hancock's Wharf (1765), near Pitts Wharf (1782).   1730–1760

Freelove, James; *Cabinetmaker*; Fish Street.   1800

French, Samuel; *Joiner*; arrived from Great Britain and warned to depart.   1715

Frogly, Henry; *Joiner*.   1712

Frost & Davis; *Cabinetmakers*; [probably James Frost] shop Ship Street.   1800

Frost, James; *Cabinetmaker*.   1798

Frothingham, Benjamin; *Cabinetmaker*; b. 1708 son of Nathaniel Frothingham, joiner of Charlestown, m. Mary Edmond 1733, m. Mildred Peck 1756, d. 1765; shop Milk Street and Battery March Street destroyed by fire (1760) and moved to Charlestown; estate £743 old tenor.   1734–1760

Frothingham, Benjamin Jr.; *Cabinetmaker*; b. 1734 son of Benjamin Frothingham, cabinetmaker, d. 1809; [probably trained by father in Milk Street shop] in Charlestown 1754; signed desk and bookcase (figs. 97, 162); other furniture originated in Charlestown shop; ref. Comstock, Spalding, Swan "Charlestown."   –1754

Fullerton, Stephen; *Chairmaker*; b. 1731 son of William Fullerton (Sr.); shop Milk Street and Battery March Street destroyed by fire (1760).   1758–1769

Fullerton, William (Sr.); *Chairmaker*; b. 1702, m. Mary Crowell 1725, i.m. Lydia Coit, widow of Job Coit (Sr.), cabinetmaker, 1742, d. 1750.   1730–1742

Fullerton, William Jr.; *Chairmaker*; b. 1727 son of William   1751–1760
   Fullerton (Sr.), m. Mary Browne 1750; shop Milk Street and
   Battery March Street destroyed by fire (1760).

Furbur (Furber), Jethro; *Joiner*; [probably m. Mary Manwaring   1728
   1728, m. Sarah ———— about 1765] d. about 1769.

Gale, Joseph; *Upholsterer*; m. Mary Alden 1736, d. 1774.   1733–1766

Gershom, Thomas; *Cabinetmaker*; Back Street.   1789

Gee, ————; *Chairmaker*.   1740

Gibbons, Peter; *Joiner*; m. Elizabeth Harrod April 1724, m.   1724–1728
   Elizabeth Warren November 1724, d. 1729; estate £529:12:6
   old tenor.

Gibbons, Thomas; *Cabinetmaker*; [probably m. Jane Hambleton   1730–1740
   1724] d. 1745; partner Lenier Kenn (1731–1739); employed
   Daniel McGregor (1740); estate £26:6:0 old tenor.

Gidding, Joseph; *Joiner*; d. 1788; inventory 1788 £126:18:1½.   1788

Gifford (Gillford), Samuel; *Upholsterer*; arrived from London   1717–1725
   (1717) and warned to depart.

Gilbert, Nathaniel; *Joiner, Housewright*; working in Hull 1714.   1712

Glen, Robert; *Joiner*; m. Margaret Rankin 1736; rented shop   1749–1753
   Mackerel Lane.

Goodwin, Thomas; *Joiner*.   1730–1740

Gookin, Edmund; *Joiner*.   1715

Gore, John; *Japanner, Painter, Shopkeeper, Gentleman*; b. 1718, m.   1741–1761
   Frances Pinkney 1743, d. 1796; apprentice John Johnston; shop
   Queen Street; estate $12,626.54.

Gore, Stephen; *Carver*.   1785

Gould (Gold), Bartholomew; *Joiner*; m. Elizabeth Lee 1728.   1729

Gould (Goold), Benjamin; *Turner*; d. 1801.   1758–1800

Grant, John; *Joiner*.   1719–1729

Grant, Joseph Jr.; *Upholsterer*.   1739–1759

Grant, Moses; *Upholsterer, Shopkeeper*; b. 1745 son of Samuel   1784–1800
   Grant, upholsterer, d. 1817; partner father (1784); shop 6 Union
   Street (1789–1800).

Grant, Samuel; *Upholsterer*; b. about 1705, m. Elizabeth Cookson   1753–1784
1729, d. 1784; apprentice John Breck Jr. (1753); partner son
Moses (1784); Grant's trade card (fig. 24).

Gray, Samuel; *Upholsterer*.   1762

Gray, William; *Upholsterer*; b. 1724, m. Elizabeth Hall 1759, d.   1748–1775
1775; inventory 1775 £2481:18:5.

Grayham, James; *Chairmaker*; rented shop Mackerel Lane.   1760–1771

Greenough, Thomas; *Cabinetmaker*.   1777

Greenwood, John; *Cabinetmaker*.   1760

Gridley, Isaac; *Cabinetmaker*.   1750

Griffin, Morris; *Chairmaker, Turner*; b. 1704, [probably m. Mary   1737–1747
Allen 1733] m. Martha Pierce 1744, m. Sarah Jones 1747,
d. 1752.

Guild & Adams; *Cabinetmakers*; Abner Guild and Elisha Adams;   1796–1798
shop 48 Orange Street.

Guild, Abner; *Cabinetmaker*; partner Elisha Adams (Guild &   1796–1800
Adams) (1796–1798); partners' shop 48 Orange Street (1796–
1798); jointly owned land on Federal Street (1798), Guild alone
at 48 Orange Street (1800).

Guild, Benjamin; *Cabinetmaker*.   1800

Hading, Mark; *Joiner*; arrived from London.   1716

Hall & Bisbe; *Cabinetmakers*; [probably Simon Hall]   1796
Washington Street.

Hall, Edward; *Cabinetmaker*; [maybe the father of, or the same   1767–1768
man as, the chairmaker listed below].

Hall, Edward; *Chairmaker*; [maybe the same man as cabinetmaker   1796–1800
listed above] shop Cross Street (1796–1798), 72 Middle Street
(1800).

Hall, John; *Cabinetmaker*; Washington Street.   1798–1800

Hall, Peter; *Upholsterer*; moved to New York by 1743.   1732

Hall, Sewel; *Cabinetmaker*; Back Street.   1796

Hall, Simon; *Cabinetmaker*; [probably partner Bisbe (Hall & Bisbe)] Battery March Street; called upon by courts as arbiter with George Bright of case involving cabinetmaker John Otis (1789); John Johnston & Daniel Rea, painters, decorated some furniture for Hall (1791). — 1780–1799

Hammatt, John B.; *Upholsterer*; 9 Union Street. — 1800

Hancock, William; *Chairmaker*; Congress Street. — 1796

Hannah, William; *Joiner*; i.m. Martha Clark 1695. — 1701–1707

Hardy, Joshua; *Chairmaker*; shop Orange Street. — 1796–1800

Hartshorne (Hartshern), Ebenezer; *Joiner*; b. 1690, m. Mary Lowden about 1712, moved to Boston from Charlestown 1743, moved to Concord 1746, d. 1781; signed high chest (fig. 19); Randall & McElman. — 1743–1746

Hay, Charles; *Chairmaker, Joiner*; m. Theodosia Napping 1724. — 1724–1726

Hay, Edmund; *Cabinetmaker*; partner William Hay (1798–1800); partners' shop Battery March Street (1798). — 1791–1800

Hay, Edmund & William; *Cabinetmakers*; Battery March Street. — 1798–1800

Hay, William; *Cabinetmaker*; partner Edmund Hay (1798–1800); partners' shop Battery March Street (1798). — 1798–1800

Hayward, Abraham; *Cabinetmaker*; d. 1796; Ann Street (1789); shop White Bread Alley; shop inventory $94.50. — 1780–1796

Hayward (Haywood), John; *Cabinetmaker*; shop Ann Street (1796); shop Ship Street (1798). — 1796–1798

Hendrick, David; *Chairmaker, Sexton*; Cow Lane. — 1796–1800

Hichborn (Hichborne), Thomas; *Joiner, (Ship Joiner)*. — 1714–1721

Hilliard, Peter; *Joiner*. — 1729

Hobart (Habbot) (Hubbard), Gabriel; *Carver*; m. Ruth ——— about 1721. — 1721–1725

Hogh, Robert; *Joiner*; arrived from Ireland 1766. — 1766

Holden, Jonah; *Cabinetmaker*; Washington Street. — 1798

Holland, Samuel; *Joiner*; i.m. Elizabeth Howard 1722, i.m. Mary Webber 1743. — 1725–1745

Holmes, Nathaniel; *Joiner, Distiller, Shopkeeper*; b. 1703 son of   1725–1740
Nathaniel Holmes, joiner and bricklayer, m. Mary Webber
1728, m. Rebecca Goodwill 1747, d. 1774; took Thomas
Sherburne as apprentice (1733), as partner (1736–1737);
employed Richard Woodward (1736); worked at distilling and
general merchandizing (1735–1774).

Homer, Andrew; [possibly *Cabinetmaker*] only evidence of Homer   [1780]
as a cabinetmaker is a questionably labelled table (*Antiques*,
XVII [May, 1930], 448, and *Antiquarian*, XIV [May, 1930], 62).
Label does not mention cabinetmaking.

Hopkins, David; *Chairmaker*.   1786

Hopkins, Thomas; *Chairmaker*.   1784–1792

Howe & Alexander; *Cabinetmakers*; 56 Back Street.   1793–1800

Howe, John & Son; *Turners*; 3 Back Street.   1796–1800

Howe, John (Sr.); *Cabinetmaker, Turner, (Joiner)*; d. 1823; worked   1776–1800
with son [probably John, possibly Thomas] as turners (1796–
1800); shop 3 Back Street.

Howe, John (Jr.); *Turner*; b. 1764, [probably m. Hannah Homer   1796–1800
1793, m. Rebecca Bass 1795, m. Mary Howland 1797] d. 1828;
[probably worked with father as John Howe & Son at 3 Back
Street].

Howe, Thomas; *Turner*; 5 Middle Street.   1796–1800

Howell, William; *Cabinetmaker, Joiner*; d. 1717; ref. Forman,   1714–1717
Singleton.

Hubbard, Richard; *Carver, Chairmaker*.   1733

Hughes, Robert; *Japanner*.   1726

Humphreys (Humphrys), John; *Joiner, Chairmaker*;   1702–1704

Hunt, Edward; *Cabinetmaker*; [probably m. Sarah Fairfield 1746].   1784

Hunt, Francis; *Cabinetmaker, Joiner*; m. Sarah Edgar 1736, d. 1752.   1740–1752

Hunt, Thomas; *Turner*; d. about 1733; estate £1042:2:0 old tenor.   1712–1733

Hunt, William; *Cabinetmaker*; m. Ruth Page 1734; [probably   1740–1741
served as servant to Edward Mirick, Charlestown cabinetmaker (1731)].

Hunting, Asa; *Cabinetmaker, Chairmaker*.   1790

Hutter, John; *Wood and Ivory Turner*; Water Street.   1798

Ivory, William; *Joiner*; m. Sarah Horton 1702.   1708

Jackson, Fyfield; *Cabinetmaker, Joiner*; m. Mary Bennet 1724,   1723–1724
  d. 1728.

Jackson, John; *Joiner*; arrived from England and warned to depart.   1716

James, George; *Picture Frame Maker, Upholsterer*; Newbury Street.   1798–1800

Jarvis, ———; *Joiner*; arrived from London 1768 [possibly John   1768
  Jarvis, cabinetmaker].

Jarvis (Jarves) (Jarvas), John Jackson; *Cabinetmaker*; b. England,   1787–1800
  m. Hannah Seabury 1788, m. Sally Cunningham 1793, d. 1823;
  shop 76 Newbury Street; ref. Swan "II."

Jenkins, John; *Joiner*; m. Margaret Snelling 1732, d. 1745; shop   1734–1745
  Green Dragon Lane; estate £2427:9:10 old tenor.

Jent, Peter; *Chairmaker*; trained by Edmund Perkins, chairmaker;   1741
  given "freedom clothes" 1741.

Johnson, James; *Chairmaker*; m. Mary Berry 1729, m. Jane   1734
  Barber 1730.

Johnson, John; *Cabinetmaker*.   1797

Johnson (Johnston), Thomas; *Cabinetmaker*; b. 1715 (Charlestown),   1736–1787
  m. Susanna McMillian 1739, d. 1787; Back Street; inventory
  1787 £340:9:0.

Johnson William; *Joiner*; brother of Thomas Johnson, cabinet-   1741–1756
  maker, bapt. 1713, m. Anna Burnell 1737, d. 1756.

Johnston, John; *Portrait Painter, Painter, (Japanner)*; b. about 1753 1773–1789
  son of Thomas Johnston (Sr.); apprenticed to John Gore,
  japanner; partner Daniel Rea (Rea & Johnston); ref. Swan
  "Johnstons."

Johnston (Johnson), Thomas (Sr.); *Japanner, Painter, Engraver,*   1732–1767
  (*Looking Glass Seller*); b. 1708 (England), m. Rachel Thwing
  1730, m. Bathsheba Thwing 1747, d. 1767; estate £912:1:10;
  ref. Fales, Downs "American Japanned," Swan "Johnstons,"
  Whitehill and Hitchings.

Johnston, Thomas Jr.; *Japanner*; b. 1731 son of Thomas Johnston   1758
  (Sr.), d. about 1776; ref. Swan "Johnstons," Whitehill and
  Hitchings.

Jones, John; *Cabinetmaker*.   1719

Kelly, James; *Joiner*; arrived from Ireland 1716.   1716

Kelsa, James; *Cabinetmaker*; Water Street.   1796

Kenn, Lenier; *Cabinetmaker*; partner Thomas Gibbons.   1730–1739

Kennedy, Quintin; *Joiner*.   1714

Kingman, Seth; *Cabinetmaker*; Fish Street.   1789

Knepton (Knapton), Joseph; *Joiner*; arrived from London 1714,   1714, 1716
went to Barbados and returned to Boston 1716.

Knight, Richard; *Carver*; North Street near Battery.   1701–1706

Knowlton, Ebenezer; *Cabinetmaker*; bapt. 1769, d. 1810; shop Ann   1796–1800
Street (1796), shop Moore's Wharf (1798–1800); labelled
tambour desk (*American Collector*, 1 [December, 1933], 1); ref.
Ormsbee "New Boston."

Lamb, Edward; *Chairmaker*.   1741

Lambert, John; *Joiner*; [probably m. Abigail Bumstead 1713].   1713–1722

Lane, John; *Chairmaker, Chair Caner*; husband of Sarah Lane, d.   1730–1736
about 1737; from London; School Street.

Lane, Sarah; *Chair Caner*; widow of John Lane, m. John Goodwin   1737–1756
1738; School Street.

Laply, George; *Joiner*; arrived in Boston 1764.   1764

Laply, Patrick; *Joiner*; arrived in Boston 1764.   1764

Larkin, Elisha; *Cabinetmaker*; Back Street.   1796

Larkin, John; *Chairmaker*; b. 1724 son of Edward Larkin, chair-   1789–1798
maker of Charlestown, m. Katherine Frothingham about 1748,
d. 1798; [probably worked in Charlestown 1746–1748 and
1756–1773] Boston shop Moore's Wharf; estate £27:3:2.

Larrabee, John; *Cabinetmaker, Joiner*; b. 1713, m. Sarah Wallis   1748–1778
1740, d. 1778; estate £227:2:0.

Latta, William; *Joiner*; arrived in Boston 1768.   1768

Lawrence, John; *Chairmaker*.   1732

Learee, Samuel; *Joiner*.   1710

Learnard (Learned), Elisha; *Cabinetmaker*; [possibly b. 1765, d.   1796–1800
1827) 50 Back Street; ref. Randall "Works 1."

Leech, James; *Joiner*; b. 1721; inherited tools from father John   1748
Leech.

Leech (Leach), John; *Joiner*; m. Ruth Miller 1713, d. 1748; left   1740–1748
joiner's tools to son James Leech; estate £2378:8:8 old tenor.

Lemon (Lemmon), William; *Upholsterer*; m. 1796, d. 1827; moved   1799–1800
from Salem (1799); 55 Marlborough Street (1800).

Lenox, David; *Cabinetmaker, House Joiner*; m. Abigail Wakefield   1731–1765
1730, d. 1765; estate £127:6:2.

Leonard, Henry; *Turner*.   1743

Lester, William; *Cabinetmaker*; Washington Street.   1800

Lilke (Lilhi), Thomas; *Cabinetmaker*.   1796

Lincoln (Linkhorn), John; *Carver*; [probably did carved work on   1722–1725
chairs for Samuel Mattocks, chairmaker] promised court
to pay Mattocks £4 worth of carving work on demand (1722).

Linsey, Thomas; *Turner*; posted as a drunkard (1728).   1728

Little, David; *Joiner*.   1724

Livermore, Thomas: *Joiner*; d. 1709.   1701–1709

Lloyd, Francis; *Carver, Gilder*; Milk Street.   1800

Lord, Robert; *Joiner*; m. Katherine Haley 1738; [possibly inn-   1735
holder (1724)].

Lord, Rupert; *Upholsterer*; shop Cornhill.   1714

Loring, John; *Turner*.   1793

Loring, Joseph; *Turner*; Pond Street (1789), School Street (1798–   1785–1800
1800).

Loring, William; *Joiner*.   1734

Love, William; *Chairmaker*.   1732

Luckis (Lucas), Benjamin; *Cabinetmaker*; Middle Street.   1768

Luckis (Lucus), Thomas; *Carver*; d. 1808; North Street (1796–   1760–1800
1800).

Lush, George; *Turner*.   1793

Lynham, George; *Cabinetmaker*; at "the Chest of Drawers in   1719
Middle Street" (*Boston News-Letter*, December 21–28, 1719).

McClure, John; *Chairmaker*.   1760

McDonald, William; *Carver, Gilder*; Essex Street (1796), Pond   1796–1798
Street or Rowe's Lane (1798).

McGregor, Daniel; *Joiner*; worked for Thomas Gibbons (1740).   1740

McKeen, Robert; *Chairmaker*.   1790

McKeller, John; *Joiner*; arrived from Scotland 1767.   1767

McKenzie, James; *Cabinetmaker*.   1750

McMillian, James; *Cabinetmaker*; m. Ann Brown 1748, d. 1769;   1749–1769
apprentice Morgan Kavanagh (1753–1757); shop and house
Back Street; estate £540:4:0; stamped desk and bookcase (fig.
101).

Marpel, Henry; *Joiner*.   1733

Marston, Daniel; *Cabinetmaker*.   1799

Martin, William; *Cabinetmaker*; 44 Newbury Street.   1798

Mason & Winslow; *Looking Glass Makers*.   1799

Mason, David (Sr.); *Upholsterer*; b. 1703, m. Susannah Steven   1726–1746
1725, d. 1746; shop Wing's Lane.

Mason, David (Jr.); *Painter, Japanner*; b. 1726 son of David   1758
Mason, upholsterer, m. Sarah Goldthwaite 1748, m. Hannah
Symmes 1751, d. after 1792; shop under Edes & Gill's Print
Office, Queen Street; shop Fore Street (1782); ref. Brazer.

Mason, Richard; *Joiner*; d. 1725; owned property Newbury Street;   1725
estate £500 old tenor.

Mattocks, James; *Joiner, Cabinetmaker*; b. 1694, brother of Samuel   1726–1735
Mattocks, chairmaker, m. Sarah Pearce 1726, moved to
Middletown, Connecticut, by 1742; Ann Street near Mill Creek.

Mattocks, Samuel; *Chairmaker, (Innholder)*; b. 1688, brother of   1720–1729
James Mattocks, joiner, m. Admonition Tucker 1712, m. Sarah
Cross, owner of inn, 1723, m. Mary Spooner 1727, d. about
1739; listed as innholder 1728; [John Lincoln probably did
carved work for Mattocks]; owned property on Ann Street near
Mill Bridge.

Maverick (Maverike), John; *Cabinetmaker, Shopkeeper*; m.   1707–1720
Elizabeth Mattocks sister of Samuel Mattocks,
chairmaker, 1710; partner George Thomas (1714); owned
property Middle Street, called shopkeeper (1729–1743).

Mellendy (Melleday), John; *Joiner*; b. 1705 (Charlestown); North Street near Winnisimmet Ferry (1725 – about 1750).   1729

Mellens, Thomas; *Joiner, Carver*; [probably m. Susanna Bill 1720, i.m. Martha Williston 1729].   1721–1723

Messenger, Ebenezer; *Turner, Joiner*; b. 1697 son of Thomas Messenger, joiner, m. Rebecca Sweetzer 1719; ref. Forman.   1718–1722

Messenger, Henry; *Turner*; ref. Forman.   1720–1721

Messenger, Simeon; *Joiner*; b. 1645, m. Bethiah Howard about 1668; ref. Forman.   1701–1710

Messenger, Thomas; *Joiner*; b. 1662, m. Elizabeth Mellowes about 1685; ref. Forman.   1701–1712

Messenger, Thomas; *Turner*; b. 1691 son of Thomas Messenger, joiner; ref. Forman.   1713–1720

Metcalfe, John; *Joiner*.   1734

Mills, George; *Cabinetmaker*; [probably b. 1721] [possibly m. Mary Baker 1750].   1759–1762

Moberly, Thomas; *Joiner*; m. Mary Howard 1731.   1732

Montgomery, Hugh; *Joiner*; [possibly m. Martha Mayo (Mayhew) 1738].   1715

More, Samuel; *Carver*; arrived in Boston 1736.   1736

Morgan, William; *Cabinetmaker*; Beacon Hill.   1795

Morris, Samuel Jr.; *Joiner*.   1718

Morse, Jonathan; *Joiner*.   –1776

Mull, James; *Joiner*; arrived from Scotland 1766.   1766

Mulligam, John; *Joiner*; m. Elizabeth ——— about 1690.   1708

Murfey (Murphy), James; *Joiner, Mariner*; arrived from Newfoundland 1739.   1739

Needham, Thomas; *Turner, Joiner, Cabinetmaker*; father, son, and grandson of same name and trade; father b. 1728; son b. 1755, d. 1787; grandson b. 1780, d. 1850; family moved to Salem (1776); in Boston by 1796; Hanover Street (1796–1798), shop North Square (1800); ref. Montgomery.   1796–1800

Nelson, William; *Cabinetmaker*; North End; advertised spinning wheels.   1754

Newcomb, Edmund; *Chairmaker*; m. Mary Emmens 1719.   1727–1729

Newell, John; *Joiner*; arrived from Ireland 1766.   1766

Nichols, Alexander; *Joiner*; arrived from Ireland 1766.   1766

Nichols (Nicholls), John; *Joiner*, (*Merchant*); b. 1654.   1709–1725

Nichols, John; *Joiner*; [probably b. 1715 son of William Nichols]   1740
d. 1764; held post of viewer and sealer of wood 1740;
inventory 1764 £10:0:0.

Nichols, William; *Joiner, Auctioneer*; b. 1692 son of John Nichols,   1719–1733
joiner, m. Bethia Webb 1714, d. after 1774; owned property
Middle Street deeded to him by father (1722); in late '30's and
'40's designated "Gentleman."

Norton, William; *Upholsterer*.   1739–1740

Nottage (Knottage), Josias; *Joiner, Housewright*; m. Elizabeth   1728
Wallis 1726.

Odell, Thomas; *Chairmaker*; m. Anna Wakefield 1710, m. Sarah   1712–1728
Peck 1737; [possibly worked with Nathaniel Breck (1724);]
rented shop Water Street near head of Oliver's Dock (1720–1721).

Orr & Sewell; *Cabinetmakers*; [probably John Orr] Back Street.   1796

Orr, John; *Cabinetmaker*; [probably Orr of Orr & Sewell].   1796

Otis, John; *Cabinetmaker*; working in Plymouth 1789.   1780

Paddock, Jonathan; *Chairmaker*.   –1777

Page, Benjamin; *Cabinetmaker*; Fish Street (1789).   1779–1794

Paige, John; *Turner*.   1702

Paine (Pain), Edward; *Upholsterer, Chaisemaker*.   1732–1741

Paine (Pain), Stephen; *Joiner*; [probably third son of William   1715–1732
Paine (Sr.), joiner] m. Mary Kennet 1709; worked with
William Paine [probably his brother] 1728; shop near Town
Dock (1727–1728).

Paine, Thomas; *Joiner*; b. 1680 son of William Paine, joiner, m.   1712–1725
Elizabeth Pierce 1703, m. Eunice Treat 1721, m. Dianer Milborn
1729; inherited one-half father's tools 1712.

Paine (Payn), William (Sr.); *Joiner*; d. about 1711; father of   1701–1711
Thomas, William, [and probably Stephen], joiners.

Paine (Payne), William (Jr.); *Joiner*; b. 1688 son of William Paine (Sr.), joiner, m. Hannah White 1709, m. Hannah Stevens 1718, m. Mary Ruggles 1734, m. Mary Lowder 1737, m. Sarah Sloley 1751, d. about 1766; inherited one-half father's tools 1712; worked with Stephen Paine [probably his brother] 1728; estate £16:7:3. 1712–1732

Parkman, Samuel; *Joiner, Shopkeeper*; b. 1695, brother William Parkman, joiner, m. Dorcas Bowes 1729, d. 1767; principally shopkeeper after 1740. 1730–1740

Parkman, William; *Joiner, Cabinetmaker*; b. 1685, brother Samuel Parkman, joiner, m. Hannah Goodwin 1705, m. Hannah Harris 1750, m. Mary Hawkins 1757, declared incompetent 1774, d. 1776; apprentice Hugh Brown (1749–1759); shop at the Case of Drawers (1723), shop Scarlet's Wharf (1750). 1714–1775

Parsons, William; *Joiner*; [probably b. 1614, m. Ruth ——— about 1644, d. 1702]. 1701

Partridge, Nehemiah; *Japanner, (Painter)*; m. Mary Ffilbrick 1718, d. about 1726; Tremont Street (1712), Mill Bridge (1713), Water Street at head of Oliver's Dock; moved to Portsmouth about 1720; ref. Brazer, Fraser "Painted," Fraser "Pedigreed," Lyon. 1712–1717

Peak, Henry; *Joiner*; i.m. Abigail Delliway 1736; rented two chambers Fish Street (1749). 1749

Peake, John; *Joiner, (Sawyer)*; b. 1685, m. Sarah White 1714, m. Margaret ——— 1721. 1723

Pearce, Benjamin; *Chairmaker*. –1776

Pearce, Joseph; *Joiner*; b. 1682, m. Mary Mellins 1718, m. Sarah Pain 1730 [probably daughter of William Paine and sister of Thomas, William, and Stephen, all joiners], d. about 1751. 1718

Pearson, James; *Chairmaker*; m. Elizabeth ——— about 1701, m. Mary Cockroft 1711, m. Priscilla Jackson 1712. 1716

Peck, Nathaniel; *Chairmaker*; m. Lydia Chaffin 1740, m. Mary Marion 1742. 1784–1790

Pendleton, Roger; *Japanner*; d. 1712. –1712

Perkins, Edmund (Edmond) (Sr.); *Joiner, Chairmaker*; b. 1683, m. Mary Farris 1709, m. Ester Frothingham 1722, d. about 1761; apprentice Peter Jent (–1741); shop Mackerel Lane destroyed by fire (1760); estate £40:13:11. 1711–1750

Perkins, Edmund Jr.; *Chairmaker*; son of Edmund Perkins (Sr.), d.   1760–1762
1773; lost tools and furniture in fire (1760); estate £6.

Perkins, Henry; *Chairmaker*; b. 1710 son of Edmund Perkins (Sr.),   1738–1783
m. Mary Kilby 1737, m. Grace Thaxter about 1745, d. 1783;
lost tools in fire (1760).

Perkins, John; *Chairmaker*; b. 1723 son of Edmund Perkins (Sr.),   1750–1760
m. Susanna Tuck about 1745, moved to Gorham, Massachusetts
(now Gorham, Maine), by 1771; loss in fire (1760) £649:7:6
old tenor; shop Battery March Street.

Perkins, William; *Chairmaker*; b. 1716 son of Edmund Perkins   1750
(Sr.), m. Mary Hind 1748, d. 1759 or 1760; estate £24:0:1.

Perring, Charles; *Joiner*; arrived from London 1768.   1768

Peters, Benjamin; *Joiner*.   1776

Pickman, Nathaniel; *Upholsterer*; rented house Marlborough   1739–1744
Street (1739–1741).

Pike, Timothy; *Chairmaker*.   1776

Pillet (Pillett), John; *Joiner*; Lynde Street (1720).   1714–1725

Pimm (Pymm), John; *Cabinetmaker, (Joiner)*; m. Jane Tout 1744,   1735–1770
m. Hannah Mower 1751, d. 1773; signed high chest (fig. 37);
ref. Fraser "Pedigreed," Randall *American Furniture*.

Poignand, David; *Cabinetmaker*; b. St. Heliers, Isle of Jersey, m.   1788
Delicia ——— about 1787; documented desk and bookcase,
chest, table (*Antiques*, XLIII [February, 1943], 87).

Powell, John; *Chairmaker*.   1775

Price, William; *Cabinetmaker, Print Seller, Merchant, Shopkeeper*; b.   1714–1730
1684 (England), m. Sarah Miles 1727, d. 1771; shop Cornhill
(1733–1737); ref. Brazer.

Prichard (Pritcherd), John; *Joiner, (Housewright)*; Marlborough   1713–1717
Street.

Prince, John; *Upholsterer*; arrived from Topsham 1716.   1716

Putnam, Joseph; *Chairmaker*; b. 1714 (Salem), brother of William   1750–1767
Putnam, m. Sarah Uran (Vran) 1735, d. 1788; apprentice James
Burton (1755–1765); shop Milk Street and Battery March
Street destroyed by fire (1760); estate £684:10:5.

Putnam, William; *Chairmaker*; b. 1717 (Salem), brother of Joseph   1749
Putnam, m. Ruth Leach, daughter of John Leach, joiner, 1740,
d. 1749; shop near Oliver's Dock, South End; estate £2511:12:0
old tenor.

Ragget, Thomas; *Joiner*; arrived from Great Britain and warned to   1715
depart 1715.

Rand, Robert; *Joiner, (Lumber Merchant)*; m. Susanna Cheever   1712–1751
1709, d. about 1752; Mill Creek and Ann Street.

Rand, Robert Jr.; *Lumber Merchant, (Joiner)*; b. 1719 son of Robert   1756–1788
Rand, joiner, m. Martha Grice 1756, m. Mary Simpkins 1773,
d. 1794; owned shop and wharf Rand's Wharf.

Randle (Randall), William; *Japanner, (Cabinetmaker)*, *Looking*   1715–1739
Glass Seller; m. Mary Butler 1714; advertised "Looking-
Glasses of all sorts, . . . Chests-of-Drawers, Tables, . . . all sorts
of Japan-work, Done and Sold by *William Randle* at the Sign of
the Cabbinett, a Looking-Glass Shop in Queen-Street near the
Town-House" (*Boston News-Letter*, April 25, 1715); shop Dock
Square (1731), shop Hanover Street (1738); signed high chest
(Adams National Historic Site, Quincy, Massachusetts); ref.
Brazer, Fraser "Pedigreed," Lyon, Randall "Boston Japanner."

Rann, John; *Cabinetmaker*.   1776

Ransom, Ebenezer; *Joiner*.   1776

Ray (Wray), Caleb; *Joiner*; m. Ann Tolman 1704, d. 1721.   1713–1715

Rea & Johnston; *Painters, Gilders, (Japanners)*; partners John   1773–1789
Johnston and Daniel Rea, brothers-in-law (1773–1789); ref.
Swan "Johnstons."

Rea, Daniel (Sr.); *Painter, (Japanner)*; m. Rachel Johnston,   1767–1800
daughter of Thomas Johnston (Sr.), 1764; [probably worked for
father-in-law (1764–1767)] took over father-in-law's business
(1767); partner John Johnston (1773–1789); partner son Daniel
Rea (Jr.) (1789–1800); ref. Swan "Johnstons."

Rea, Daniel (Jr.); *Painter, Japanner*; partner father Daniel Rea (Sr.);   1789–1800
ref. Swan "Johnstons."

Read (Reed), Bridges; *Joiner*; [probably m. Mary Ventiman 1725]   1728–1735
rented shop Fish Street in North End.

Redin (Redden), Henry; *Carver*.   1714–1728

Reed (Read), Richard; *Cabinetmaker*; father and son of same name and trade; father m. Hannah Walker 1705; son b. 1708.   1732

Richards, Edward; *Joiner*; [probably brother of William Richards, carver] m. Mary Kidder 1703, m. Hannah Copp 1722.   1715–1733

Richards, Edward Q.; *Chairmaker*; Devonshire Street or Pudding Lane.   1796–1798

Richards, William; *Carver*; [probably brother of Edward Richards, joiner].   1739

Ridgway (Ridgeway), Ebenezer; *Chairmaker*; b. 1739 son of Samuel Ridgway Sr., m. Mary West 1762; shop Fish Street (1789).   1773–1800

Ridgeway, Nathaniel; *Chairmaker*; b. 1729 son of Samuel Ridgway Sr., i.m. Rebecca Gooding 1754.   1754

Ridgway, Samuel Sr.; *Chairmaker*; b. 1700 (Charlestown), m. Naomi Reynolds 1724, d. 1773; apprentices Miles Hubbard (1749–1761), Samuel Allen (1758–1764), John Taylor (1759–1771); shop Ann Street with son Samuel; estate £193:16:7.   1748

Ridgway (Ridgeway), Samuel Jr.; *Chairmaker*; b. 1726 son of Samuel Ridgway Sr., m. Elizabeth Gedney 1754, m. Mary ——— by 1784, d. 1799; shop Ann Street (1786), shop Fish Street (1789); estate $14,089.05.   1773–1790

Righton (Wrighton), Francis; *Upholsterer, Shopkeeper*; m. Elizabeth Royal 1706; still had shop 1743.   1712–1716

Roberts, ———; *Joiner*; arrived from London 1765.   1765

Roberts, Joshua; *Japanner*; d. 1719; employed by William Randle, japanner.   1714–1719

Roberts, Samuel; *Chairmaker*.   1783–1784

Robins, James; *Joiner*; Ward 4.   1780

Robinson, George; *Carver*; father and son of same name and trade; son b. 1680, m. Sarah Maverick 1698, d. 1737.   1706–1720

Robinson, Richard; *Cabinetmaker*; m. Abigail Medeenor 1733, m. Sarah Powell 1748.   1747

Robinson, William; *Cabinetmaker*; earlier of Arrowsic Island.   1715–1717

Rogers, James; *Chairmaker*; m. Elizabeth Phillips 1756, d. 1793; Friends Street; estate £215:0:0.   1766–1793

Rogers, Nathaniel; *Joiner, Cabinetmaker.*   1720–1749

Ross, Benjamin; *Cabinetmaker.*   –1775

Salisbury, Benjamin; *Joiner*; b. 1699, m. Deborah Sterns 1732;   1720–1760
apprentice Samuel Wood (1743–1752); Bangs Alley (1751),
Mackerel Lane, where personal possessions destroyed by fire
(1760).

Salisbury, John; *Cabinetmaker*; in Hingham 1793.   1768

Samber, Samuel; *Upholsterer.*   1734

Sanborn (Sanburn), Reuben; *Windsor Chair Maker*; Lendell's Row   1796–1800
(1796), shop Leverett's (or Quaker's) Lane (1798), shop Doane's
Wharf (1800).

Sandford (Sanford), John; *Carver, Gilder*; 39 Cornhill.   1789–1798

Saxton, William; *Grocer, Crockery Seller*; [possibly *Cabinetmaker*]   [1785]
85 Newbury Street; sold groceries and crockeryware (1789),
shop 2 Dock Square. Only mention of Saxton as cabinetmaker
is a questionably labelled desk (*Antiquarian*, XIV [May, 1930], 62).
Label does not mention cabinetmaking.

Scott & Willard; *Windsor Chair Makers*; [probably Edward Scott   1800
and Josiah Willard] Water Street.

Scott, Edward; *Cabinetmaker, Windsor Chair Maker*; [probably   1800
partner Josiah Willard (Scott & Willard)].

Scottow, John; *Cabinetmaker*; b. about 1701, m. Elizabeth Lock   1764
about 1726, d. 1790.

Seaver & Frost; *Windsor Chair Makers*; [probably William Seaver]   1800
57 State Street.

Seaver, William; *Windsor Chair Maker, Cabinetmaker*; Vose's   1796–1800
Wharf (1796), shop Liberty Square (1796–1798), Battery
March Street (1800).

Seymour, John; *Cabinetmaker*; b. England; arrived Portland 1785,   1796–1800
Boston 1794; worked with son Thomas; Creek Square; labelled
desk (Montgomery no. 184), labelled desk (Stoneman nos. 4–8);
ref. Hipkiss, Montgomery, Ormsbee, Randall *American Furniture*,
Randall "Seymour," Stoneman, Swan "Seymour."

Seymour, Thomas; *Cabinetmaker*; b. 1771 (England) son of John   1799–1800
Seymour, cabinetmaker; arrived Portland 1785, Boston 1794;
worked with father, John Seymour, Creek Square; for
documented pieces and bibliography see John Seymour.

Sherburne, Thomas (Sr.); *Cabinetmaker*; b. 1713 (Portsmouth), m.   1736–1784
Margaret Goldthwait 1739, i.m. Abigail Elwell 1757, d. 1784;
apprenticed to Nathaniel Holmes (1733); partner Holmes (1736–
1737); shop Back Street; ref. Dow.

Sherburne, Thomas (Jr.); *Cabinetmaker*; b. 1741 son of Thomas   1784–1796
Sherburne, cabinetmaker, d. 1806.

Shove, Theophilus; *Joiner, Glazier*.   1736–1740

Shute, William; *Carver*; m. Martha Budd daughter of Edward   1716–1721
Budd, carver, 1690, d. 1746; worked with Jacob Crouch (1719).

Simms (Symmes), Andrew; *Joiner, Shipjoiner*; b. 1704, d. after   1739–1764
1780.

Simpkins, John; *Upholsterer, (Shopkeeper)*; b. 1740, m. Elizabeth   1760–1789
Grant, daughter of Samuel Grant, upholsterer, 1764, d. 1831;
Cornhill (1789).

Simpson, Jehabed; *Joiner*; arrived from North Carolina 1768.   1768

Simpson, John; *Joiner*; b. 1668 (Charlestown), m. Rely Holmes   1706–1709
1695; Union Street and Creek Lane.

Simpson, Josiah; *Cabinetmaker*; Exchange Lane (1782–1789).   1780–1793

Skilling (Skillin), John; *Carver*; b. 1746 son of Simeon Skilling   1780–1800
(Sr.), carver, m. Mary Fowle 1795, d. 1800; partner Simeon
Skilling (Jr.) (1780–1800); apprentices Isaac Fowle, Edmund
Raymond (1800); shop on wharf north of Governor Hancock's,
Skilling's Wharf (1796–1798); documented pediment figures on
chest-on-chest by Stephen Badlam of Dorchester Lower Falls
(*Antiques*, xx [December, 1931], 341); ref. Swan "Revised,"
Swan "Orrery," Swan "Skillin," Thwing.

Skilling (Skillin), Samuel; *Carver*; b. 1742 son of Simeon Skilling   1780–1800
(Sr.), carver, d. 1816; Barret's Wharf (1796–1798); for
bibliography see Simeon (Sr.).

Skilling (Skillin), Simeon (Sr.); *Carver*; b. 1716, d. 1778;   1767–1778
Salutation Alley; inventory 1786 £181:0:7; ref. Swan "Orrery,"
Swan "Skillin," Thwing.

Skilling (Skillings) (Skillin), Simeon (Jr.); *Carver*; b. 1757 son of   1780–1800
Simeon Skilling, carver, m. Margaret Casheau 1782, d. 1806;
partner John Skilling (1780–1800); shop on wharf north of
Governor Hancock's, Skilling's Wharf (1796–1798); for
documented pieces and bibliography see John Skilling.

Smibert, William; *Cabinetmaker*.   1750

Smith, Benjamin; *Chairmaker*; arrived from New York 1716.   1716

Smith, Mathias; *Turner*.   1714

Smith, Thomas; *Chairmaker*.   1742

Smithen, Joseph; *Turner*.   1728

Snelling, Joseph; *Joiner*; Ward 2.   1780

Snow, Henry; *Cabinetmaker, Joiner*; m. Lillie Poor (Power) 1743,   1743–1778
    m. Elizabeth Shirley 1776, d. 1778; damages from fire (1760)
    £88, inventory 1778 £259:10:0.

Snowden (Snoden), David; *Chairmaker*; b. 1705, m. Margaret   1727–1739
    Gallop 1734, d. about 1745; estate £1890:3:6 old tenor.

Spear, John; *Cabinetmaker*.   1798

Spear, Paul; *Innkeeper*, (*Chairmaker*); m. Clemence Weld 1756, d.   1760–1767
    1792; estate £626:15:4.

Sprague (Sprage), Ebed (Ebenezer); *Chairmaker*; shop Liberty   1796–1798
    Square (1796), Battery March Street (1798).

Stafford, Samuel; *Cabinetmaker*; Kilby Street.   1789

Starr, Eleazer; *Joiner*; employed other joiners (1718); shop   1712–1723
    Mackerel Lane (1723).

Stelling, Peter; *Joiner, Cabinetmaker*; Wentworth's Wharf (1731),   1728–1733
    Corn Court (1732).

Stevens, Erasmus; *Joiner, Wharfinger, Gentleman*; m. Persis Bridges   1707–1729
    1707, m. Susanna Pinkney 1739, d. 1750; rented shop Clark's
    Wharf (1707), rented wharf from Clark (1730-1739).

Stevens, John (Sr.); *Joiner*; [possibly b. 1671 brother of Erasmus   1740
    Stevens] d. 1745.

Stevens, John Jr.; *Joiner, Housewright*; son of John Stevens (Sr.),   1743
    joiner.

Stevens, Place; *Joiner*; b. 1696, twin brother Thomas Stevens (Jr.),   1729–1732
    joiner, son of Thomas Stevens (Sr.), joiner.

Stevens, Thomas (Sr.); *Joiner*; m. Sarah Place 1695, d. by 1724;   1701–1718
    estate £212:10:16 old tenor.

Stevens, Thomas (Jr.); *Joiner, Housewright*; b. 1696, twin brother   1729–1732
    Place Stevens, joiner, son of Thomas Stevens (Sr.), joiner, m.
    Elizabeth Martin 1729.

Stokes, Joseph; *Carver, Gilder*; Milk Street (1798), Federal Street (1800).   1798–1800

Stone & Alexander; *Cabinetmakers, Chairmakers*; partners Samuel Stone and Giles Alexander; Prince Street corner of Back Street (1796); labelled chair (Montgomery no. 31), labelled desk (Swan "II," fig. 3), two labelled chairs (Henry Ford Museum); ref. Montgomery, Swan "II."   1792–1796

Stone, Ebenezer; *Windsor Chair Maker*; b. 1763, brother of Samuel Stone, cabinetmaker.   1786–1800

Stone, Samuel; *Cabinetmaker*; b. 1760, brother of Ebenezer Stone, chairmaker; partner Giles Alexander (1792–1796); Ann Street (1800); for labelled furniture see Stone & Alexander.   1794–1800

Storer, Joseph; *Joiner*.   1776

Stratford, Samuel; *Cabinetmaker*; employed Thomas Aimer (1791–1795); shop Lendall's Row (1798).   1791–1798

Sumner, Ebenezer; *Chairmaker*; m. Lydia Britton 1757.   1763

Sutton, William; *Joiner*; b. 1667, m. Mary Johnson 1695, d. about 1721.   1714–1715

Swaney, William; *Cabinetmaker*; Newbury Street.   1798

Swanton, Samuel; *Cabinetmaker*; d. 1777.   –1777

Syvert, Elias; *Joiner*.   1724–1725

Terutch, Richard; *Joiner*; arrived from Ireland 1767.   1767

Thacher, Joseph W.; *Paper Hanging Dealer, Upholsterer*; 2 Cornhill.   1798

Thayer, William; *Upholsterer, Merchant*; partner William Brown (Brown & Thayer); shop Hanover Street.   1798

Thayer, Ziphion; *Upholsterer, Trader*; 4 Cornhill (1789), Water Street (1796); Thayer's trade card (fig. 174).   1764–1799

Thomas, George; *Cabinetmaker*; father and son of same name and trade; father m. Rebecca ——— about 1680; son b. 1698; son working by 1712; [father] partner John Maverick (1714).   1706–1717

Thorpe (Thorp), Henry; *Chairmaker*.   1797–1798

Tippin (Tippen), Thomas; *Joiner*; worked with Thomas Bennett (1723).   1723–1729

Todd, Joshua; *Joiner*; m. Sarah Chamberline 1713.   1710–1718

Todd, William; *Cabinetmaker*; m. Rebecca Fearing 1797, d. 1800;   1796–1798
[probably partner Isaac Vose or possibly Stephen Vose (Vose &
Todd) (1796)] partner Samuel Adams (Adams & Todd) (1798);
for labelled table see Adams & Todd; ref. Randall "Works II."

Tolman, William; *Gilder*.   1800

Tookey (Tuckey), John (Joshua); *Chairmaker*; m. Sarah Scot 1718;   1717–1719
arrived from England and warned to depart 1717.

Torrey, William; *Joiner*; d. by 1786.   1728

Toult, Frederick; *Joiner*; Frog Lane.   1796

Townsend, Davis; *Joiner*; m. Sarah Snelling 1732, m. Mary   1729
Forbes 1743.

Trenchard & Dixon; *Carvers, Engravers, Gilders*; Milk Street.   1798

Trevett (Trevet), John; *Chairmaker*; m. Esther Perkins, daughter   1749
of Edmund Perkins, chairmaker, 1749; [probably worked with
brother-in-law John Perkins, chairmaker] co-owner with John
Perkins of property on Battery March Street, site of Perkin's
shop.

Tuck, Joseph; *Chairmaker*; worked with Samuel Tuck (1798);   1795–1798
shop Battery March Street.

Tuck (Tucke), Samuel Jones; *Chairmaker, Windsor Chair Maker,*   1794–1800
Windsor Chair Manufacturer; Gentleman; worked with Joseph
Tuck (1798): manufactory Battery March Street (1796–1800);
Windsor chair stamped "S. J. Tucke" (Colonial Williamsburg),
Windsor chair stamped "S. J. Tucke" (Winterthur), set of six
Windsor chairs stamped "S. J. Tucke" (Gore Place).

Tucker, James; *Turner*; loss in fire (1760) £10:9:0.   1760–1769

Tucker, Joshua; *Turner*; arrived from London 1717 and warned   1717
to depart.

Tufts, Samuel Putnam; *Chairmaker*.   1794–1800

Turner, Joseph; *Joiner*; i.m. Deliverance Hazelton 1736, m.   1738–1740
Elizabeth Kenley 1738.

Turner, Matthew; *Joiner*.   1701–1716

Underwood, Anthony; *Chairmaker*; b. 1680, m. Jane Place 1703,   1709–1717
d. 1749; estate £2011:5:0 old tenor.

Underwood, David; *Cabinetmaker*.	1780
Underwood, John; *Chairmaker, Turner*; d. 1758; Middle Street 1743	1732–1743
Veasey (Veazie), Benjamin; *Chairmaker*; Ward 12.	1780–1784
Veasey, John; *Chairmaker*; Ward 12.	1780–1782
Vergoose, Isaac; *Joiner, Ship Joiner*; m. Elizabeth Pain 1731.	1734–1738
Vincent, Clement; *Chairmaker*; i.m. Mercy Langdon 1741, m. Ann Durant 1769; fire (1760) destroyed tools and unfinished furniture worth £4:6:2½.	1751–1760
Vincent, William; *Joiner;* arrived from Bristol 1716.	1716
Vinton (Vintenan) (Vintenon), John Lewis; *Joiner, Housewright*; i.m. Margaret Mooney 1742.	1725
Vose & Todd; *Cabinetmakers*; [probably William Todd and Isaac and/or Stephen Vose] Cambridge Street.	1796
Vose, Isaac; *Cabinetmaker*; [probably partner William Todd (Vose & Todd)] worked with Stephen Vose (1798–1799); John Johnston & Daniel Rea, painters, decorated some furniture for Vose (1785); Orange Street (1789).	1785–1800
Vose, Stephen; *Cabinetmaker*; worked with Isaac Vose (1798–1799).	1798–1799
Wade, Thomas; *Upholsterer*; d. by 1757; inventory 1757 £39:4:10.	1739–1747
Waghorne, John; *Japanner, Teacher of Psalmody*; South End; ref. Brazer.	1739–1740
Wakefield, Obadiah (Sr.); *Joiner*; b. about 1677, m. Rebecca Waters 1701, d. 1733.	1709–1718
Wakefield, Obadiah Jr.; *Joiner*; b. 1702, m. Elizabeth Willis 1713.	1714
Walker, Richard; *Cabinetmaker*.	1761
Ward, Moses; *Cabinetmaker, Shop Joiner*; partner James Campbell (Campbell & Ward) (1791); Leverett's (or Quaker's) Lane (1796).	1791–1796
Warham (Wareham), Charles; *Cabinetmaker, Joiner*; b. 1701 (London), m. Martha Giles 1722, d. 1779; shop near Dock Square; moved to Charleston, South Carolina, by 1733; ref. Singleton.	1724–1731

Warner, Nathaniel; *Japanner*; Fish Street. 1764–1796

Waters, Ebenezer; *Chairmaker*; Orange Street (1789), Moon Street (1796–1800). 1789–1800

Waters, Samuel; *Chairmaker*; shop Kilby Street. 1800

Watson, William; *Joiner*; m. Elizabeth Indecott 1715, m. Abigail Trott 1723. 1715

Webb, John; *Cabinetmaker*; m. Hannah Burrill 1740, m. Christian Bailey 1741, d. about 1761; estate £6. –1761

Webb, Thomas; *Joiner*; d. 1728. 1723–1728

Webber, William Jr.; *Joiner*; b. 1707, m. Rebecca Thomas 1731. 1733

Webster, Francis; *Cabinetmaker*. 1793

Welch, John; *Carver*; b. 1711, m. Sarah Barrington 1735, m. Dorcas Gatecombe 1741, m. Elizabeth Hall 1753, d. 1789; carved codfish for House of Representatives; Dock Square; ref. Brown, Swan "1," Swan "Johnstons." 1734–1789

Welch, John Jr.; *Carver*; b. 1735 son of John Welch, carver. 1780

Wharton, Thomas; *Joiner*. 1733

Wheeler, Samuel (Sr.); *Joiner, Chairmaker*; b. 1689, m. Mary How 1726, d. about 1748; shop Orange Street; estate £942:5:0 old tenor. 1720–1747

Wheeler, Samuel (Jr.); *Chairmaker*; [probably b. 1728 son of Samuel Wheeler (Sr.)] Orange Street. 1757

Wheeler, Thomas; *Turner*; [possibly b. 1731 son of Samuel Wheeler (Sr.), chairmaker] Pleasant Street. 1800

Wheelwright, Theodore; *Upholsterer*. 1750

Whetcomb (Whetcombe), William; *Upholsterer*. 1707–1727

Whitehorne, George; *Ship Carpenter, Shipwright, Joiner*; d. by 1728. 1724

Whitehorne, John; *Carpenter, Joiner*; m. Hannah Kettle 1723; apprenticed to John Courser March 1714 – September 1721. 1721–1724

Whiting, Stephen (Sr.); *Japanner, Looking Glass Maker, Print Seller*; b. 1720; declared bankrupt 1758; shop Union Street opposite Cornfield; labelled looking glass (Israel Sack, Inc.); ref. Brazer, Dow. 1743–1773

Whiting, Stephen Jr.; *Looking Glass Maker, Picture Frame Seller,* 1767–1773
Japanner; shop Union Street below Cornfield (1771), near Mill-
Bridge (1773); ref. Dow.

Whitwell, Samuel; *Joiner*; m. Abigail Champney 1701, m. 1721
Elizabeth Archer 1712, d. 1727; estate £75:10:0 old tenor.

Wilkins, John; *Joiner*; m. Ester Walker 1723, d. 1724 or 1725; 1724
estate, in joiner's tools and "stuff," £35:4:1 old tenor.

Wilkinson, Thomas; *Chairmaker*; shop 18 Winter Street. 1796–1800

Willard, Josiah; *Chairmaker, Windsor Chair Maker*; [probably 1799–1800
partner Edward Scott (Scott & Willard)] High Street.

Willcox (Wilcox), Jesse Barber; *Joiner*; m. Beulah Meriam 1792. 1798

Williams, Daniel; *Cabinetmaker*; d. 1778. –1777

Williams, John; *Joiner*; [probably the John Williams, joiner, who 1743
arrived from Ireland 1715].

Williams, Oliver; *Upholsterer*; b. 1679, [possibly m. Hannah 1703–1708
Adams 1724].

Wilson, William; *Turner*; d. 1732; estate £389:12:8 old tenor; 1701–1732
inventory 1732 included "6 Carved foreparts for Chairs –
0:6:0."

Winston, Stephen; *Joiner*; arrived from Long Island 1716. 1716

Wittemore (Whittemore), Daniel; *Joiner*; m. Mary Turell 1715, 1715–1718
m. Mary Chamberlain 1719, m. Elizabeth Townsend 1746.

Woodward, Nathaniel; *Joiner, House Joiner*; m. Priscilla Alley –1744
1710, m. Elizabeth Hunt 1739, d. about 1744; estate £135:13:6.

Woodward, Richard; *Joiner*; m. Susanna Luce 1747; worked for 1736–1751
Nathaniel Holmes 1736; Fish Street 1751; moved to Dedham
by 1752.

Young, John; *Joiner*. 1715–1717

Appendix B

READINGS ON INDIVIDUAL CRAFTSMEN

Brazer, Esther Stevens. "The Early Boston Japanners." *Antiques*, XLIII (May, 1943), 208–211.

Brown, May Louise. "John Welch, Carver." *Antiques*, IX (January, 1926), 28–30.

Comstock, Helen. "Frothingham and the Question of Attributions." *Antiques*, LXIII (June, 1953), 502–505.

Decorative Arts Photographic Collection (DAPC). Henry Francis du Pont Winterthur Museum.

Dow, George Francis. *The Arts and Crafts in New England 1704–1775*. Topsfield: The Wayside Press, 1927.

Downs, Joseph. *American Furniture, Queen Anne and Chippendale Periods in the Henry Francis du Pont Winterthur Museum*. New York: The Macmillan Company, 1952.

———. "American Japanned Furniture." *Metropolitan Museum of Art Bulletin*, XXVIII (March, 1933), 42–48.

———. "John Cogswell, Cabinetmaker." *Antiques*, LXI (April, 1952), 322–324.

Evans, Nancy Goyne. "The Genealogy of a Bookcase Desk." *Winterthur Portfolio 9*. Charlottesville: University Press of Virginia, 1974. Pp. 213–222.

Fales, Dean A. *American Painted Furniture 1660–1880*. New York: E. P. Dutton & Company Inc., 1972.

Forman, Benno. "Urban Aspects of Massachusetts Furniture in the Late Seventeenth Century." *Winterthur Conference Report 1969: Country Cabinetwork and Simple City Furniture*. Charlottesville: University Press of Virginia, 1970. Pp. 1–33.

Fraser, Esther. "Painted Furniture in America." *Antiques*, V (June, 1924), 302–306.

————. "A Pedigreed Lacquered Highboy." *Antiques*, xv (May, 1929), 398–401.

Hipkiss, Edwin J. *Eighteenth-Century American Arts: The M. and M. Karolik Collection*. Cambridge, Massachusetts: Harvard University Press, 1950.

Lyon, Irving Whitall. *The Colonial Furniture of New England*. Boston: Houghton Mifflin Company, 1891.

Montgomery, Charles F. *American Furniture, The Federal Period in the Henry Francis du Pont Winterthur Museum*. New York: The Viking Press, 1966.

Mooz, H. Peter. "The Origins of Newport Block-Front Furniture Designs." *Antiques*, xcix (June, 1971), 882–886.

Ormsbee, Thomas Hamilton. *Early American Furniture Makers*. New York: Thomas Y. Crowell Company Publishers, 1930.

————. "A New Boston Worker Identified." *American Collector*, i (December, 1933), 1.

Randall, Richard H., Jr. *American Furniture in the Museum of Fine Arts, Boston*. Boston: Museum of Fine Arts, 1965.

————. "George Bright, Cabinetmaker." *Art Quarterly*, xxvii (1964), 134–149.

————. "Seymour Furniture Problems." *Museum of Fine Arts, Boston, Bulletin*, lvii (1959), 102–113.

————. "William Randall, Boston Japanner." *Antiques*, cv (May, 1974), 1127–1131.

————. "Works of Boston Cabinetmakers, 1795–1825, Part i." *Antiques*, lxxxi (February, 1962), 186–189.

————. "Works of Boston Cabinetmakers, 1795–1825, Part ii." *Antiques*, lxxxi (April, 1962), 412–415.

————, and McElman, Martha. "Ebenezer Hartshorne, Cabinetmaker." *Antiques*, lxxxvii (January, 1965), 78–79.

Rhoades, Elizabeth, and Jobe, Brock. "Recent Discoveries in Boston Japanned Furniture." *Antiques*, cv (May, 1974), 1082–1091.

Singleton, Esther. *The Furniture of Our Forefathers.* New York: Double-day, Page, and Company, 1901.

Smith, Susan Augusta. *Ancestors of Moses Belcher Bass.* Boston, 1896.

Spalding, Dexter E. "Benjamin Frothingham of Charlestown, Cabinet-maker and Soldier." *Antiques,* XIV (December, 1928), 536–537.

Stoneman, Vernon C. *John and Thomas Seymour, Cabinetmakers in Boston, 1794–1816.* Boston: Special Publications, 1959.

Swan, Mabel M. "Boston's Carvers and Joiners, Part I." *Antiques,* LIII (March, 1948), 198–201.

———. "Boston's Carvers and Joiners, Part II." *Antiques,* LIII (April, 1948), 281–285.

———. "Furnituremakers of Charlestown." *Antiques,* XLVI (October, 1944), 203–206.

———. "John Seymour and Son, Cabinetmakers." *Antiques,* XXXII (October, 1937), 176–180.

———. "The Johnstons and the Reas—Japanners." *Antiques,* XLIII (May, 1943), 211–213.

———. "Orrery by Joseph Pope of Boston." *Antiques,* XXXI (March, 1937), 112–115.

———. "A Revised Estimate of McIntire." *Antiques,* XX (December, 1931), 338–343.

———. "Simeon Skillin, Senior: The First American Sculptor." *Antiques,* XLVI (July, 1944), 21.

Thwing, Leroy. "The Four Carving Skillins." *Antiques,* XXXIII (June, 1938), 326–328.

Whitehill, Walter Muir, and Hitchings, Sinclair. *Boston Prints and Print-makers 1670–1775.* Boston: Colonial Society of Massachusetts, 1973.

Winchester, Alice. "Frontispiece." *Antiques,* LXXXVI (October, 1964), 430–431.

Young, M. Ada. "Five Secretaries and the Cogswells." *Antiques,* LXXXVIII (October, 1965), 478–485.

Index

HAEC OLIM MEMINISSE JUVABIT

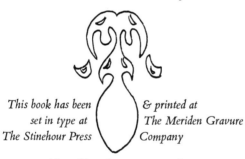

This book has been set in type at The Stinehour Press & printed at The Meriden Gravure Company and bound by The New Hampshire Bindery